GAETANO DONIZETTI

COMPOSER RESOURCE MANUALS
VOLUME 51
GARLAND REFERENCE LIBRARY OF THE HUMANITIES
VOLUME 1983

GAETANO DONIZETTI
A GUIDE TO RESEARCH

JAMES P. CASSARO

GARLAND PUBLISHING, INC.
A MEMBER OF THE TAYLOR & FRANCIS GROUP
NEW YORK & LONDON
2000

Published in 2000 by
Garland Publishing, Inc.
A member of the Taylor & Francis Group
29 West 35th Street
New York, NY 10001

10 9 8 7 6 5 4 3 2 1

Library of Congress Cataloging-in-Publication Data

Cassaro, James P.
    Gaetano Donizetti : a guide to research / James P. Cassaro.
    p. cm. — (Composer resource manuals ; v. 51) (Garland
reference library of the humanities ; v. 1983)
    Includes discographical references and index.
    ISBN 0-8153-2350-6 (alk. paper)
    1. Donizetti, Gaetano, 1797–1848—Bibliography.   I. Title.
II. Garland composer resource manuals ; v. 51.   III. Garland
reference library of the humanities ; vol. 1983.

ML134.D66 C37 2000
016.7821'092—dc21   00-029426

Cover: Gaetano Donizetti. Taken from Leonhard Stierlin, *Biographie von
Gaetano Donizetti*. Zürich: Druck von Orell, Füssli und Comp., 1852 (By
permission of the Cornell University Library, Music Library Collection)

Printed on acid-free, 250-year-life paper.
Manufactured in the United States of America

Contents

Composer Resource Manuals

In response to the growing need for bibliographic guidance to the vast literature on significant composers, Garland is publishing an extensive series of research guides. This ongoing series encompasses more than 50 composers; they represent Western musical tradition from the Renaissance to the present century.

Each research guide offers a selective, annotated list of writings, in all European languages, about one or more composers. There are also lists of works by the composers, unless these are available elsewhere. Biographical sketches and guides to library resources, organizations, and specialists are presented. As appropriate to the individual composer, there are maps, photographs or other illustrative matter, glossaries, and indexes.

Preface

Composers who are transitional figures within the operatic traditions have always held an uneasy place in both history and the scholarly literature that formulates such history. Their works are constantly evaluated, reevaluated, and ultimately discussed in terms of either what came before them or what came after them. Such is the case for the operatic works of Gaetano Donizetti.

It is true that the composer's earlier works in this genre are clearly in the Rossinian tradition. However, as his art evolved, finding inspiration in the works of Bellini and other contemporaries, Donizetti broke free of many of the formulaic approaches in vogue in the early nineteenth century, thereby allowing the form of the drama to suggest musical form. This technique was to find fruition later in the century in the work of Giuseppe Verdi. Not merely a figure of transition but an innovator as well, Donizetti produced a vast and varied output.

To date, the majority of scholarly publications on Donizetti have focused on the composer's operatic output. Indeed, this volume reflects that interest; the literature on the operas is at the core of this annotated bibliography. However, Chapter 10 provides citations to the available scholarly literature on the composer's works in other genres: instrumental music, vocal chamber music, and sacred music. Inclusion of these works should demonstrate that these forgotten works deserve more than a cursory glance.

This volume is not comprehensive in scope, but is highly selective. It is designed, however, to be as useful to the beginning researcher as it is to the more experience scholar. The organization of this bibliography is, in part, modeled on that of other published bibliographies of literature on Donizetti, most notably those that appear in the *New Grove Dictionary of Music and Musicians* (London: MacMillan, 1980) and its spinoff publication, *The New Grove Masters of Italian Opera: Rossini, Donizetti, Bellini, Verdi, Puccini* (New York: W. W. Norton, 1983). This approach will be familiar to many and therefore will aid in efficiently accessing the pertinent information found in this volume. Further, an arrangement from the general to the more specific allows the user of this book to find most of the essential literature on a given work in one place. Understandably, there will be some articles that focus on more than one work. In such instances, the reader should look to the name and subject indexes to find these citations. Each item within a section is numbered, with numbering consecutive throughout the volume.

This volume is not intended to be an exhaustive survey of the available literature on Donizetti and his works. It includes citations for books, articles, and disertations that are readily available to the scholar or novice researcher within the collections of various kinds of libraries. Published literature in English, Italian, French, and German may be found within the volume. Fully analyzed in this work are the proceedings of the two international conferences devoted to Donizetti (Bergamo 1983, 1993), as well as important collections of essays devoted to the composer's life and works (for example, *Gaetano Donizetti* [Milan: Nuove Edizioni, 1983]). In addition, the two journals dedicated to Donizetti, the *Donizetti Society Journal* and *Studi donizettiani*, are selectively analyzed. Further, citations for critical editions, libretti, and other contemporary sources are included. Citations for libretti include not only those recently published but also nineteenth-century publications that are held in the Albert Schatz Collection at the Library of Congress. Microfilm copies of these particular sources may be found at the University of Virginia Music Library. The contemporary sources cite the publication of nineteenth-century vocal scores but do not attempt to work out the publication history of these sources—that is, their reprinting by other publishers or by the original publishers. This volume provides the information necessary to begin to undertake research on various aspects of the composer's life and works, and also includes a highly selective discography and videography. The discography cites recordings currently available in compact disc format (including remasters from long-playing discs), but only notable LPs. The reader should look to *Schwann Opus* or to any of the myriad trade discographies for a fuller listing of available recordings. The discography listing in each sections is not fully annotated.

Excluded from the work are ephemeral publications such as playbills, programs from various productions and revivals, newspaper articles, reviews of productions (both contemporary and modern), and recordings in all formats. RISM sigla are used for all manuscript locations.

Acknowledgments

This volume would not have been possible without access to the wonderfully rich collections held by the Cornell University Library and, in particular, the Cornell Music Library. I am eternally grateful to the Interlibrary Services Department of the Cornell University Library (Julie Copenhagen, administrative supervisor), which quickly and efficiently found several publications needed to complete this volume. Several individuals also must be thanked: foremost Roger Parker, for setting me onto this project; then, a number of people who provided me with leads to some of the literature cited within, or offered support and suggestions along the way: Emanuele Senici, Rebecca Harris-Warrick, and David Rosen. It is to these colleagues that I dedicate this work.

James P. Cassaro
University of Pittsburgh

GAETANO DONIZETTI

Chronology

1797   Born in Bergamo, 29 November 1797, the fifth child of Andrea Donizetti, a porter in a pawnshop, and Domenica Nava, a weaver. The family lives in extreme poverty in the Borgo Canale, in the old section of the city.

1806   Donizetti is enrolled in a free music school conducted by Giovanni Simone Mayr, who is the maestro di cappella at Santa Maria Maggiore in Bergamo. Attending the school until 1814, Donizetti studies a broad range of music, mostly by composers of the Viennese School. In addition to Mayr, Donizetti is instructed as well by Francesco Salari, who gives him singing lessons, Antonio Gonzales, and Giuseppe Antonio Capuzzi.

1811   Mayr arranges and partially subsidizes Donizetti's travel to Bologna to study counterpoint with Padre Mattei. His first attempts at composing opera are undertaken in Bologna, producing the works *Il Pigmalione* and *L'ira d'Achille,* neither of which is performed, and *Olimpiade,* which he does not complete.

1817   Donizetti returns to Bergamo where Mayr arranges a contract for him with the impresario Zancla for a series of operas to be produced in Venice. These operas include *Enrico di Borgogna, Una follia,* and *Il falegname di Livonia.*

(None of these works may be considered remarkable, but they reveal the young Donizetti's process as he developed his skills at portraying drama onstage.)

1817– In this period, Donizetti composes many nonoperatic works,
1821   including cantatas, several short sacred pieces, some orchestral sinfonias, and assorted works for the piano. The influence of study with Mayr on Donizetti's early style may be seen in the series of string quartets that are composed during this time.

1822   Mayr turns over to Donizetti a contract for an opera. This commission results in Donizetti's first real operatic success: *Zoraide di Granata*, which premieres January 28 at the Teatro Argentina in Rome. After this initial success, Donizetti receives an offer from Domenico Barbaja to write an opera for the Teatro Nuovo in Naples. His first opera for this theater is *La zingara,* which premieres on May 12.

1822– In this productive but not overly successful period, Doni-
1827   zetti composes two to five operas per year. His tremendous focus of attention and speed in composing dramatic works will remain a hallmark of his compositional method. These operas are created mainly for houses in Naples, but also for La Scala in Milan, where his *Chiara e Serafina* premieres in 1822. Works for Rome, Palermo, and Genoa are produced during this period as well. Donizetti meets with some success with these works, especially in the latter cities, but does not achieve the international fame that he ardently desires. After 1827, Donizetti is regularly conducting and preparing operas by other composers for production in Naples.

1828   Donizetti marries Virginia Vasselli, the daughter of a Roman lawyer. None of the three children of this marriage survives infancy. This year sees the premieres of four new operas: *L'esule di Roma, Gianni di Calais,* and *Il giovedì grasso* in Naples, and *Alina, regina di Golconda* in Genoa.

1830   The premiere and ultimate success of *Anna Bolena* in Milan at the Carcano on August 23 marks a turning point in Donizetti's career, as well as in his compositional style.

1832   Increasingly dissatisfied with the limitations that Naples places on the broadening of his career, Donizetti breaks his contract there to accept offers from other theaters. His first major success after this break is with *L'elisir d'amore,* which premieres at the Canobbiana in Milan on May 12.

1833   Two operas are produced in Rome during this year: *Il furioso all'isola di San Domingo* and *Torquato Tasso.* The experience leads to an interaction with the young Italian baritone Giorgio Ronconi, whose forceful dramatic power gives Donizetti the opportunity to exploit this particular type of voice within his works. This relationship between composer and performer provides both singer and composer with some of the most fulfilling moments of their respective careers. The well-received premiere of *Lucrezia Borgia* at La Scala in Milan, on December 26, begins a performance history of this work that is to span the next half century.

1834   Donizetti signs a new contract with the Teatro San Carlo in Naples for one new opera per year. The first of these was to have been *Maria Stuarda,* based on Schiller's play, but censors blocked its premiere. The composer reworks the opera to a new libretto and retitles it *Buondelmonte.* The premiere of this version of the opera is not successful.

1835   At Rossini's insistence, Donizetti travels to Paris to supervise a production of *Marino Faliero* at the Théâtre-Italien. Although the production is not well received, this visit exposes Donizetti to the genre of French "grand" opera as practiced by Meyerbeer and Halévy. Donizetti returns to Naples for the premiere of *Lucia di Lammermoor* on September 26 at the San Carlo. It is a resounding success, spearheaded by the performances of Carla Persiani as Lucia and Gilbert Duprez as Edgardo. The public reception of this work establishes Donizetti as a competitive force among contemporary operatic composers. At year's end, this high point in the composer's career is somewhat diminished by the failure of *Maria Stuarda* in a revised version at La Scala on December 30.

1836   *Belisario* premieres in Venice on February 4. The first of three operas that Donizetti is to write for this city, the work marks the composer's first attempt at interpolating attributes of French grand opera into his personal style. Later in this year, Donizetti composes two one-act comic operas to libretti of his own devising: *Il campanello* and *Betly,* both for the Teatro Nuovo in Naples. For San Carlo that autumn, he produces *L'assedio di Calais,* reviving an antiquated tradition of including a male role written for a female contralto voice.

1837   In this year, Donizetti is offered the directorship of the Naples Conservatory, but the appointment is delayed and ultimately falls through (the post eventually goes to Saverio Mercadante). The death of Donizetti's wife on July 30 devastates the composer, but he soon rouses himself for the rehearsals of a new work. The premiere of this opera, *Roberto Devereux*, in Naples on October 29 is a complete success.

1838–   The banning of Donizetti's opera *Poliuto* by the Neapoli-
1840   tan censors provides the catalyst for the composer to leave Naples and pursue a career in Paris. He arrives in Paris in October 1838, eager to take the city by storm. And indeed he does. During the next two years, Donizetti has operas performed at four theaters in Paris, much to the amazement of his French colleagues. Ultimately, this success leads to an attack by Berlioz in the *Journal des débats*. The operas produced include *Lucie de Lammermoor*, the French version of *Lucia*, for the Théâtre de la Renaissance in 1839, *La fille du régiment* for the Opéra-Comique in February 1840, *Les martyrs*, the original *Poliuto* expanded into four acts to a French libretto by Scribe, for the Opéra in April 1840, and *La favorite* for the Opéra in December. This last work, after an uncertain beginning, is quickly established in the repertoire.

1841– Donizetti hopes his success in Paris will earn him
1842   enough money to allow him to retire from the taxing world
of composing opera, but this is not to be. His health begins
to decline. Nevertheless, Donizetti pours himself into composing with an intensity unsurpassed until he can no longer
concentrate sufficiently to produce large-scale works. His
Adelia is a fiasco at its premiere in Rome in February 1841.
The work of the censors in Milan color the performances of
Maria Padilla in December of the same year. At Rossini's in-
vitation, Donizetti goes to Bologna to conduct the elder
composer's *Stabat Mater*. Rossini urges Donizetti to accept
the post of maestro di cappella at San Petronio in Bologna,
but instead he travels to Vienna to seek an appointment as
Kapellmeister to the Austrian court. This post would allow
Donizetti six months' leave annually so that he could pursue his career in other arenas. The success of his *Linda di
Chamounix* at its Viennese premiere in May 1842 assures
his appointment to this position.

1843– *Don Pasquale* premieres at the Théâtre-Italien in Paris to
1844   unparalleled success, thanks to the talents of Grisi, Mario,
Tamburini, and Lablache. Donizetti's comic masterpiece
firmly establishes itself in the repertoire. However, the exterior effervescence of this opera gives little indication of
the composer's deteriorating state of health. In June 1843,
the successful premiere of *Maria di Rohan* in Vienna gives the
baritone Ronconi another opportunity to display his acting
ability. While Donizetti is preparing his last opera, *Dom
Sébastien, roi de Portugal,* for the Paris Opéra in November,
his erratic behavior raises some concern about his abilities.
Although several passages of this work contain some of the
composer's finest music, the opera ultimately fails.

1845– At the close of the 1845 opera season in Vienna, Doni-
1846   zetti returns to Paris; the decline of his mental state continues to affect him. On 28 January 1846, his doctors diag-
nose him as suffering from a degeneration of the brain and
spine, a condition of syphilitic origin. They recommend that
Donizetti be institutionalized, and the composer is moved
to the sanatorium at Ivry, where he resides until June 1847.

1847– With the aid of his family, Donizetti, now paralyzed and
1848   unable to speak, moves back home to Bergamo. He arrives
        there in October 1847. Here family and friends tend to him
        until his death on the morning of 8 April 1848. After an au-
        topsy, which confirms his doctor's earlier diagnosis, Doni-
        zetti is laid to rest in the Pezzoli family vault in Bergamo's
        Valtesse Cemetery. In 1875, his remains, along with those of
        his beloved mentor, Mayr, are moved to Santa Maria Mag-
        giore in Bergamo.

General Sources

Here are cited general information sources that provide brief articles on Donizetti's life and works as contained in various dictionaries, encyclopedias, and spinoff publications, as well as guides to recorded sound, plot summaries, and collections of libretti.

A. Dictionaries, Encyclopedias, and Indexes

1. Ashbrook, William, and Julian Budden. "Gaetano Donizetti." In *The New Grove Masters of Italian Opera*, 93–152. The New Grove composer biography series. New York: W. W. Norton, 1983. ISBN: 0-393-30089-7. LC: ML 390.N466 1983.

Covers the life and works of the composer, including the findings of recent research, by revising the entry that originally appeared in *The New Grove Dictionary of Music and Musicians* (Macmillan, 1980). The bibliography is also updated.

2. Ashbrook, William, John Black, and Julian Budden. "Donizetti, Gaetano." In *The New Grove Dictionary of Opera*, 1206–1221. London: Macmillan, 1992. ISBN: 0-935859-92-6. LC: ML 102.O6 N5 1992.

Unlike *The New Grove Masters of Italian Opera* previously cited, the discussion of works in this resource is limited to the operas.

After a short biographical sketch, which includes an overview of Donizetti's character, a listing of the operas (with the usual date and place of premiere, librettist, genre [buffa, semiseria, etc.] and location of autograph manuscript), and a bibliography up to 1992 follow. This dictionary also includes separate articles (mainly extended plot summaries) on most of the composer's operas. In general, this publication is an excellent resource for information on singers, theaters, and other topics that relate to the genre of opera.

3.   Ashbrook, William. "Donizetti, Gaetano." In *International Dictionary of Opera*, vol. 1, 354–359. Detroit: St. James Press, 1993. ISBN: 1-558-62081-8. LC: ML 102.O6 I6 1993.

Includes a short biography, but predominantely contains a worklist of the operas and a bibliography up to 1990.

4.   Barblan, Guglielmo. "Donizetti, Gaetano." In *Die Musik in Geschichte und Gegenwart*, vol. 3, 676–683. Kassel: Bären-reiter, 1954. LC: ML100 .M92.

Until the revised edition (Kassel: Bärenreiter, 1994–) produces its projected twelve volume *Personenteil*, this remains the major German-language music encyclopedia. The article on Donizetti consists mostly of a biography of the composer, with a very short discussion of his works and popular reception. The worklist is not as complete as in later publications, and the bibliography is highly selective.

5.   _____. "Donizetti, Gaetano." In *Dizionario enciclopedico universale della musica e dei musicisti*, vol. 2, 522–537. Turin: Unione Tipografico-Editrice Torinese, 1985. ISBN: 8-802-03931-3 (v. 2).

An expanded and updated version of the entry for Donizetti that Barblan provided in *La Musica* (Turin: Tipografico Sociale Torinese, 1966–1971, 259–283). Contains an extended biographical sketch of the composer, with an overview of his works and of his personality. A complete list of works and a select bibliography (divided into categories by form and function) appears at the end.

6.   Cohen, H. Robert. *Les gravures musicales dans "L'illustration," 1843–1899*. La vie musicale en France au dix-neuvième siècle: études et documents. Québec: Les Presses de l'Univer-

sité Laval, 1983. ISBN: 2-763-76833-4. LC: ML 270.4.G7
1983.

A three-volume set of iconographical evidence covering the period
1843–1899. The original engravings run the gamut from set designs, costumes, caricatures, orchestras, audiences, and portraits.
The third volume is the index to the work.

7.   Loewenberg, Alfred. *The Annals of Opera, 1597–1940.* 3rd
      ed., rev. and corrected. Totowa, N.J.: Rowman and Littlefield,
      1978. ISBN: 0-87471-851-1. LC: ML 102.O6 L6 1978.

Chronological arrangement. An alphabetical index of operas (pp.
756–785), composers (pp. 786–827) and librettists (pp. 828–851)
is included. Does not list any subsequent performances within a
country other than the premiere, and contains some inaccuracies.
Dates supplied often conflict with the source cited next.

8.   Manferrari, Umberto. *Dizionario universale delle opere melo-
      drammatiche.* Contributi alla biblioteca bibliografica italica,
      4, 8, 10. Florence: Sansoni, 1954–1955. 3 vols. LC: ML
      102.O6 M3.

A chronology of operatic performances compiled from information
predominantly found in Italian theatrical journals and arranged alphabetically by composer. Coverage is up to 1950. Supplies less information than the previously cited source (no cast lists, for
example), and sometimes conflicts with, it. A bibliography of
sources consulted appears on pp. 8–16. Entries for Donizetti are
found in the first volume, pp. 321–335.

9.   Meloncelli, Raoul. "Donizetti, Gaetano." In *Dizionario bio-
      grafico degli Italiani*, vol. 41, 185–200. Rome: Istituto dell'
      Enciclopedia Italiana, 1992. LC: CT 1123.D5.

An extended biographical article in a general Italian dictionary.
The composer's life and works are assessed, and quotations from
the published literature underscore the facts presented in the text.
At the end is a worklist, complete for the operas, but not for works
in other genres. Here, selected works are given, with citations
to the publications in which full listings appear. A bibliography is
included.

10.   Miller, Norbert. "Gaetano Donizetti." In *Pipers Enzyklo-padie des Musiktheaters,* vol. 1, 737–766. Munich: Piper, 1986. ISBN: 3-492-02411-4 (v. 1). LC: ML 102.O6 P5 1986.

Essentially a collection of plot summaries for selected Donizetti operas written between 1826 and 1835. The difference between this publication and the plot summary sources cited in subsequent entries is that this article includes performance duration, orchestra requirements, and a short overview of each work's genesis and reception. Selected bibliographies appear at the end of each discussion of a particular work.

11.   Parsons, Charles H. *Opera Premieres: An index of casts,* vol. 1, 328–340. The Mellen Opera Reference Index, v. 13–14. Lewiston, N.Y.: Edwin Mellen Press, 1992. ISBN: 0-88946-412-X (v. 1). LC: ML 102.O6 P25 1986.

Alphabetically arranged by composer and then by title, this source lists the place and date of the opera's premiere and the singers who created the various roles.

12.   Pitou, Spire. *The Paris Opéra: An Encyclopedia of Operas, Ballets, Composers, and Performers.* New York: Greenwood, 1990. ISBN: 0-313-26218-7. LC: ML 1727.8.P2 P5 1983.

Essential source for basic information of a historical nature on ballet and opera at the Academie Royal de Musique (the Paris Opéra). Vols. 3–4, "Growth and Grandeur, 1815–1914," include entries in alphabetical order on operas, ballets, singers, dancers, composers, choreographers, librettists, and set designers. A brief bibliography appears at the end of each entry.

13.   Raeburn, Michael. *The Chronicle of Opera.* London: Thames and Hudson, 1998. ISBN: 0-500-01867-7. LC: ML 1700.R34 1998.

Presents the premieres of Donizetti's operatic works in context with other composers of the period, thereby characterizing his career as a successor to Rossini and precursor to Verdi. Lavishly illustrated, with sidebar information on composers, singers, and theaters, the chapters covering 1817–1821 (Weber and German Romanticism),

1822–1828 (Romantic Opera), 1829–1835 (Bel Canto), 1836–1841 (Successors to Rossini), and 1842–1850 (Verdi and Wagner) give a vivid, if brief, account of Donizetti's career.

14. Sartori, Claudio. "Donizetti, Gaetano." In *Enciclopedia dello spettacolo*, 858–866. Rome: Le Maschere, 1954–1957. LC: PN 1625.E7.

A short biography of the composer in Italian. As the title of the dictionary suggests, the article is well illustrated with scenes from nineteenth- and early-twentieth-century productions of Donizetti's operas. It contains a full worklist, including titles of projected operas never composed. A bibliography of important literature up to 1955 follows the entry.

15. Warrack, John, and Ewan West. *The Oxford Dictionary of Opera*, 198–200. Oxford: Oxford University Press, 1992. ISBN: 0-198-69164-5. LC: ML 102.O6 W37 1992.

A short biographical sketch with worklist, perfect for the reader who wants a brief overview of Donizetti's life and works. A very short bibliography of important literature is included.

B. Discographies

16. Ashbrook, William. "Gencer and Donizetti." *Opera Quarterly* 6/3 (Spring 1989): 135–137.

The Turkish soprano, Leyla Gencer, played an important role in the renaissance of interest in Donizetti. Hers was an uneven voice, but her intense involvement with the characters she portrayed allowed her to communicate far beyond the footlights. She was a singing actress in the vein of Maria Callas for whom she was understudy for *Anna Bolena* at La Scala in 1957. This article reviews four live recordings of *Anna Bolena*, *Lucrezia Borgia*, *Maria Stuarda*, and *Roberto Devereux* that have been remastered onto compact discs. Each set includes complete libretti as well as essays on the soprano and her art.

17. Bollert, Werner. "Gaetano Donizetti: Opéra comique und opera buffa." *Musica* 23/4 (July–August 1969): 343–345.

A discographical essay on the operas *Il campanello, Don Pasquale, L'elisir d'amore, La fille du régiment,* and *Rita.* Citations for long-playing albums are given.

18.   Fairman, Richard. "Donizetti's Tudor Queens." In *Opera on Record* 3, 52–67. Dover, N.H.: Longwood Press, 1984. ISBN: 0-89341-531-6. LC: ML 156.4.O64 O553 1984.

Following a brief discussion of the history of a particular opera, a critical discographical essay is given for *Anna Bolena, Maria Stuarda,* and *Roberto Devereux.* At the end, bibliographical citations and cast lists for recordings of these works released between 1957 and 1983 are given.

19.   Giudici, Elvio. "Discografia del Donizetti napoletano," In *Donizetti e i teatri napoletani nell'Ottocento,* 236–238. Napoli: Electa, 1997.

Discography primarily of compact disc recordings of the Neapolitan operas, with listings of selected long-playing pressings as well. Arranged alphabetically by title of the works and then chronologically by date of release.

20.   Gray, Michael. *Classical Music Discographies, 1976–1988: A Bibliography.* Discographies, 34. New York: Greenwood, 1989. ISBN: 03-132-5942-9. LC: ML 128.D56 G7 1989.

The first cumulative supplement to *Bibliography of Discographies.* Volume 1: *Classical Music, 1925–1975* (New York: Bowker, 1977). It covers discographies that appear in books and in journal articles. Arranged alphabetically, entries for Donizetti may be found on pp. 71–73.

21.   Lanzani, Gaetano. "Discografia donizettiana." In *Gaetano Donizetti,* 275–278. Milan: Nuove Edizioni, 1983.

A discography of long-playing discs of Donizetti's works, arranged alphabetically under each category: operas, religious music, instrumental music, and vocal music.

22. Mordden, Ethan. "Donizetti." In *A Guide to Opera Record-ings*, 87–94. New York: Oxford University Press, 1987. ISBN: 0-19-504425-8. LC: ML 156.4.O46 M7 1987.

A critical review of opera recordings issued in the twentieth century. A chronological arrangement from opera's beginnings to the late twentieth century provides information on the development of per-forming styles, as well as measuring the quality of the recorded per-formances under discussion here. A brief history of opera on disc (pp. 3–15) is essential reading for those unfamiliar with discographical techniques. For Donizetti, the most well-known operas are examined.

23. Parker, Roger. "The Case of Donizetti: Some Recordings." *Opera Quarterly* 2/1 (Spring 1984): 171–179.

The seven recordings reviewed here of performances of *Mary Stu-art, Maria de Rudenz, L'esule di Roma, Fausta, Il furioso all'isola di San Domingo, Belisario,* and *Poliuto* demonstrate the inexhaustible variety of which Donizetti was capable. His use of fixed forms rarely lapses into formula or a mechanical adherence to tradition. Several aspects of performance practice are discussed here, most notably unauthorized cuts which can skew the work's reception and the lack of proper performing materials, such as scores and parts that do not conform to modern-day standards of editorial practice. In addition, the issue of recording Italian opera in English translation is also discussed.

24. Parsons, Charles H. *Opera Discography,* 88–111. The Mellen Opera Reference Index, v. 10–12. Lewiston, N.Y.: The Edwin Mellen Press, 1990. ISBN: 0-889-46410-3 (v. 10); 0-889-46411-1 (v. 11); 0-889-46497-9 (v. 12). LC: ML 102.O6 P25 1986.

Cites opera recordings produced up to 1989 that are "substan-tially" complete, although some abridged recordings are included. "Pirate" and other "off-air" recordings are also included. Alpha-betical arrangement by composer, with listing of singers, conduc-tors, and orchestras. Citations for both long-playing and compact disc recordings are given.

25. Rossi, Nick. "European Opera for the Record." *Fanfare* 8/5 (May–June 1985): 47–52.

A discography of Donizetti opera recordings.

26. Steiner-Isenmann, Robert. "Diskographie." In *Gaetano Donizetti: Sein Leben und seine Opern,* 523–532. Bern: Hallwag, 1982. ISBN: 3-444-10272-0.

A discography of long-playing albums of Donizetti's works. The list is divided into several sections: complete operas, opera highlights, arias on recital discs, songs, sacred music, and instrumental music.

C. Plot Summaries

27. Ashbrook, William. "Gaetano Donizetti." In *The Viking Opera Guide,* 267–291. London: Penguin Books, 1993. ISBN: 0-670-81292-7. LC: ML 102.O6 V55 1993.

Following a short biographical sketch of the composer, plot summaries for the majority of Donizetti's operas are given. Also included is information on librettists, date of composition, date and place of premiere, and available recordings.

28. Bourne, Joyce. *Who's Who in Opera: A Guide to Opera Characters.* Oxford: Oxford University Press, 1998. ISBN: 0-192-10023-8. LC: ML 102.O6 B68 1998.

An index to characters in various operas, which includes short plot summaries to provide context for the dramatic portrayal of operatic roles. For Donizetti, provides information on characters in *Anna Bolena, Don Pasquale, L'elisir d'amore, La favorite, La fille du régiment, Linda di Chamounix, Lucia di Lammermoor, Maria Stuarda,* and *Roberto Devereux.*

29. Czerny, Peter. *Opernbuch,* 221–241. Berlin: Henschelverlag, 1958. LC: MT 95.C985 O6 1958.

In German; includes a short biography of the composer, plot summaries for six mature works by Donizetti, and a most useful glossary of musical terms used in the book (pp. 974–1000).

30. Davidson, Gladys. *The Barnes Book of the Opera,* 179–198. New York: Barnes, 1962. LC: MT 95.D2 B4.

Provides plot summaries for six operas by Donizetti: *Anne Boleyn* (*Anna Bolena*), *The Daughter of the Regiment* (*La fille du régiment*), *Don Pasquale, The Favorite* (*La favorite*), *Lucia di Lammermoor,* and *Lucrezia Borgia.*

31. Drone, Jeanette M. *Musical Theater Synopses: An Index.* Lanham: Scarecrow Press, 1998. ISBN: 0-8108-3489-8. LC: ML 128.O4 D76 Suppl.

An index of citations to plot summaries of various operas, arranged alphabetically by title. A listing of sources indexed provides the key to the citations given. A composer index lists all of the Donizetti operas (pp. 325–326).

32. Jacobs, Arthur, and Stanley Sadie. *The Opera Guide,* 72–80. London: Hamish Hamilton, 1964.

Provides plot synopses for *L'elisir d'amore* and *Lucia di Lammermoor.* The brief analyses that follow the plot summary include musical examples to illustrate the effect intended by the composer.

33. Kobbé, Gustav. *The Definitive Kobbé's Opera Book,* 354–387. New York: G. P. Putnam's Sons, 1987. ISBN: 0-399-13180-9. LC: MT 95.K52 1987.

The standard source for opera plot summaries. The articles on individual operas contain not only a synopsis of the plot but include musical examples from the most memorable arias and ensembles. For Donizetti, ten of his mature and most well-known works are included.

34. Leopold, Silke, and Robert Maschka. *Who's Who in der Oper.* Kassel: Bärenreiter; Munich: Deutscher Taschenbuch Verlag, 1997. ISBN: 3-7618-1268-X (Bärenreiter); 3-423-32530-5 (DTV).

An index in German to characters in various operas, including short plot summaries that provide context for the dramatic portrayal of operatic roles. For Donizetti, provides information on characters in *Il borgomastro di Saardam, Il castello di Kenilworth, Don Pasquale, L'elisir d'amore, La fille du régiment, Il furioso nell'isola di San Domingo, Lucia di Lammermoor, Lucrezia Borgia, Maria Stuarda,* and *Roberto Devereux.*

35. Morley, Alexander F. *The Harrap Opera Guide*, 78, 84, 154. London: George G. Harrap, 1970.

Includes short plot summaries for *Don Pasquale, L'elisir d'amore,* and *Lucia di Lammermoor.* Entries are arranged alphabetically by title of the opera. An index by composer at the end of the listings helps to facilitate access to the plot synopses.

36. Sadie, Stanley, ed. *The New Grove Book of Operas*. London: Macmillan, 1996. ISBN: 0-333-65107-3.

Includes plot summaries; date, place, and cast of the premiere; and a brief performance history for *Anna Bolena* (p. 30), *Don Pasquale* (p. 165), *L'elisir d'amore* (p. 181), *La favorite* (p. 213), *La fille du régiment* (p. 225), *Lucia di Lammermoor* (p. 367), *Lucrezia Borgia* (p. 372), and *Maria Stuarda* (p. 398). A glossary of operatic terms is included, as well as indexes of role names and text incipits of arias and ensembles.

D. Libretti

Here are listed compilations of the libretti used for various performances of Donizetti's operas. Libretti for individual works from the Albert Schatz Collection in the Library of Congress or those published in this century are listed under the particular work.

37. Dorsi, Maria Letizia. *I libretti d'opera dal 1800 al 1825 nella Biblioteca del Conservatorio "G. Verdi" di Milano*. Musica e teatro. Milan: Associazione Amici della Scala, 1987.

Bibliographical citations for libretti in the conservatory's collection that include those for Donizetti's cantata *Aristea* (p. 41) and the operas *Chiara e Serafina* (p. 66), *Emilia di Liverpool* (p. 100), *Il fortunato inganno* (p. 128), and *La zingara* (p. 295).

38. Fabbri, Paolo. "I testi teatrali." In *Donizetti e i teatri napoletani nell'ottocento*, 61–64. Naples: Electa, 1997.

In order to study the texts set by Donizetti during his time in Naples (1822–1838), one must look at the libretti from the work's premiere, as well as potential changes and original titles that were suppressed by the censors. New versions of the works also add to the complexities of textual criticism in Donizetti studies.

39. Fuld, James J. *The Book of World-Famous Libretti: The Musical Theater from 1598 to Today*. New York: Pendragon, 1994. ISBN: 0-945-19348-3. LC: ML 128.O4 F8 1994.

Revised edition of the 1984 publication. Includes facsimiles of the title pages from the libretti for *Anna Bolena, Don Pasquale, L'elisir d'amore, La favorite, La fille du régiment, Linda di Chamounix, Lucia di Lammermoor, Lucrezia Borgia,* and *Maria Stuarda*. Each libretto has a complete bibliographical description and RISM sigla are included for collections that hold a copy.

40. Massa, Maria Rosa. *Libretti di melodrammi e balli nella Biblioteca Palatina di Caserta*. Ancilla musicae, 5. Lucca: Libreria Musicale Italiana, 1992. ISBN: 88-7096-064-1. LC: ML 136.C28 B536 1992.

Cites librettos for the following operas: *Alahor in Granata, Alfredo il Grande, Emila di Liverpool, Il fortunato inganno,* and *Lucrezia Borgia*.

41. Saracino, Egidio, ed. *Tutti i libretti di Donizetti*. Italy: Garzanti, 1993. ISBN: 8-8114-1056-8. LC: ML 49.D66 S2 1993.

A compilation of almost all the libretti texts set by Donizetti, with facsimiles of the original title pages. The introductory essays cover several topics, including biographical information on the librettists, the poetical changes Donizetti made to some of the texts (using *Le convenienze* and *Il campanello* as examples), the effects of censorship on the libretti (for example, with *Maria Stuarda*), and the composer's self-borrowings (as in the case of *La favorite*). The reasons that some libretti are left out of this publication are adequately discussed in the preface. One drawback to this source is that the editor chose in some instances to use libretti from performances other than the premiere.

Catalogs

42. Albinati, G. "Prospetto cronologico delle opere di Gaetano Donizetti." *Rivista musicale italiana* 4 (1897): 736–743.

Originally appeared in the *Gazzetta musicale* (Milan). Gives in chronological order the season, place, theater, and title of each opera; the genre of the work (semiseria, buffo, etc.); the librettist; and the performers of the premiere. There are also sections that cover the cantatas, sacred music, vocal chamber music, and instrumental works. Bibliographic footnotes are included.

43. Campana, Alessandra, Emanuele Senici, and Mary Ann Smart. *Donizetti a Casa Ricordi: Gli autografi teatrali*. Le fonti donizettiane, 1. Bergamo: Fondazione Donizetti, 1998.

An analytical catalog of all the manuscript musical sources for twenty-two of Donizetti's operatic works that are conserved in the archives of the publisher Ricordi in Milan. The sources are divided into three categories: autograph manuscripts, manuscripts that are partially autograph, and copies of parts with or without autograph corrections. The analytical descriptions of the sources are based on the division of the manuscript into musical numbers.

44. *Donizetti: Itinerari di un artista europeo*. Milan: Mazzotta, 1997. ISBN: 88-202-1243-9.

Catalog of an exhibition held at the Palazzo della Ragione, Bergamo, in 1997, and published on the occasion of the second centenary of the birth of Donizetti.

45. Emerson, John. *Catalog of Pre-1900 Vocal Manuscripts in the Music Library, University of California at Berkeley*. Berkeley: University of California Press, 1988. ISBN: 0-520-09703-3. LC: ML 136.B382 U63 1988.

Arranged alphabetically by composer, this catalog cites not only single manuscripts from a particular opera, but also analyzes the contents of manuscript anthologies held by this library. The single manuscripts that pertain to Donizetti may be found in nos. 191–196 (pp. 40–41) [for excerpts from *La fille du régiment*, *La favorite*, *Roberto Devereux*, *Marino Faliero*, *L'elisir d'amore*, and a substitute duet for Rossini's *La siège de Corinthe*] and the manuscript anthologies in no. 578 (p. 161) and no. 584 (p. 164).

46. Hughes-Hughes, Augustus. *Catalogue of Manuscript Music in the British Museum*. London: The Museum, 1908. LC: ML 136.L8 B72.

A catalog with entries arranged by genre or form. This may warrant the user to look in several places for the contents of manuscripts that have been separated and distributed throughout this three-volume set. Volume 2, "Secular Vocal Music," contains several entries for Donizetti. These include manuscript sources for *Le convenienze ed inconvenienze teatrali*, *Il furioso nell'isola di San Domingo*, *Lucia di Lammermoor*, *L'elisir d'amore*, and *Anna Bolena*. A reprint was issued in 1964.

47. Inzaghi, Luigi. "Catalogo generale delle opere." In *Gaetano Donizetti*, 133–278. Milan: Nuove Edizioni, 1983. LC: ML 410.D7 G23 1983.

The works are arranged in either chronological order (operas and oratorios) or alphabetical order (all other works). Alphabetical order does not exclude initial articles, so that "Il cavallo arabo" files under "I," not under "C." Includes locations of autographs and other contemporary printed editions. A title index of arias and ensembles in the operas, and for the solo songs, follows the

catalog. At the end may be found a short bibliography and selected discography.

48. Lajarte, Théodore de. *Bibliothèque musicale du Théatre de
    l'Opéra: Catalogue.* Paris: Librairie des Bibliophiles, 1878.

A catalog arranged chronologically in order of first performance at
the Paris Opéra in which a descriptive list of the various sources
held by the library for each particular work is given. For Donizetti,
the following operas are represented: *Les martyrs, La favorite,
Dom Sébastien, Roi de Portugal, Lucie de Lammermoor,* and *Betly.*
Reprint, Hildesheim: Olms, 1969.

49. Lindner, Thomas. "An Integral Catalog of Donizetti's Oper-
    atic Works." *Opera Quarterly* 14/3 (Spring 1998): 17–23.

A short catalog of the operas and cantatas. The listing of operas is
divided into two categories, "Completed and Performed Operas"
and "Unfinished Operas, Fragments, Dubia." Each citation gives
the genre of the work, the number of acts, the librettist, and the
date and place of the premiere.

50. Longyear, Rey M., comp. "Gaetano Donizetti." In *The Sym-
    phony, 1720–1840.* Reference volume: contents of the set and
    collected thematic indexes. New York: Garland, 1986. ISBN:
    0-8240-3860-6. LC: ML 128.O5 S95 1986.

Includes incipits for fourteen symphonies arranged by key. Dates
of composition, manuscript sources, instrumentation, and references to modern published scores, orchestral parts, and recordings
are included.

51. Malherbe, Charles. *Centenaire de Gaetano Donizetti: Cata-
    logue bibliographique de la section française à l'exposition
    de Bergamo.* Paris: Impr. de la Cour d'Appel, 1897. LC:
    Z 6817.D68 M25.

Not examined.

52. *The Mary Flagler Cary Music Collection.* New York: Pierpont
    Morgan Library, 1970. ISBN: 87598-000-9. LC: ML 136.N52 P5.

A catalog of the printed books and music, manuscripts, autograph letters, documents, and portraits in the collection of the Pierpont Morgan Library. Full bibliographic citations are supplied for the manuscript sources, and those that pertain to Donizetti may be found in nos. 102–104 (pp. 23–24) of the catalog. These include the manuscript of an unpublished song, "J'aime trop pour être heureux," a manuscript score for a recitative and aria from _Lucezia Borgia_ written for the tenor Nicholas Ivanoff, and the manuscript full score to a "Qui tollis" for tenor, chorus, and orchestra. Four autograph letters are included in the catalog for Donizetti. This entry is on p. 64.

53. Parsons, Charles H. _Opera Composers and Their Works_. The Mellen Opera Reference Index, vol. 1–4. Lewiston, N.Y.: Edwin Mellen Press, 1986. ISBN: 0-88946-401-4. LC: ML 102.O6 P25 1986 vol. 1–4.

A catalog arranged alphabetically by composer and then chronologically under each composer which supplies information on the genre, number of acts, premiere, librettists, and location of the autograph manuscript. There are some errors, and the user would be wise to compare information given here with that of the more authoritative catalog cited earlier compiled by Inzaghi. Entries for Donizetti may be found on pp. 483–488.

54. _Ricordi di Gaetano Donizetti esposti nella mostra centenaria tenutasi in Bergamo nell'agosto–settembre 1897, raccolti da Giuseppe e Gaetano Donizetti, collezione di proprietà dei fratelli Giuseppe e Gaetano Donizetti_. Bergamo: Istituto italiano d'arti grafiche, 1897, enlarged 2/1897.

Not examined.

55. Sacchiero, Valeriano. "Contributo ad un catalogo donizettiano." In _Atti del 1° convegno internazionale donizettiano_, 835–942. Bergamo: Azienda Autonoma di Turismo, 1983.

Presents the works of Donizetti that can be found in various European libraries. Locations are indicated using RISM sigla for the libraries and collections contained in the catalog. Not meant to be exhaustive, the catalog is divided into four categories: 1) autograph and manuscript copies of the stage works; 2) nineteenth-century vocal scores for the stage works; 3) autograph and manuscript copies of the sacred music, and 4) autograph and manuscript copies of the instrumental music (further divided into the categories of orchestral music, piano music, and chamber music).

56. Sacchiero, Valeriano and others. *Il Museo donizettiano di Bergamo*. Bergamo: Centro di Studi Donizettiani, 1970. LC: ML 136.B34 M84.

First published in 1936, this edition has a historical introduction, followed by a list of important performances of Donizetti's works between 1946 and 1969. The catalog contains six sections covering autographs and manuscripts, musical publications, theatrical publications, letters and documents, iconography, and artifacts.

57. Turner, J. Rigbie. *Four Centuries of Opera: Manuscripts and Printed Editions in The Pierpont Morgan Library*. New York: Pierpont Morgan Library/Dover Publications, 1983. ISBN: 0-486-24602-7. LC: ML 141.N4 P57 1983.

A chronologically arranged catalog of holdings in the Pierpont Morgan Library, with many facsimile illustrations, that is meant to illustrate the history of opera. The 1834 entry (pp. 54–56) covers the additional music composed by Donizetti to turn *Maria Stuarda* into *Buondelmonte*. On pp. 121–123, a selective checklist of opera manuscripts in the library's collections includes additional citations for excerpts from *Anna Bolena* and *Lucrezia Borgia*. The checklist of printed opera scores and libretti on pp. 124–127 includes a citation for the first edition of the piano-vocal score to *Torquato Tasso*.

58. _____. *Nineteenth-Century Autograph Music Manuscripts in the Pierpont Morgan Library*. New York: Pierpont Morgan Library, 1982. ISBN: 0-875-98077-5. LC: ML 136.N5 P56 1982.

An alphabetically arranged list of the nineteenth-century music manuscripts held in the Pierpont Morgan Library. In addition to the items listed in the preceding entry, the catalog includes citations for the songs *Chant bedouin, Io soffrirò tacendo*, and *J'aime trop pour être heureux*, as well as the manuscript to a *Qui tollis* for tenor, chorus, and orchestra.

Correspondence

59. Alborghetti, Federico, and Michelangelo Galli. *Gaetano Donizetti e G. Simone Mayr: Notizie e documenti*. Bergamo: Gaffuri e Gatti, 1875. LC: ML 390.A33.

An important collection of documents concerning the relationship of the composer to his teacher, Giovanni Simone Mayr, that includes many letters. These letters may be found on pp. 5–101. A list of works by Donizetti is included (pp. 143–151), as well as a work list for Mayr (pp. 153–158).

60. Allitt, John S. "A Recently Discovered Letter of Donizetti to Agostino Rovere." *Donizetti Society Journal* 1 (1974): 137–140.

A reproduction of the actual letter, which documents Donizetti's despair with singers, appears in *Studi donizettiani* 2; an English translation by Allitt is provided here.

61. Barblan, Gugliemo, and Frank Walker. "Contributo all'epistolario di Gaetano Donizetti." *Studi donizettiani* 1 (1962): 1–150.

One of the important collections of Donizetti's letters to appear after the 1948 publication by Zavadini. All of the letters are carefully transcribed.

62.   Cametti, Alberto. *Donizetti a Roma: Con lettere e documenti inediti.* Turin: Fratelli Bocca, 1907.

A compilation of the individual articles on Donizetti's career in Rome originally published from 1904 to 1907 in *Rivista musicale italiana*, vol. 11–14. The study is divided chronologically: part 1 covers 1822, and the years leading up to the premiere of *Zoraide di Granata*; part 2, 1823–1824; part 3, 1825–1827, including the premiere of *Olivo e Pasquale*; part 4, 1833 and *Il furioso nell'isola di San Domingo*; part 5, 1833 and *Torquato Tasso*; part 6, 1833–1841, from *Torquato Tasso* to *Adelia*; part 7, 1841 and *Adelia*; part 8, 1841–1869 from *Adelia* to *Il duc d'Albe*, and part 9, 1882 and *Il duc d'Albe*.

63.   Chesi, Marcella, ed. "Lettere inedite." *Studi donizettiani* 4 (1988): 7–120.

An additional collection of letters that were left out of the Barblan and Walker continuation of Zavadini. The letters were brought together by Barblan's wife, Marcella Chesi, in a joint project with the Centro di Studi Donizettiani in Bergamo. The letters are divided into categories: those that are dated; those that are without dates or have incomplete dates; letters written to Donizetti; letters of others that speak about Donizetti, and letters that concern Donizetti's final illness. An index to the letters appears on pp. 121–126 of the volume.

64.   Commons, Jeremy. " Una corrispondenza tra Alessandro Lanari e Donizetti (45 lettere inedite)." *Studi donizettiani* 3 (1978): 9–74.

Zavadini's monumental collection of letters of Donizetti, while exhaustively covering the composer's music, does not contain correspondence with others besides the musicians with whom the composer often worked. This collection focuses on Donizetti's interaction with the Italian impresario Alessandro Lanari. Lanari is mainly associated with the Teatro della Pergola in Florence. However, he also oversaw the premieres of several operas by Donizetti in other Italian houses.

65.   Eisner-Eisenhof, Angelo, ed. *Lettere di Gaetano Donizetti.* Bergamo: Istituto Italiano d'Arti Grafiche, 1897. LC: ML 410.D7 E4.

A collection of letters compiled on the occasion of the centenary of Donizetti's birth. The letters written by Donizetti are addressed to numerous people. The collection, however, also includes letters written to the composer by others (most notably, Rossini, Scribe, Dumas, Spontini, Adam, and Verdi.)

66. Galeati, Paolo, ed. *Lettere inedite di G. Rossini e G. Donizetti*. Imola: Tipografia del Galeati e Figlio, 1889.

A selection of letters of Rossini and Donizetti.

67. Lippmann, Friedrich. "Autographe Briefe Rossinis und Donizettis in der Bibliothek Massimo, Rom." *Analecta musicologica* 19 (1979): 330–335.

Discusses several autograph manuscripts from the collection of the princely house of Massimo in Rome. The documents include previously unknown letters from Rossini to several recipients, as well as a previously unknown autograph letter from Donizetti to Scribe dated 20 September 1843. This single letter in French is fully transcribed.

68. Marchetti, Filippo, and Alessandro Parisotti. *Lettere inedite di Gaetano Donizetti*. Rome: Unione Cooperative Editrice, 1892. LC: ML 410.D7 C28.

One of the first important publications devoted entirely to Donizetti and probably issued in anticipation of the centenary of the composer's birth. This collection of letters covers the period from 1837 to 1845, with the greater part of the letters addressed to Donizetti's father-in-law, Antonio Vaselli.

69. Pugliese, Giuseppe. "Appunti per uno studio sui motivi letterari e poetici dell'epistolario di Donizetti." In *Atti del 1° Convegno Internazionale di Studi Donizettiani*, 699–720. Bergamo: Azienda Autonoma di Turismo, 1983.

One of the many gaps in the bibliography of Italian music is the lack of a history of the correspondence of the great musicians. As such, the published correspondence of Rossini, Bellini, Verdi, and Donizetti is briefly described. Critical readings of these letters are based on what the reader is looking for. A critical reading of Donizetti's correspondence results in the identification of some important characteristics:

the consistent poeticism in many parts, as well as the becoming and maturing of the composer's style. This latter characteristic is paralleled in the maturing of Donizetti's personality as a man and as an artist.

70. Schlitzer, Franco. "Curiosità epistolari inedite nella vita teatrale di Gaetano Donizetti." *Rivista musicale italiana* 50 (1948): 273–283.

Reproduces several interesting letters, unpublished at the time this article appeared, that shed light on Donizetti's theatrical life. Perhaps the most important of these letters are those from Alexandre Dumas concerning a libretto to a projected opera, and from Donizetti to Salvatore Cammarano concerning the time it took to compose *Lucia di Lammermoor*.

71. Speranza, Francesco, ed. "Lettere inedite di Donizetti." *Studi donizettiani* 2 (1972): 97–132.

A continuation of the letters presented by Barblan and Walker cited in item 61. The same care is given to providing accurate transcriptions of the correspondence.

72. "An Unpublished Donizetti Letter." *Donizetti Society Journal* 2 (1975): 271–274.

Includes a facsimile of a letter from Donizetti to Sig. G. Peluti postmarked 24 February 1838 discussing the fate of the composer's *Maria de Rudenz* and *Parisina*. A partial English translation is given, but the letter is not fully transcribed.

73. Zavadini, Guido. *Donizetti: Vita, Musiche, Epistolario.* Bergamo: Istituto Italiano d'Arte Grafiche, 1948. LC: ML 410.D7 Z3.

A veritable landmark of Donizetti scholarship in the twentieth century, this publication contains a short biography of the composer, a work list, and a collection of 726 letters. Many of the letters had been previously published, but Zavadini reedited a majority of them, correcting misreadings, restoring uncited cuts and words that had been censored, and included 246 hitherto unknown letters. The location of the letters, whether previously published or newly edited, is given.

Biographical Sources

This section includes memoirs.

74. Allitt, John. *Donizetti in the Light of Romanticism and the Teaching of Johann Simon Mayr*. Shaftesbury, Dorset [England]; Rockport, MA: Element, 1991. ISBN: 18-523-0299-2. LC: ML 410.D7 A7 1992.

Within the research that has resulted from the Donizetti Renaissance of the 1950s and 1960s, an essential aspect of Donizetti's life and works was ignored, that of Giovanni Simone Mayr as key to a fundamental understanding of the composer. Mayr was a member of the Bavarian "Illuminati" and traveled to Italy in hopes of "reforming" Italian music. This book gives insight into Donizetti's art that resulted from the quality of teaching he received from Mayr, which was basic to his creative life. Each chapter in this book essays a particular aspect of the composer, ranging from his relationship to the Romantic movement to his relationship to Christian tradition and religious thought of the period. The various aspects surveyed are then synthesized as the key to six operas—*Linda di Chamounix, Maria Stuarda, L'elisir d'amore, Lucia di Lammermoor, Poliuto,* and *Don Pasquale*—which the author feels reveals all there is to know about the composer. At the end, a catalog of works arranged by genre indicating manuscript sources, premiere performance information, and published scores is included (pp. 189–289). A select bibliography can be found on pp. 291–295.

75. Angeloni, Giuseppe. "Gli anni della prima èta." In *Gaetano Donizetti*, 11–18. Milan: Nuove Edizioni, 1983.

A biographical essay that attempts to give context to the environment that Donizetti was exposed to during his early childhood. As such, it covers the demographics of Bergamo in the late eighteenth century, describes the neighborhood and house the composer lived in, and provides genealogical information on Donizetti's ancestors and siblings. Interestingly, all of the composer's brothers survived while the sisters all died at an early age of either epilepsy or tuberculosis. Donizetti's early education and training at the Capella Musical of Santa Maria Maggiore is also covered and a description of the intensity with which he pursued his studies is given. At the end may be found a biography of Donizetti's mentor, Giovanni Simone Mayr and his method of instruction.

76. Antonini, Giuseppe. "Un episodio emotivo di Gaetano Donizetti." *Rivista musicale italiana* 7 (1900): 518–535.

At the time this article was published, no biography of Donizetti from a psychological point of view had been written. The author attempts to fill this gap by exploring the clinical and anthropological elements of the composer's nature, thereby presenting a more complete picture of Donizetti's personality and genius.

77. Ashbrook, William. *Donizetti*. London: Cassell, 1965. LC: ML 410.D7 A8.

The first 350 pages of this book furnish a standard biography of the composer. The second part, more analytical in tone, provides essays on the formal structures Donizetti used in his operas, aspects of his compositional style, and the composer's revisions and self-borrowings. There is also a discussion of the librettists Donizetti worked with and the librettos they produced. An extensive bibliography appears on pp. 521–532.

78. Barblan, Guglielmo. "Donizetti in Naples." *Donizetti Society Journal* 1 (1974): 105–119.

There are no extant documents to indicate why in 1822 Donizetti decided to leave the success he found in Rome after the premiere of

Zoraide di Granata and go to Naples. Perhaps the void created by Rossini's departure from Naples to find additional success in Paris partially explains this move. Once in Naples, Donizetti wasted little time in convincing the public that he was a worthy successor to Rossini. The first step was to "Neapolitanize" himself, learning about the musical as well as the social climate of the city. By doing so, Donizetti could then understand the proper scansion of the local dialect and infuse the proper idiomatic flavor into his operas. The twenty-one operas written during Donizetti's thirteen-year tenure in Naples are discussed. Translated into English by Derek Turner.

79. Bonesi, Marco. "Note biografiche su Donizetti." *Bergomum* 40/3 (1946): 81–89.

In a letter dated 16 July 1861 now in the collection of the Biblioteca Civica in Bergamo, Bonesi, a fellow student of Donizetti at Mayr's school, reveals his understanding of Donizetti's compositional style, especially in regard to instrumental music. Bonesi describes the composer's ease at producing music, the power of his concentration when involved in a project, and the rapidity with which he worked. These are the exact traits that Mayr saw in his gifted student. Other biographical information may be found here, including a discussion of Donizetti's ability in the area of musical caricature.

80. Brindicci, Monica. "Cenni biografici." In *Donizetti e teatri napoletani nell'ottocento,* 254–256. Naples: Electa, 1997. ISBN: 88-435-8698-X.

A chronology of Donizetti's life and works in the context of other cultural events of the period.

81. Cicconetti, Filippo. *Vita di Gaetano Donizetti.* Rome: Tipografia Tiberina, 1864.

The earliest known biography of Donizetti, which contains many facts overlooked in more recent surveys of the composer's life.

82. Cottrau, Guillaume. *Lettres d'un mélomane.* Naples: A. Morano, 1885.

A musical history of Naples from 1829 to 1847.

83.   Dent, Edward. "Donizetti: An Italian Romantic." *Donizetti Society Journal* 2 (1975): 249–270.

Out of the hundreds of composers who produced operas between 1800 and 1850, only three names survive—Rossini, Bellini, and Donizetti. Biographers have often centered their efforts on the more interesting aspects of Rossini's and Bellini's personal lives rather than on any analysis of their music. Donizetti's life as well as his music has hardly been found as interesting. This article, in its own way, attempts to rehabilitate the composer's reputation and reception by fusing a brief discussion of biographical information with analyses of several of Donizetti's operas. Reprinted from *Fanfare for Ernest Newman*, pp. 86–107 (London: A. Baker, 1955).

84.   Donati-Pétteni, Giuliano. *Donizetti*, 3rd edition. Milan: Garzanti, 1947.

An important Italian biography of the composer.

85.   Everett, Andrew. "Illness, Caught at Paris." *Donizetti Society Journal* 4 (1980): 241–246.

There are numerous inaccuracies in biographies of Donizetti concerning his final illness and his place in the development of Italian opera. This article examines some of the facts in the composer's medical history and disputes quasi-psychological explanations of his condition, which was clearly caused by a specific kind of microorganism known today as "cerebral syphillis."

86.   Fayad, Samy. *Vita di Donizetti*. Storia & Storie. Milan: Camunia, 1995. LC: ML 410.D7 F39 1995.

An Italian-language biography of the composer, written in a more popular vein, by an author famous in Italy as a radio playwright and writer of comedies.

87.   Franken, Franz H. *Die Krankheiten* grosser Komponisten, Band 2, 201–244. Taschenbücher zur Musikwissenschaft, 105. Wilhelmshaven: F. Noetzel, 1989. ISBN: 3-7959-0420-X.

A medically oriented biographical study of Donizetti and several other composers, which provides information on the diseases and treatments of these artists as well as insights into their personalities and the stresses of everyday life. Includes a short bibliography of sources consulted in compiling the biography.

88. "Gaetano Donizetti: Elementi biografici e cronologia delle opere." In *Teatro alla Scala: Stagione 1983–84*, 80–81. Milan: Edizioni del Teatro alla Scala, 1984.

A chronology of Donizetti's life and operatic works.

89. Geddo, Angelo. *Donizetti (l'uomo, le musiche)*. Bergamo: Edizioni della Rotonda, 1956.

The first critical Italian-language biography of the composer, much like that in English written by William Ashbrook. A thorough biographical study is found in the first section, while the second section is a critical assessment of the music. A catalog of the operas and the string quartets appears on pp. 105–108. The short bibliography at the end (p. 233) cites Italian-language sources only.

90. Giazotta, Remo. "Donizetti ospite d'onore fra i dementi di Ivry." *Nuova rivista musicale italiana* 2/4 (July–August 1968): 725–734.

Discusses three unpublished documents (preserved in the Archivio di Stato in Milan) which shed some light on Donizetti's circumstances and illness in the last part of his life: 1) a petition dated 15 June 1846 from the Austrian charge d'affaires in Paris to Count Spaur, governor of Lombardy; 2) a report to the Milan Tribunal (dated 3 November 1847), and 3) a medical certificate.

91. Illo, John. "Donizetti in Decline: Another Memoir." *Opera Quarterly* 14/3 (Spring 1998): 55–64.

This particular memoir of Donizetti in his last years was penned in 1854 by Charles George Rosenberg, music critic for the London *Morning Post*. It originally appeared as "Gaetano Donizetti, the Composer" in a collection of essays entitled *You Have Heard of Them*, published by Rosenberg under his pseudonym "Q." Rosenberg's visit with Donizetti occurred in early 1844 or 1845 in Vienna and shows the composer in good humor despite his declining state of health.

92.   Mikoletzky, Lorenz. "Gaetano Donizetti und der Kaiserhof zu Wien: Neue Dokumente." *Analecta musicologica* 14 (1974): 411–413.

Discusses the financial aspect of the appointment of Donizetti as master of chamber music and court composer at Vienna. Also discusses the dispatch of a Viennese doctor to Paris in connection with the onset of Donizetti's severe illness.

93.   Northcott, Roger. "A Sketch of his Life and a Record of his Operas." *Donizetti Society Journal* 2 (1975): 229–248.

A rather popularized account of the composer's life and works reprinted from a pamphlet of the same title published in 1916 (London: The Printer's Press). Most useful for Donizetti studies is the author's description of the composer's physical and social nature. At the end is an alphabetical listing of the operas, citing original casts and the casts of the first performances in London.

94.   Oliario, T. "La malattia ed i medici di Gaetano Donizetti." *Minerva medica* 29/2 (October 1938): 4–30. LC: R 61.M48.

In August 1845, Donizetti was examined by two well-known Parisian physicians, Gabriele Andral and Luigi Leone Rostan. Andral was noted for his research on blood diseases, while Rostan's specialty was in diseases of the brain and arteriosclerosis. These physicians first thought that Donizetti's illness was brought on by fatigue. Other medical consultations revealed otherwise. This article, using correspondence, medical records, and an autopsy report thoroughly covers the extent and seriousness of the composer's illness. An interesting comparison of the changes in Donizetti's signature from 1816 to 1847 helps to illustrate the deterioration of the composer's health.

95.   Pougin, Arthur. "Donizetti." In *Musiciens du XIXe siècle*, 87–116. Paris, Fischbacher, 1911.

Pougin, trained as a violinist, also had a career as a writer on music and was one of the pioneers of French musicology. Although he published several separate biographies of French nineteenth-century musicians, Donizetti was not one of them. Here in this

anthology of short biographies, he fills that gap. Includes a facsimile of a letter by Donizetti.

96. Ragni, Sergio. "Le note in mostra." In *Donizetti e i teatri
    napoletani nell'ottocento,* 131–148. Naples: Electa, 1997.

A bibliographical essay arranged chronologically which provides
citations for primary and secondary sources (including iconographical) for the study of Donizetti's life and works.

97. Rowbotham, John F. "Donizetti." In *The Private Lives of the
    Great Composers,* 272–293. London: Ibister, 1892. LC: ML
    390.R87.

A popular biographical sketch of the composer, full of descriptive
passages written in the late-Victorian-era style, which paints a lively
portrait of the composer, his physical appearance, and his musical
output. As such, it is appropriate as a basis for historical criticism
as opposed to historical truth. At the end of the sketch, a synopsis
of Donizetti's life and works by James D. Brown is included.

98. Schlitzer, Franco. "Interessi ereditari: La dote di Virginia." In
    Mondo teatrale dell'ottocento, 109–120. Naples: Fausto
    Fiorentino Libraio, 1954.

Describes the correspondence and legal documents that pertain to
the process undertaken by Antonio Vasselli, Donizetti's brother-in-
law, to reclaim the dowry of his sister, Virginia, Donizetti's late
wife, from the composer's co-heir, Andrea Donizetti.

99. _____. "L'ultima pagina della vita di Donizetti." In
    Mondo teatrale dell'ottocento, 58–97. Naples: Fausto Fio-
    rentino Libraio, 1954.

Describes a group of letters in the possession of Giuseppe Donizetti
at the time of the composer's death. These letters came into the
hands of Guido Chigi Saracini who then donated them to the Accademia Musicale in Bergamo. The correspondence is between Donizetti's brothers, Giuseppe and Francesco, Giuseppe's son Andrea,
Gaetano's brother-in-law Antonio Vasselli, and the conductor Antonio Dolci. The author uses these letters to describe the final years
of Donizetti's life and the disease he succumbed to. Also published

as part of the series Quaderni dell'Accademia Chigiana, 28 (Siena: Ticci, 1953).

100. Steiner-Isenmann, Robert. *Gaetano Donizetti: Sein Leben und seine Opern*. Bern: Hallwag, 1982. ISBN: 3-444-10272-0.

A biography which utilizes almost all of the previously published Donizetti correspondence. It is written from the perspective of the composer using, however, linguistic means that provide objectivity. For the first time, it portrays Donizetti as a tragic, romantic personality. The author discusses the repertoire of forms in Donizetti's operas, their development from copies of Rossini to models for Verdi, and the strong mutual influences between Donizetti and Bellini. The book includes a guide to the operas (detailed lists of the individual numbers in relation to the content) as well as a glossary of technical terms.

101. Stierlin, Leonhard. *Biographie von Gaetano Donizetti*. Neu-jahrstück der Allgemeinen Musikgesellschaft in Zürich, 40. Zürich: Druck von Orell, Füssli und Comp., 1852. LC: ML 5.N48 no. 40.

An early German-language biography of the composer. In a short amount of space (eleven pages), the author outlines the composer's life and works and assesses his reception in German-speaking countries. As is usual in nineteenth-century literature of this type, a physical description of the man is given. At the end, a chronological table of Donizetti's operas is given.

102. Tintori, Giampiero. "L'uomo Donizetti." In *Gaetano Donizetti*, 19–24. Milan: Nuove Edizioni, 1983.

Reading Donizetti's letters, splendidly collected by Zavadini, reveals a perfect picture of the Lombardian workingman: a man very preoccupied with a quest for glory. These letters also provide important information on the composer's relationship with his brothers, Giuseppe and Francesco, as well as the profound effect of his illness on his personality and career.

103. Weinstock, Herbert. *Donizetti and the World of Opera in Italy, Paris, and Vienna in the First Half of the Nineteenth Century*. New York: Pantheon Books, 1963. LC: ML 410.D7 W4.

Written to fill the gap in available English-language books on Donizetti, this standard biography offers a historical account of the composer's life and works. A strength of this publication is found in the appendices, which include genealogical tables for the Donizetti and Vasselli families, English translations of Donizetti's baptismal and marriage certificates, and documents which pertain to the diagnosis of the composer's illness and the autopsy that was conducted after his death. Legal documents that offer insight into the history of *Lucrezia Borgia, Maria Stuarda,* and *Le duc d'Albe* are included. The scenario for a projected opera, , as well as a very useful table of present-day value of nineteenth-century Italian currency is given. The reader will also find biographical information on Donizetti's brothers, Giuseppe and Francesco, in this book.

Critical Studies

Here are cited critical studies that cut across Donizetti's life and works; studies that pertain to one work will be found later in the volume under the specific work.

104. Allitt, John. *Donizetti and the Tradition of Romantic Love: A Collection of Essays on a Theme.* London: Donizetti Society, 1975. LC: ML 410.D7 A53.

This book is not concerned with biographical facts about the composer, but strives to create a picture and an interpretation of Donizetti by attempting to answer several fundamental questions, including "What is the tradition that formed the composer's soul?" "Who was Giovanni Simone Mayr, Donizetti's beloved teacher and mentor?" and "What was the secret of Donizetti's beautiful music?" Starting with a biography of Mayr, the remainder of this work focuses on aspects of Donizetti the composer, the man, his relationship to the Romantic age, and his religious faith. The author then uses these themes to discuss the operas *L'elisir d'amore* and *Poliuto*.

105. _____. "Donizetti e Dante, un incontro." *Studi donizettiani* 3 (1978): 81–99.

Donizetti was introduced to Dante's works by his teacher, Giovanni Simone Mayr. Mayr considered this literature, as well as a knowledge of mythology, as essential to every musician. This article looks at Donizetti's works from a metaphysical perspective, one richly interpreted by Dante in *La vita nuova* and *La divina commedia*.

106. _____. "L'importanza di Simone Mayr nella formazione culturale e musicale di Gaetano Donizetti." In *Atti del 1° Convegno Internazionale di Studi Donizettiani*, 333–349. Bergamo: Azienda Autonoma di Turismo, 1983.

This article outlines Giovanni Simone Mayr's qualities: his participation with a group of philosophers, his religious devotion, and his involvement with the Freemasons. As such, the author looks at the principles upon which Mayr founded his music school at Santa Maria Maggiore in Bergamo, as well as his method of education. Finally, Mayr's *Dissertazione sul genio e sulla composizione* and its impact on Donizetti's compositional style and method is examined. Some of Mayr's thoughts have been translated by Allitt and appear as "The Notebooks of Giovanni Simone Mayr" (*Donizetti Society Journal* 1 [1974]: 141–148) and "Mayr Expresses Some Thoughts on Italian Opera" (*Donizetti Society Journal* 2 [1975]: 316–317).

107. _____. "The Mayr+Donizetti Collaboration: Rediscovering Donizetti through Discovering Mayr." In *L'Opera teatrale di Gaetano Donizetti: Atti del Convegno Internazionale di Studio*, 423–428. Bergamo: Comune di Bergamo, 1993.

Although Donizetti has been recently acknowledged as a major composer, there is still much work to accomplish in the renaissance of Donzietti studies. Giovanni Simone Mayr is probably even less well known than his prized pupil, but his significance for those interested in Donizetti is great. It was Mayr who led Italian opera on its path from the late eighteenth-century techniques of Cimarosa, Galuppi, and Paisiello into the new Romantic stylings of the early nineteenth century. His role as a reformer of the operatic genre, alongside Gluck, Haydn, and Mozart is also virtually unacknowledged. This article outlines the sources in the collection of the Biblioteca Civica in Bergamo that are available to research the life and works of Mayr. Such study would help us learn more about the elder composer's influence on Donizetti.

108. Allorto, Riccardo. "Bergamo e la rinascita donizettiana." In *L'Opera teatrale di Gaetano Donizetti: Atti del Convegno*

Internazionale di Studio, 27–33. Bergamo: Comune di Bergamo, 1993.

The annual festival given in Bergamo, "Donizetti e il suo tempo," has made considerable contributions to furthering our knowledge of the composer's life and works. This festival has its roots in the city's efforts to celebrate the centennial of Donizetti's death in 1948, and which now can be deemed the beginnings of this century's "Donizetti Renaissance." The scholarly aspects of the festival have forged a rebirth of musicological interest in Donizetti, and reconstruction of little-known or forgotten works has placed the composer's originality as separate from that of Rossini and early Verdi. Under the artistic direction of Bindo Missiroli and Adolfo Camozzo, the instrumental and chamber works of Donizetti were given center stage alongside the operas. An important outcome of this special mixture of performance and scholarship is the critical edition of Donizetti's operas sponsored by the city of Bergamo and the publisher Casa Ricordi. Recently, the festival has begun to include discussions and performances of other Bergamasc composers, chief among them Giovanni Simone Mayr. In Italian; with English summary.

109. Angermüller, Rudolph. "Il periodo viennese di Donizetti." In *Atti del I° Convegno Internazionale di Studi Donizettiani*, 619–697. Bergamo: Azienda Autonoma di Turismo, 1983.

An exhaustive account of Donizetti's stay in Vienna, a period noteworthy not for its length but for its importance to the composer's career. Using information found in several newly discovered local documents, the facts known about this period of Donizetti's creative life can be better organized and, as such, integrated into a complete history of the time. A critical assessment of two operas Donizetti wrote for Vienna, *Linda di Chamounix* and *Maria di Rohan,* is also provided. At the end, appendices provide excerpts from the contemporary critical press that help us to understand the reception of these two works.

110. Antonini, Giacomo. "Donizetti and Byron." *Donizetti Society Journal* 1 (1974): 91–104.

At the time Donizetti was writing the most important of his operas, the works of Byron were enjoying similar success across the European continent. It was, therefore, inevitable that Donizetti would be influenced by the poet, mainly through the librettists the composer utilized. Donizetti wrote three operas directly based on works by Byron and a fourth that uses Byron's poem "The Lament of Tasso" as a source of inspiration. The operas that show a direct influence are *Il diluvio universale*, based on Byron's *Heaven and Earth; Parisina; Marino Faliero*, based on Byron's play; and *Torquato Tasso*. However, Byron also had an indirect influence on the composer, one that can be seen in the characters in *Pia de' Tolomei, Belisario*, and *La favorite*.

111. Arruga, Franco Lorenzo. "Appunti e prospettive sulla drammaturgia di Donizetti." In *Atti del 1° Convegno Internazionale di Studi Donizettiani*, 743–774. Bergamo: Azienda Autonoma di Turismo, 1983.

A discussion of Donizetti's dramaturgical style, one which stresses that a firm understanding of the language of Italian Romantic opera is necessary to undertake research like this.

112. Ashbrook, William. "Acquisizioni culturali e scientifiche della Donizetti Renaissance." In *L'Opera teatrale di Gaetano Donizetti: Atti del Convegno Internazionale di Studio*, 43–53. Bergamo: Comune di Bergamo, 1993.

Donizetti never achieved the full glory he was due in his own lifetime. The recent renaissance of interest in his life and works has produced many worthy studies. Scholars must now assess the impact of this interest and think about future developments in the area of Donizetti studies. Certainly one of the most important results of this renewed interest in the composer is the separation of the former Rossini-Bellini-Donizetti entity into three distinct historical figures. This allows scholars to speak of Donizetti in his own right, without comparing his oeuvre to the other two composers. There are still many aspects of Donizetti's career that need investigating, including his relationship to his cultural context, and the clarification of his place in the theatrical hierarchy of the period, as well as comparative studies that concern Donizetti's audience and the social function of the theater.

113. _____. *Donizetti and His Operas*. Cambridge: Cambridge University Press, 1982. ISBN: 9-521-23526-X. LC: ML 410.D7.

An indispensable expanded version of the author's earlier book published by Cassell in 1965, which discusses the life and operatic output of Donizetti from a cultural and formal point of view. Arranged chronologically, the composer's use of operatic conventions, as well as his relationship to his forerunners, contemporaries, and successors—in particular, Rossini, Bellini, and Verdi—are thoroughly assessed. The various appendices cover plot synopses of the operas, information on projected and incomplete works, and biographical information on the various librettists that Donizetti worked with. A bibliography (pp. 701–707) points to other useful sources, and the index (pp. 709–744) helps the reader to quickly find information.

114. _____. "Donizetti and Romani." *Italica* 64/4 (Winter 1987): 606–631.

Of the approximately 125 composers who set the more than 80 librettos produced by Felice Romani, tradition most closely associated his name with Vincenzo Bellini, but the working relationship of Donizetti and Romani is of equal importance artistically and more representative of theatrical conditions in Italian opera houses during the 1820s and 1830s. If the directions toward which Donizetti's talent ultimately led him caused him to outgrow the sort of well-tailored, rather self-consciously literate texts that Romani could provide and to move into a climate at once more intense and less stable, his associations with the librettist had brought him, with *Anna Bolena, Parisina,* and *Lucrezia Borgia,* into his full maturity.

115. _____. *Donizetti: La vita.* Turin: EDT, 1986. ISBN: 88-7063-041-2.

An Italian translation by Fulvio Lo Presti of item 113 in this volume. The translator provides additions and annotations, as well as corrections of dates, details, and names found in Ashbrook's original work.

116. _____. *Donizetti: Le opere.* Turin: EDT, 1987. ISBN: 88-7063-047-2.

A continuation of item 115, also in Italian translation by Fulvio Lo Presti. The same kinds of alterations and corrections of information in Ashbrook's original work are evident.

117. _____. "La struttura drammatica nella produzione musicale di Donizetti dopo il 1838." In *Atti del 1° Convegno Internazionale di Studi Donizettiani*, 721–741. Bergamo: Azienda Autonoma di Turismo, 1983.

The basis of this essay is the analysis of those operas that Donizetti wrote for theaters in Paris and Vienna after 1838. Discussion centers on the dramatic structure of the works as demonstrated in the aria forms. The operas examined are *Les martyrs, La fille du régiment, La favorite, Linda di Chamounix, Maria di Rohan,* and *Dom Sébastien.* These works in particular show an expansion of the composer's ability to be expressive, as well as his movement away from the conventional constraints of recitative and aria.

118. Attardi, Francesco. "L'opera comica." In *Gaetano Donizetti*, 81–95. Milan: Nuove Edizioni, 1983.

After a brief discussion of opera seria form, this essay provides an analysis (structural, harmonic, and formal) of Donizetti's most important comic operas composed between 1824 and 1843. In addition, the issues of versification and rhyme scheme of the texts are considered, comparing Donizetti's style with earlier models. Further, the function of rhythmic gestures to portray comedy and the elements of both Donizetti's Italian and French comedies are examined.

119. Baldacci, Luigi. "Donizetti e la storia." In *Atti del I° Convegno Internazionale di Studi Donizettiani*, 5–27. Bergamo: Azienda Autonoma di Turismo, 1983.

The core aspect of Donizetti's dramaturgy is history. By this is meant that Donizetti is the only author of historical stories that Italy would ever know. Italian cultural circles knew well the historical romance, but not the historical story. The historical romance in Italy was a literary genre, but there was no real genre of historical story. The author discusses Donizetti's operatic output from this point of view: whether the work is historical romance or story. Also covers the genres of buffo and semiseria.

119a._____. *La musica in italiano: Libretti d'opera dell'ottocento*. Milan: Rizzoli, 1997. ISBN: 88-17-66072-8.

Full of great observations on linguistic and cultural aspects of the libretti to *Linda di Chamounix, Gemma di Vergy, Lucrezia Borgia, Parisina, Maria Stuarda, Belisario,* and *Pia de' Tolomei,* among other Donizetti works, this book covers aspects of situations, history versus nonsense, and the relationship of fathers and sons.

120. Balthazar, Scott L. *Evolving Conventions in Italian Serious Opera: Scene Structure in the Works of Rossini, Bellini, Donizetti, and Verdi, 1810–1850.* Ph.D. diss., University of Pennsylvania, 1985.

Study of arias, duets, and central finales from thirty-seven operas of Rossini, Bellini, Donizetti, and Verdi suggests that in the past we may have overestimated the conventionality of scene structures in Italian operas from the period 1810–1850. While Bellini, Donizetti, and Verdi clearly retained the outlines of Rossini's layouts for these types of scenes, they moved away from the relative stasis of Rossini's archetypes in several ways. Rossini himself led the way in many of these changes by experimenting in his late operas with new variations on formats he had popularized. In short, operatic structure did not stagnate during the period 1820 to 1850. Those years saw Bellini, Donizetti, Verdi, and even Rossini moving toward a freer, more active musical drama. Abstract abridged from *Dissertation Abstracts Online.*

121. _____. "The *Primo ottocento* Duet and the Transformation of the Rossinian Code." *Journal of Musicology* 7/4 (Fall 1989): 471–497.

The procedures codified by Rossini for the organization of lyric numbers in opera governed operatic practice in the early nineteenth century. By studying the operatic duets written between 1815 to 1850 by Rossini's contemporaries and successors, in particular those of Bellini, Donizetti, and Verdi, the changes in musical, poetic, and dramatic designs point to a disintegration of archetypal schemas and give rise to the structural continuity prevalent in the latter part of the century. Abstract abridged from *RILM Abstracts Online.*

122. Barblan, Guglielmo. "Attualità di Donizetti." In *L'opera italiana in musica: Scritti e saggi in onore di Eugenio Gara,* 59–73. Milan: Rizzoli, 1965. LC: ML 1733.O64.

An appraisal of research on Donizetti from 1948 (the beginning of the first Donizetti Renaissance and centenary of the composer's death) to 1965. Performances of works by the composer during this period are also assessed.

123. _____. "Donizetti in Naples." *Donizetti Society Journal* 1 (1974): 105–119.

Few documents survive that indicate why the young Donizetti decided to leave Rome after the success of his opera *Zoraide di Granata* and travel to Naples. The Neapolitan lyric theater had just seen the departure of Rossini, and the younger composer had a tremendous amount of work to do to fill the elder composer's shoes. Donizetti did not waste time in this effort, taking as his first step to learn as much as he could about the musical and social climate of the city. In addition, musically adjusting himself to the proper scansion of the local dialect lent a certain idiomatic flavor to his works. The author surveys the formalistic innovations that Donizetti created during his stay in Naples, as well as his use of music as a symbol of a character's pyschological state.

124. _____. "Gaetano Donizetti mancato direttore dei conservatori di Napoli e di Milano." In *Il melodramma italiano dell'ottocento*, 403–411. Saggi, 575. Turin: G. Einaudi, 1977. LC: ML 1733.4.M5.

Outlines the events that precipitated Donizetti's departure from Naples in 1838. Although originally thought to have been a result of the composer's problems with the local censors concerning the subject of his opera, *Poliuto*, the two other issues that forced the decision were Donizetti's lack of action in accepting the post of director of the Naples Conservatory and also that of the Conservatory in Milan.

125. _____. *L'opera di Donizetti nell'età romantica*. Bergamo: Banca Mutua Popolare, 1948.

Discusses how the Romantic streak manifests itself in the works of Donizetti's contemporaries, especially those of Spontini, Rossini, and Bellini. In Donizetti, a Romantic individualism manifests itself in the moral characteristics of the composer's personality, which, instead of stimulating a feeling of pride, leads to a loving, elegiac analysis of the "I." Studying the human conflicts that may be found in the libretti set by Donizetti allows for a mediation of the inherent pathological atmosphere that permeates these works.

126. Bezzola, Guido. "Aspetti del clima culturale italiano nel periodo donizettiano." In *Atti del 1° Convegno Internazionale di Studi Donizettiani,* 29–42. Bergamo: Azienda Autonoma di Turismo, 1983.

Donizetti's creative activity took place exclusively in a time that saw the birth, affirmation, and initial crisis of Romanticism. The characteristics peculiar to this period deal not so much with aesthetics, but more with sociopolitical issues. This article underscores the essential elements of nineteenth-century Italian melodrama and the possibilities they offer to better understand Donizetti's works.

127. Bini, Annalisa. "Donizetti, Napoli e le farse in un atto." In *Donizetti e i teatri napoletani nell'ottocento,* 51–60. Naples: Electa, 1997.

A revision of an article that originally appeared in *Gioachino Rossini, 1792–1868: Il testo e la scena* (Pesaro: Fondazione Rossini, 1994: pp. 565–585). The author defines the term "farsa" and outlines the term's usage in various musical centers of the eighteenth and nineteenth centuries. Primary examples of the form may be found in the works of Mayr, Rossini, and Carlo Coccia, among others. From this perspective, the operatic farces of Donizetti are examined, including some works in the genres of semiseria and opéra-comique. A list of the works discussed, including information on librettist, date and place of premiere, and cast is included.

128. Black, John. "Cammarano's Libretti for Donizetti." *Studi donizettiani* 3 (1978):115–131.

Salvatore Cammarano began his career as a librettist only in 1834, when he was in his mid-thirties and already had a reputation as a dramatist. This article summarizes a biography of the dramatist and his early experiences with producing libretti. Cammarano's libretto for *Ines de Castro,* set by Persiani, was the work that brought the poet to the attention of Donizetti. Their first collaboration produced *Lucia di Lammermoor,* one of the greatest successes in the history of the San Carlo theater. This success was key to the continued collaboration of the two. From 1835 to 1838, Donizetti set only libretti by Cammarano, and likewise, Cammarano produced libretti for no one but Donizetti. This article examines the sources of Cammarano's inspiration for six operas by Donizetti, arranged by date of production. As such, it is noted that during this collaborative period, under Donizetti's experienced tutelage, Cammarano was able to work out many technical problems, and to develop a trait that was to become a hallmark of his style as a librettist: the pathetic closing scene. Includes a summary in Italian.

129. _____. "Donizetti a Napoli." In *Gaetano Donizetti,* 25–32. Milan: Nuove Edizioni, 1983.

The sixteen years Donizetti spent in Naples saw a profound transformation in the composer, from a neophyte artist wanting to perfect his craft into a completely mature musician. During this period, he broke free from the conventional models that preceeded him (ones he closely imitated in his early works) and developed a powerful compositional style. This style was one of great originality and ultimately brought him international fame. This article provides an overview of this period in Donizetti's life and career, and reproduces several title pages from libretti for works that premiered during these years.

130. _____. "Donizetti and His Contemporaries in Naples, 1822–1848: A Study in Relative Popularity." *Donizetti Society Journal* 6 (1988): 11–27.

It is difficult to assess the popularity of the various composers of Italian opera in the nineteenth century due to the lack of comprehensive chronicles for the opera houses in Naples. The author has assembled a chronology of the five theaters that were regularly used for opera in Naples during the period from 1822 to 1848. Eight composers were selected as the basis of this study in popularity: Donizetti, Rossini, Bellini, Mercadante, Pacini, Raimondi, Luigi Ricci, and Vincenzo Fioravanti. From this study, the following conclusions are drawn: 1) Bellini's operas were extremely popular in the smaller theaters; 2) Donizetti was by far the most frequently performed; 3) Fioravanti, who composed opere buffe in Neapolitan dialect, was performed mainly at the Teatro Nuovo; 4) Mercadante had a comparative lack of success during this time; 5) Pacini was the least performed; 6) Raimondi had outstanding successes with opere buffe in the smaller theaters and with opera seria in the royal theaters: and 7) Ricci, another "vernacular" composer, was also more successful in the smaller theaters. Rossini is not well represented here as his departure from Naples in 1822 caused a substantial decline in performances of his works.

131. _____. *Donizetti's Operas in Naples, 1822–1848*. London: Donizetti Society, 1982. LC: ML 410.D7 B55 1982.

Discusses dates of performance (through the end of 1848) and censorship problems concerning the librettos. For each opera, gives the number of performances at the various theaters. Includes a calendar of all operas performed in Naples during the 1830s and 1840s.

132. Blier, Steven. "Waiting for Gaetano." *Opera News* 62/5 (November 1997): 36–43.

Donizetti is often thought of as a composer whose music is more fluff than substantive and much less interesting than Rossini and Bellini. His operas in particular are viewed by many as mediocre, with a few good roles or scenes that are vehicles for the singer. Clearly, Donizetti suffers from an image problem. This article chronicles the Donizetti revival of the late 1950s, spearheaded by singers such as Maria Callas, Virginia Zeani, and Leyla Gencer. Part of this image problem is that the recent interest in Donizetti's operas has come at a time when productions are dominated by a realism based on "verismo" techniques, and which makes the composer's romantic melodramas look ridiculous. However, our thoughts on Donizetti will change when we understand how he sought to overturn conventions and change the musical construction and dramatic intensity of nineteenth-century opera.

133. Brindicci, Monica, and Franco Mancini. "Cronologia degli spettacoli (1822–1860)." In *Donizetti e i teatri napoletani nell'Ottocento*, 239–246. Naples: Electa, 1997.

A performance history of Donizetti's operas given in Naples from 1822 to 1860. Includes the place and date of premiere, original cast lists, and dates of subsequent performances, as well as the names of set and costume designers.

134. Budden, Julian. "Aspects of the Development of Donizetti's Musical Dramaturgy." In *L'Opera teatrale di Gaetano Donizetti: Atti del Convegno Internazionale di Studio*, 121–133. Bergamo: Comune di Bergamo, 1993.

Mad scenes in opera, a long-established tradition in Italian opera, seem credited solely to Donizetti based primarily on one work: *Lucia di Lammermoor*. Using this work as a point of departure, the author surveys several dramaturgical elements of Donizetti's operas, including his diverse synthesis of formal structures, his narrative procedures that differ significantly from that of Bellini and Verdi, and his ability to express emotion using harmonic nuance rather than melodic contour. Stressing Donizetti's role as an element of transition between Rossini and Verdi the author concludes that Donizetti influenced Verdi but was also influenced by him. Summary in Italian (pp. 132–133).

135. Buldrini, Yonel. "Donizettti e il 'mélodrame' francese." *Studi donizettiani* 4 (1988): 183–186.

The evolution of Donizetti's operatic style parallels that of the history of the rebirth of French theater. Limiting this study to the French theatrical models that inspired libretti which Donizetti set, the characteristics of the genre, and the possibilities afforded in transforming spoken plays into opera libretti are examined.

136. Casini, Claudio. "Il decennio della fortuna critica di Donizetti a Parigi." In *Atti del 1° Convegno Internazionale di Studi Donizettiani*, 571–593. Bergamo: Azienda Autonoma di Turismo, 1983.

The death of Bellini and the early retirement of Rossini left a gap in the Parisian theater world, one that Donizetti would ultimately fill. The road to Donizetti's artistic fulfillment in the musical capital of Europe was not an easy one. First, the French would need to realize that the Italians were actually a force in the musical world of Paris, and then that they were actively being integrated into the life of this vibrant city. In an effort to examine the continuity of Italian opera in Paris, the author discusses the three major theaters in the city from 1831 to 1845 and demonstrates how Donizetti successfully penetrated their rigid organizational structures. At the end, Donizetti's fall from the pinnacle of success with the Parisian public, paving the way for Verdi's conquest of the city, is outlined.

137. Cella, Franca. "Donizetti novellatore." In *L'Opera teatrale di Gaetano Donizetti: Atti del Convegno Internazionale di Studio*, 219–227. Bergamo: Comune di Bergamo, 1993.

Donizetti was always interested in a good story that might assuage his voracious appetite for more provocative and variegated subjects for stage works. Unlike Rossini, Donizetti was more interested in narratives that would give greater emphasis to the emotional content of the drama. Donizetti was concerned with a character's pyschological profile, and as such he delved more deeply into their emotions, often placing them into new dramaturgical areas as they interacted with one another. The composer viewed his role as narrator as one that was responsible on both moral and aesthetic levels. He employed traditional structures that were flexible and used the orchestra as the primary agent to connect the dramatic action. Donizetti often appropriated oral tradition models, using a strophic structure that lends a ballad-like character to an aria. These models could also be used to create a story within the story as in *L'elisir d'amore*.

138. _____. "Il donizettismo nei libretti donizettiani." In *Atti del 1° Convegno Internazionale di Studi Donizettiani*, 43–50. Bergamo: Azienda Autonoma di Turismo, 1983.

The author examines the plots of several libretti that Donizetti set from a poetical and theatrical standpoint. Doing so reveals the relationships, coincidences, common characteristics, and other recognizable elements that comprise the composer's dramaturgical style.

139. _____. "Indagini sulle fonte francesi dei libretti di Gaetano Donizetti." *Contributi dell'Istituto di Filologia Moderna, Serie francese* 4 (1966): 343–590.

An exhaustive study that balances biographical information with a comparative study of the French models for libretti set by Donizetti.

The essay covers the composer's entire career from *Il Pigmalione* (1816) to *Dom Sébastien* (1843), selecting passages from the original source and comparing them with the text as transformed in the opera libretto. The introduction to this study argues for critical analyses of libretti akin to that of critical editions of the corresponding music. As such, the author outlines the published literature that has already attempted work of this nature.

140. Celletti, Rodolfo. "La vocalità di Donizetti." In *Atti del I° Convegno Internazionale di Studi Donizettiani,* 107–147. Bergamo: Azienda Autonoma di Turismo, 1983.

Donizetti's technique in the construction and use of vocal melodies differs from that of Rossini, Bellini, and Verdi, regardless of whether these composers provided a point of departure for him. This article surveys the kinds of voices and vocal qualities that Donizetti preferred to use in his operatic works. Voice types, from coloratura soprano to basso cantante, are individually discussed, and numerous musical examples illustrate the mastery with which Donizetti constructed his melodies.

141. Chorley, Henry F. "Donizetti's Operas." In *Thirty Years' Musical Recollections,* 153–165. London: Hurst and Blackett, 1862. Reprint, Da Capo Press Music Reprint Series. New York: Da Capo, 1984. ISBN: 0-306-76216-1. LC: ML 423.C55 C5 1983.

A short assessment of Donizetti's life and works, albeit mostly in comparative terms with Rossini and Bellini, covering the composer's choice of subjects, instrumentation, melodic invention, and dramatic structure. The two volumes of this publication also offer biographical and technical information on many of the singers who created roles in Donizetti's operas. These include Maria Malibran, Louis Lablache, Giambattista Rubini, Giulia Grisi, Giuditta Pasta, Madame Persiani (Fanny Taccinardi), Giovanni Matteo Mario, and Giorgio Ronconi.

142. Commons, Jeremy. "Un contributo ad uno studio di Donizetti e la censuranapoletana." In *Atti del 1° Convegno Internazionale di Studi Donizettiani,* 65–106. Bergamo: Azienda Autonoma di Turismo, 1983.

The press and the theater were controlled by the official censors of the different states that made up pre-unified Italy in the nineteenth century. The author poses several questions concerning the censorship of stage works at this time, chief among them whether the censor was truly a negative force or not. In addition, Commons gives a face to these virtually unknown persons by answering questions such as, "Who were the censors?" "Does anyone remember their names?" "What were the qualifications to become a censor?" Working in the Archivi di Stato di Napoli, the author has identified documents that provide a new way to look at Donizetti's works that fell prey to the censors.

143. _____. "Donizetti a Napoli." In *Donizetti e i teatri napoletani nell'ottocento,* 15–18. Naples: Electa, 1997.

Donizetti arrived in Naples in 1822 when he was just twenty-four years old. This city provided a stable environment in which the composer thrived until 1838, when Donizetti left Italy for Paris. The author briefly describes the operas that were written during this twenty-six year period, and outlines the additional work that must now be done in the area of Donizetti studies. These include a critical study of the autograph sources, the compilation of a thematic catalog, and the publication of the numerous alternative readings that resulted from subsequent performances of the works.

144. _____. "Donizetti e l'opera semiseria." In *L'Opera teatrale di Gaetano Donizetti: Atti del Convegno Internazionale di Studio,* 181–196. Bergamo: Comune di Bergamo, 1993.

The genre of opera semiseria is perhaps the most confusing of all of the various forms of Italian opera at the beginning of the nineteenth century. Adapted from the French opéra-comique, this genre juxtaposed light and serious elements but found little respect because it possessed neither the seriousness of opera seria, nor the pure humor of opera buffa. This mixture generally featured contemporary themes, often of a sentimental nature, and realistic characters that audiences could identify with. Censorship laws made political themes rare in the semiseria genre, but themes that essayed moral problems or the social predicament of young women in conflict with parental demands were common. Ferdinand Paër and Giovanni Simone Mayr, Donizetti's teacher and mentor, were the most important composers of this kind of opera. Donizetti's *Emilia di Liverpool* (1824) was strongly influenced by Paër's *Agnese* (1809). His other works in the genre include *Alina, regina di Golconda* (1828), *Gianni di Calais* (1828), and *Otto mesi in due ore* (1827). Although semiseria as a genre declined in fashion during the 1830s due to a renewed, more emotionally charged approach to opera seria, Donizetti would compose another work in this genre late in his career, *Linda di Chamounix* (1842). In Italian; summary in English.

145. _____. "Unknown Donizetti Items in the Neapolitan Journal *Il sibilo*." *Donizetti Society Journal* 2 (1975): 145–160.

The premiere of Donizetti's *Caterina Cornaro* in 1844 was something of a fiasco. In an effort to clarify the reasons the opera failed, whether an issue of performance quality or of the music itself, the author looks to contemporary Neapolitan theatrical journals, most notably *Il sibilo* ("The Hiss"). Mercadante had been entrusted by Donizetti to oversee this production, and letters between the two composers concerning such may be found in this particular journal. Also discovered here are printed scores of songs by popular composers of the period that appeared every two weeks in the journal. Seven of these songs are by Donizetti, and the author discusses the character of the songs, as well as their melodic and harmonic invention. At the end, the songs as originally published in the journal are reproduced.

146. Comuzio, Ermanno. "*Attraverso il fuoco mi son fatto strada*: Le vite fiammeggianti dei musicisti sullo schermo e in televisione." *Chigiana* 42/22 (1990): 245–287.

This article looks at the problems of musical historiography in the context of Carl Dahlhaus's theories. Further, it assesses film biographies of several composers, whether factual or fictionalized, including Donizetti (pp. 255–258). At the end of the article, a list of composer film biographies produced between 1913 and 1992 is provided.

147. Conati, Marcello. "La novella scuola musicale." *Studi musicali* 21/1 (1992): 191–208.

The image of nineteenth-century Italian opera may be synthesized into a four-sided object that is delineated by the figures of

Rossini, Bellini, Donizetti, and Verdi. A homogeneity of style and an affinity of artistic intent codifies the relationship between these four composers. Further, the dramaturgical style of these figures is based on a well-known narrative structure, one developed by Rossini. This structure underwent considerable variation and radical transformation from Rossini's *Semiramide* to Verdi's *Aida*. As such, this article, a revised and corrected version of an essay that first appeared in *Atti del Convegno Internazionale di Studi Belliniani* (Catania: Giuseppe Maimone Editore, 1990), attempts to illustrate the discontinuity of style in Bellini in respect to that of Rossini, and the effect this has on Donizetti's opera seria style.

148. Cronin, Charles. *The Comic Operas of Gaetano Donizetti and the End of the Opera Buffa Tradition*. Ph.D. diss., Stanford University, 1993.

Despite the dominance of serious and tragic genres through opera's history, comic idioms have almost always occupied a significant place in the world of musical theater. Donizetti's *Don Pasquale* (1843) is the last widely recognized work of importance in this form. The objective of this study is to examine Donizetti's works as the last exemplars of opera buffa to determine how and why the demise of this once-popular genre occurred. We can best understand Donizetti's opera buffa style, and assess his contribution to the evolution of this genre, with knowledge of the formal and stylistic conventions that he inherited.

Accordingly, this study first considers the comic operas of Rossini and Mayr, but also focuses on Donizetti's buffa works of the 1820s to learn how they incorporate turn-of-the century buffa norms while they abandon others in favor of a more Romantic style. The greater portion of this project is devoted to Donizetti's most important opere buffe and semiserie, as well as the opera comique *La fille du régiment*.

Inquiry into these works leads to the conclusion that Donizetti's talent for opera buffa was not that of a reformer, but rather that of a resourceful composer with enough musical imagination to produce innovative and durable works in a genre on the wane. We learn that the overtly sentimental style, which came naturally to Donizetti, infiltrates his comic works and expresses emotions that lie as near to the world of Romantic melodrama as to that of Classical opera buffa. Abstract condensed from *Dissertation Abstracts Online*.

149. Dean, Winton. "Donizetti's Serious Operas." In *Essays on Opera*, 187–203. Oxford: Clarendon Press, 1990. ISBN: 0-19-315265-7. LC: ML 1700.D4 1990.

Approximately half of Donizetti's operas are in the genre of opera seria. The majority of these serious works were produced after 1828, the year designated by scholars as to when the composer reached artistic maturity. This article looks at the foundations of Donizetti's style in the teachings of Giovanni Simone Mayr and assesses the criticisms of the composer as a "lightweight." Three main reasons to take a closer look at Donizetti's serious operas are provided: 1) they are extremely moving onstage; 2) they demonstrate innovative approaches to, and expansion of, operatic forms; and 3) they actively influence Verdi's style. Originally appeared in the *Proceedings of the Royal Musical Association* 100 (1973–1974): 123–141.

150. _____. "Some Echoes of Donizetti in Verdi's Operas." In *Atti dei III° Congresso Internazionale di Studi Verdiani*, 122–147. Parma: Istituto di Studi Verdiani, 1974. LC: ML 36.C769 1972.

The influence of Donizetti is more obvious in Verdi's mature operas than in those of his youth. Echoes of Donizetti may be found not so much in the individual melodies, as in the general ambience of the melody, rhythm, accompanimental figures, and harmonic scheme. This often occurs in relation to dramatic situations that have certain similarities, as can be seen in examples drawn from *Nabucco* and *Maria Stuarda, Luisa Miller* and *Belisario,* as well as *Rigoletto* and *Anna Bolena*.

151. Döhring, Sieghart. "La forma dell'aria in Gaetano Donizetti." In *Atti del 1° Convegno Internazionale di Studi Donizettiani*, 149–178. Bergamo: Azienda Autonoma di Turismo, 1983.

The author's preliminary observations in this article survey the formal development of the operatic aria from its beginnings around 1600 to 1900. These remarks predominantly look at the eighteenth-century antecedents of the double aria form, a convention that prevailed over much of nineteenth-century Italian opera. This exhaustive study examines the different aria forms found in Donizetti: arias in one movement, double aria forms and transformations, and the concept of "scena." As such, the author provides structural and harmonic analyses of several arias from Donizetti's vast operatic output.

152. Fischler, Alan. "Gilbert and Donizetti." *Opera Quarterly* 11/1 (Autumn 1994): 29–42.

Examines Donizetti's influence on William S. Gilbert, the librettist, beginning with Gilbert's early English burlesques. Gilbert's *Dulcamara, or, The little duck and the great quack* (1866) is based on Donizetti's *L'elisir d'amore*; Gilbert's *La vivandiere, or, True to the corps!* (1867) is based on Donizetti's *La fille du régiment*. Gilbert's later librettos reflect his knowledge of Donizetti's characters, styles, and organization of scenes. His libretto for *Patience* (1881) is based on ideas from Donizetti's *L'elisir d'amore*.

153. Gavazzeni, Gianandrea. "Anticipazioni della Donizetti Renaissance nella prima metà del nostro secolo." In *L'Opera teatrale di Gaetano Donizetti: Atti del Convegno Internazionale di Studio*, 35–41. Bergamo: Comune di Bergamo, 1993.

Spearheading the "Donizetti Renaissance" were two important performance events that took place in Bergamo: a 1907 production of *Poliuto* given at the Teatro Rubini and conducted by Gino Marinuzzi, and an 1897 performance of *La favorita* under the baton of the young Italian conductor Toscanini. The former was a brilliant success while the latter was poorly cast and received. The interaction of performers and scholars to produce the operatic works of Donizetti has ensured in the recent past that fiascos of the Toscanini type do not occur. Revivals of little-known works like *Torquato Tasso* and the influence of singers like Leyla Gencer and Maria Callas have fueled the interest in Donizetti's art.

154. _____. "Brogliaccio donizettiano." In *Il melodramma italiano dell'ottocento*, 425–435. Saggi, 575. Turin: G. Einaudi, 1977. LC: ML 1733.4.M5.

Looks at the various aspects that would make a complete study of Donizetti's life and works, as well as his artistry. Examines in some detail previously published attempts at doing so, pointing out errors that have occurred and that have been perpetuated in other sources.

155. Gazzaniga, Arrigo. "Appunti di Donizetti per una conferenza." *Nuova rivista musicale italiana* 19/2 (April–June 1985): 291–297.

Publication of a manuscript by Donizetti housed in the Biblioteca Civica Angelo Mai in Bergamo. The document contains reflections on music and was probably written for a conference held in Vienna.

156. Gossett, Philip. "Donizetti: European Composer." *Opera Quarterly* 14/3 (Spring 1998): 11–16.

Italian composers have held a preeminent position in the history of opera, from its modest beginnings in the seventeenth century right up until today. As such, these composers have been actively involved in the musical theater of their homeland, as well as of the entire European continent. Donizetti's activity outside of Italy began around 1835, rather late in his career. Rossini was the catalyst for the composer's first operatic experience in Paris, resulting in *Marino Faliero* given at the Théâtre-Italien that year. The time Donizetti spent in Paris on that first visit was to have tremendous impact on his life and career, as well as on his musicodramaturgical style. This article also appeared in *Amadeus* under the title "Donizetti: Compositore europeo," and has been translated into English by E. Thomas Glasow.

157. Gualerzi, Giorgio. "Aspetti della rinascita di Donizetti nella vita musicale del dopoguerra." In *Atti del I° Convegno Internazionale di Studi Donizettiani*, 961–1012. Bergamo: Azienda Autonoma di Turismo, 1983.

On 8 April 1948, a performance of Donizetti's *Messa da Requiem* (composed in memory of Bellini) at the Teatro Donizetti in Bergamo, and led by Gianandrea Gavazzeni, marked the beginning of the first revival of interest in the composer's life and works. This article provides an overview of the artists (singers, conductors, and stage directors) and the musical works they brought to the stage and to the audience. At the end, a chronological table (compiled by Gualerzi and Carlo Marinelli Rosconi) of twentieth-century performances of Donizetti's operas (with cast lists and date and place of performance) is included.

158. _____. "Fermata obbligatoria per la Donizetti Renaissance." In *Donizetti e I teatri napoletani nell'ottocento,* 71–73. Naples: Electa, 1997.

The progress of the renaissance of interest in Donizetti's stage works has been halted by an interesting phenomenon: the lack of appropriate singers to adequately perform the various roles. This article looks at the vocal qualities of the original interpreters of the Donizettian repertoire and compares them to those of present-day singers.

159. Guastoni, Mimma. "Il compositore Donizetti e l'editore Ricordi: Un lungo rapporto." In *L'Opera teatrale di Gaetano Donizetti: Atti del Convegno Internazionale di Studio,* 111–117. Bergamo: Comune di Bergamo, 1993.

Donizetti's relationship with Giovanni Ricordi is marked by a certain frankness, and their correspondence centers on matters of a professional nature: unauthorized use of the composer's music, quality of performances, and matters of finance. This is in stark relief to the correspondence and relationship that Giulio Ricordi, Giovanni's grandson, was to have with Verdi and Puccini. Before the legislation of copyright, the piracy of music was commonplace. Simple piano reductions of a opera could be reorchestrated by a theater with no penalty. Some of these pirate copies of Donizetti's music, although full of errors and alterations, have taken on a misplaced authority in the area of primary sources for the composer.

160. Guccini, Gerardo. "Drammaturgia d'espressione: Una nota." In *L'Opera teatrale di Gaetano Donizetti: Atti del Convegno Internazionale di Studio,* 363–369. Bergamo: Comune di Bergamo, 1993.

The French Romantic theater in the 1830s may be characterized by spectacular and complex stagings of relatively simplistic narrative structures. This phenomenon is linked to the influence of mélodramme in which scripts were constructed by alternating scenes that moved the action forward with those that were for display only. For Italian theaters, this flexible arrangement of scenes was not easily superimposed on the rigid system of opera production. A combination of short production runs and staging time forced librettists to adhere to formulas and conventions. Composers could also serve in the role of dramaturge. Verdi is probably the most noted proponent of this situation, but Donizetti was as well.

161. Inzaghi, Luigi. "Donizetti a Parigi." In *Gaetano Donizetti,* 39–48. Milan: Nuove Edizioni, 1983.

Donizetti's Parisian "adventures" began several years before he ever set foot in the city. In 1832, after a success with *L'elisir d'amore,* Donizetti was approached by Rossini to write an opera for the Théâtre des Italiens. The composer did not initially jump at the chance, but in 1835, produced *Marino Faliero* for his Parisian debut in March of that year. This article, after a short discussion of the genre of French grand opera, provides an overview of the operas Donizetti composed for Paris from 1839 to 1843: *Les martyrs, La fille de régiment, Le duc d'Albe, La favorite, Rita,* and *Dom Sébastien.*

162. Jennings, Norman Lyle. *Gaetano Donizetti (1797–1848): The Evolution of His Style Leading to the Production of Anna Bolena in 1830.* Ph.D. diss., Michigan State University, 1986.

During the thirty-two years that Gaetano Donizetti wrote for the musical theater, he produced seventy operas, which until 1825 were produced only in Italy. Between 1825 and 1830, the year in which he wrote his thirty-fifth opera, *Anna Bolena,* he began to receive recognition from abroad and to develop a style which expressed his own individuality. This study investigates the changes Donizetti made in his musical style during the years 1822–1830 while he was living and working in Naples. These changes are considered from musical, historical, and theatrical standpoints in order to ascertain how and why *Anna Bolena* was different from Donizetti's earlier operas. The idea is to show the conditions under which Donizetti had to compose, and the numerous contributing factors which influenced his style.

163. Kantner, Leopold. "Donizetti a Vienna." In *Gaetano Donizetti*, 49–59. Milan: Nuove Edizioni, 1983.

For Italian musicians, an appointment as court composer was an indication of complete success. In the nineteenth century, Paris and Vienna were the musical centers that composers set their sights on. Of the two, only Vienna retained an active royal court. Donizetti's operas were already well known in Vienna, productions of his works given annually during the Italian opera season in the Austrian capital. This familiarity placed Donizetti in a good position to win a court appointment. This article looks at the operas written specifically for Vienna, as well as providing the programs for concerts conducted by Donizetti in Vienna from 1843 to 1845.

164. Kaufman, Thomas G. "Italian Performances in Vienna, 1835–1859." *Donizetti Society Journal* 4 (1980): 53–71.

In 1835, Italian opera companies began a long association with the Kärntnertor theater in Vienna. These regular performances of works by Italian opera composers of the day, including Donizetti, lasted until 1847. After a three-year hiatus, due to political strife, the performances started again in 1851 and lasted until 1859. The author chronicles performances in Vienna during this period, using listings found in several contemporary journals, such as *La fama, La moda,* and *La gazzetta musicale di Milano*. He provides cast lists and any changes in cast that may have occurred.

165. Keys, Robert. "Donizetti the Master Craftsman." *Opera Canada* 20/1 (Spring 1979): 14–15, 40.

An article, popular in tone, which outlines the beginnings of the Donizetti Renaissance under the guidance of conductor Tullio Serafin, and singers Maria Callas and Joan Sutherland. The author stresses that there is still much to be rediscovered about Donizetti and his position in the history of Italian opera, including his abandonment of traditional structures, his expansion of the scope and role of the opera orchestra, and his influence on Verdi.

166. Landini, Giancarlo. "Persistenze belcantistiche nella produzione di Gaetano Donizetti." In *L'Opera teatrale di Gaetano*

Donizetti: Atti del Convegno Internazionale di Studio, 310–328. Bergamo: Comune di Bergamo, 1993.

The term "bel canto" has been defined by Rodolfo Celletti in his *Storia del Belcanto* (Fiesole: Discanto; Firenze: Distribuzione, La nuova Italia editrice, 1983) as a pleasing, moving tenderness of sound that displays virtuosity in a language both florid and improvisational. Further, the style permits a certain abstraction between gender and role (as when a female voice plays a male part, or a male voice performs *en travesti* in a female role) and demonstrates a penchant for voices of a stylized or unusual quality. These attributes do not coexist in Donizetti's operatic output. By examining what of Celletti's criteria is applicable to defining bel canto in Donizetti, the result is not very satisfying. However, another perspective and definition of bel canto has been formulated by Józef Sandelewski that better applies to what Donizetti envisioned. For Sandelewski, bel canto is a gradual emanicipation of melody but at the expense of clear declamation. This is supported by Donizetti in that he created the dramatic and pyschological aspects of a character through musical sounds— trills, scales, arpeggios, and other embellishments—creating an autonomous style. This style, although based on the techniques used by Rossini, abandoned the heavy emphasis on imitation, thus defining a new and original vocabulary.

167. Lang, Paul Henry. "Donizetti and Bellini." In *Critic at the Opera*, 119–123. New York: W. W. Norton, 1971. ISBN: 393-02163-7. LC: ML 1700.L26.

Donizetti possessed an infallible sense of the beauty of the human voice. His career was in that age where the singer was glorified (especially the prima donna and primo uomo), their force often molding the form of an opera. As such, Donizetti was able to serve two masters: the audience (hungry for infectious melodies) and the singers (hungry for suitable works to showcase their talents). This essay, drawn from reviews and articles on opera written during the author's tenure as music critic for the *New York Herald Tribune* (1954–1963), provides a critical overview of Donizetti's operatic output and their relative quality. It assesses the works of Bellini in the same manner.

168. Lippmann, Friedrich. "Donizetti e Bellini: Contributo all'interpretazione dello stile donizettiano." In *Atti del I° Convegno Internazionale di Studi Donizettiani,* 179–199. Bergamo: Azienda Autonoma di Turismo, 1983.

One cannot speak of Donizetti's style without referring to Rossini and Bellini. While the composer's earliest works pay homage to Rossini's style, Donizetti and Bellini were real contemporaries, that is, the mature works of both composers date from around 1830 to 1844. The author uses this focus to outline the characteristics of Donizetti's style that distinguish it from that of Bellini's.

169. _____. "Verdi und Donizetti." In *Opernstudien: Anna Amalie Abert zum 65. Geburtstag,* 153–173. Tutzing: H. Schneider, 1975. LC: ML 55.A15 1975.

Investigates several aspects of Donizetti's stylistic affinity to Verdi, such as the structuring of ensembles, handling of rhythm and meter, and essentials of melodic writing. In the course of the study, the styles of Rossini and Bellini are also constantly compared.

170. Messenger, Michael F. "Donizetti, 1840: 3 'French' Operas and Their Italian Counterparts." *Donizetti Society Journal* 2 (1975): 99–115.

The year 1840 saw three premieres of Donizetti operas in Paris, *La fille du régiment, La favorite,* and *Les martyrs.* Each of these works has held an uncertain place in the operatic repertory and has usually been performed in versions different from the composer's original scores. This adaptability demonstrates the flexibility and versatility of Donizetti's invention. For each of these works, the author tabulates the differences between the versions and evaluates their effect on the dramatic structure of the work.

171. Mioli, Piero. *Donizetti: 70 melodrammi.* Realtà musicali. Turin: EDT, 1988.

An analytic discussion of all of Donizetti's operas (relatively brief for the earliest works), including their musical structure and summaries of the librettos. Particular attention is given to dramatic nuclei of plot structure (the confrontation between innocent and guilty love, family, society, civil and political rivalry, landscape) and to the structural characterization of closed forms (bipartite aria, duet, concertato, romance, and so forth). A list of works (pp. 507–527) and a discography (pp. 535–546) are included.

172. _____. "L'opera seria." In *Gaetano Donizetti,* 61–80. Milan: Nuove Edizioni, 1983.

In 1816, when Donizetti began his career as an opera composer, the Italian musical climate was completely dominated by Rossinian conventions. This article surveys Italian opera seria during this period, the formation of Donizetti's dramaturgical style, and the sociological function of the operatic genre. Also included is a detailed discussion of the opere serie that Donizetti wrote in the various phases of his career.

173. _____. "*Il segreto per esser felici*: alcune osservazioni sulla voce di contralto nell'opera di Donizetti e dei contemporanei." *Donizetti Society Journal* 6 (1988): 153–161.

This article begins by examining the tradition of the contralto and how this voice type was utilized up to the Rossinian era. It then looks at the role of the contralto in the Italian melodrama tradition and assesses several roles Donizetti created for this particular voice. At the end, it briefly examines how the contralto voice was used by other nineteenth-century composers, and how this differs from Donizetti.

174. Morey, Carl. "Donizetti Revised the Rules." *Opera Canada* 23/2 (Summer 1982): 24–26.

Popular in approach, this article summarizes the influence of Mayr on Donizetti and its result in the formal structure of the numerous songs, chamber music, and sacred pieces composed under the elder composer's tutelage. Donizetti's study with Mayr, therefore, helped to crystallize his melodic inventiveness and enrich his ideas about musical texture. The multicolored aspect of Donizetti's orchestration is also a result of Mayr's influence and allows for the equality of voice and orchestra in his operas. The author also summarizes the Canadian performance history of selected works by Donizetti from the mid-nineteenth century to 1982.

175. Olivieri, Guido. "L'Archivio Storico del Banco di Napoli: Barbaja, Donizetti, l'opera napoletana." In *Donizetti e i teatri napoletani nell'ottocento,* 123–126. Naples: Electa, 1997.

An economic history of stage works in the nineteenth century. Documents pertaining to studies of this kind are typically preserved in both public and private archives, but most importantly in the archives of several financial institutions. The Banco di Napoli maintains such an archive, and within it may be found important documents concerning financial agreements between Donizetti and the Neapolitan impresario Domenico Barbaja.

176. Osborne, Charles. *The Bel Canto Operas of Rossini, Donizetti, and Bellini.* Portland, OR: Amadeus, 1994. ISBN: 0-931340-71-3. LC: ML 390.O82 1994.

"Bel canto," by definition, is a method of singing taught by Italian masters of the seventeenth and eighteenth centuries characterized by a smooth emission of tone, a beauty of timbre, and an elegance of phrasing. Today, the term is most often used to describe the predominant style of Italian opera in the first half of the nineteenth century. This book is a guide to the composer's operas, blending biographical information with plot summaries for sixty-five works by Donizetti. It includes characters in the operas and their vocal types, as well as information on the librettist, the setting of the work, and the premiere performance (theater and cast). The bibliography is minimal, but the selected discography (pp. 359–364) covers the most important recorded releases of Donizetti's operas up to 1994.

177. Parker, Roger. "A Donizetti Critical Edition in the Postmodern World." In *L'Opera teatrale di Gaetano Donizetti: Atti del Convegno Internazionale di Studio,* 57–66. Bergamo: Comune di Bergamo, 1993.

Editors of critical editions of Italian opera are keenly aware of the criticism that may befall them from scholars and performers alike concerning the criteria upon which their edition is based. The guidelines for the Donizetti edition owe a considerable debt to those of the Verdi and Rossini collected works. As such, these editions take on the uneasy task of balancing the needs of performers with the responsibilities of the text critic. Although most critical editions take the composer's autograph as a point of departure, a number of features of Donizetti's compositional and notational practice warrant special treatment. These features include missing notes, slurs, and the articulation of rhythmic gestures. Often the editor's choice creates a clash between the lack of notational precision of the past with modern sensibilities.

178. Portinari, Folco. "Dal melodramma 'storico' alla commedia romantica." In *Gaetano Donizetti*, 97–105. Milan: Nuove Edizioni, 1983.

Using the structure of Donizetti's *Gabriella di Vergy* (1826) as a primary example of his dramaturgical style, other dramatic works the composer set to music in collaboration with various librettists are examined. The operas written to texts by Felice Romani and Salvatore Cammarano are given the most consideration.

179. Ragni, Sergio. "Cronache musicali napoletane dall'epistolario di Donizetti." In *Donizetti e i teatri napoletani nell'ottocento*, 19–50. Naples: Electa, 1997.

An exhaustive chronicle of the musical life of Naples from 1822 to 1838 and Donizetti's place within this milieu. The author uses the composer's correspondence as a basis for this study.

180. Ringer, Alexander L. "Aspetti socio-economici dell'opera italiana nel periodo donizettiano." In *Atti del 1° Convegno Internazionale di Studi Donizettiani*, 943–960. Bergamo: Azienda Autonoma di Turismo, 1983.

Demonstrates that economic considerations were largely responsible for shaping the nature and direction of Donizetti's operatic output, as well as for that of other composers of his generation. By comparing salaries and working conditions of both composers and singers, the author concludes that composers fared quite poorly. Contractual agreements between impresarios and composers, as well as performance rights, are also covered. An English version of this article was subsequently published in *Analecta musicologica* 22 (1984): 229–247.

181. Roccatagliati, Alessandro. *Felice Romani librettista.* Musica/ Realtà, 37. Lucca: Libreria Musicale Italiana, 1996. ISBN: 88-7096-157-5.

Although predominantly about the librettist, a tremendous amount of information on Romani's relationship with Donizetti is covered.

182. Rosselli, John. "Verdi e la storia della retribuzione del compositore italiano." *Studi verdiani* 2 (1983): 11–28.

Investigates the underlying economic conditions of the operatic industry of the eighteenth and nineteenth centuries and makes observations on the earnings of Johann Simone Mayr and Donizetti as well as others. From this, the author can look more closely at Verdi's financial situation and at the impact of copyright legislation on his payment as an opera composer.

183. Sala, Emilio. "Women Crazed by Love: An Aspect of Romantic Opera." *Opera Quarterly* 10/3 (Spring 1994): 19–41.

The theme of women rendered insane by love in operas of the late eighteenth and nineteenth centuries is examined in regard to *Nina* by Nicolas-Marie Dalayrac, *Il pirata* and *I puritani* by Vincenzo Bellini, *Anna Bolena* and *Lucia di Lammermoor* by Gaetano Donizetti, and *Edmea* by Alfredo Catalani. Contemporary French plays of the boulevard theaters, commonly intermediaries between the original literary works and the opera libretto, are also discussed. Translated into English by William Ashbrook.

184. Scudo, Paul. "Donizetti et l'école italienne depuis Rossini." In *Critique et littérature musicales,* 75–100. Paris: Amyot, 1850. LC: ML 60.S434.

Written during July 1848, only three months after Donizetti had died in Bergamo, this essay offers perhaps the earliest biographical sketch of the composer (pp. 76–83). It also includes a discussion of his works, with emphasis on *Anna Bolena, Lucia di Lammermoor, L'elisir d'amore,* and *Don Pasquale* (pp. 84–91) and of his use of instrumentation (pp. 91–92). The remainder of the essay places Donizetti in relation to the careers and dramatic art of Rossini, Bellini, and Verdi.

185. Smart, Mary Ann. *Dalla tomba uscita: Representations of Madness in Nineteenth-century Italian Opera*. Ph.D. diss., Cornell University, 1994.

Chapter 2 considers Donizetti's *Lucia di Lammermoor* in the context of recent feminist and psychoanalytic writings on "the gaze" and the potential to free women from societal constraints; Chapter 4 looks at *I pazzi per progetto* in the context of comic madness and the nineteenth-century popular genre of operas set in madhouses; Chapter 5 looks at the tradition of male madness, focusing on the mad father in *Maria Padilla*.

186. Sorce Keller, Marcello. "'Gesunkenes Kulturgut' and Neapolitan Songs: Verdi, Donizetti, and the Folk and Popular Traditions." In *Trasmissione e recezione delle forme di cultura musicale: Atti del XIV Congresso della Società Internazionale Musicologia, Bologna, 1987,* 401–405. Turin: Edizioni di Torino, 1990.

Discusses Italian operatic tunes, folk tunes, opera tunes transmitted by brass bands, and operatic folk tunes and contrasts all these with the role of middle-class popular songs.

187. Steiner, Robert. "Donizetti's Marien: Ein rudimentären Vorgleich." *Studi donizettiani* 3 (1978): 75–80.

This article examines the figure of Maria in four Donizetti operas: *Maria di Rohan, Maria di Rudenz, Maria Padilla,* and *Maria Stuarda*. As such, our understanding of the dramaturgy and the diverse meanings of the works is broadened. The author proposes a pairing of these works, based on emotional and spiritual issues in the operas. Includes a summary in Italian (pp. 79–80).

188. Tomlinson, Gary. "Italian Romanticism and Italian Opera: An Essay in Their Affinities." *19th Century Music* 10/1 (Summer 1986): 43–60.

Examines the politics of the period in which Donizetti was composing operas and its effect on the compositional choices he made within his stage works.

189. Turner, Derek. "Donizetti and the Victorian Musical Machine." *Donizetti Society Journal* 1 (1974): 129–135.

Melodies from popular operas were often recreated in the salon or front parlor of a home in arrangements by several nineteenth-century piano virtuosi, among them Liszt and Thalberg. Amateur performers, for whom these arrangements were often too difficult, relied on mechanical music boxes to recreate the tunes they loved. These machines juxtaposed classical airs and operatic melodies with popular tunes of the day. Melodies from Donizetti's operas were well represented in this Victorian phenomenon, including tunes from *Lucia di Lammermoor, La fille du régiment, Lucrezia Borgia,* and *Anna Bolena.* The author hypothesizes whether the demand for this mechanization of opera coincided with the demand to see these works on stage. A short history of the pianola, the successor to music boxes and mechanical organs, is also given, as well as a table of all mechanized versions of tunes from Donizetti's operas.

190. Weatherson, Alexander. "Donizetti in Revival 1978–1980." *Donizetti Society Journal* 4 (1980): 13–26.

Discusses the renewed interest in Donizetti in opera houses around the world, focusing on the production of works other than *Don Pasquale* and *L'elisir d'amore.* Includes a performance history for the period covered.

191. Wiklund, Anders. "The Nydahl Collection of Stockholm and Its Importance for Nineteenth-century Opera." In *L'Opera teatrale di Gaetano Donizetti: Atti del Convegno Internazionale di Studio,* 69–73. Bergamo: Comune di Bergamo, 1993.

After the publication of critical editions of Donizetti's *Maria Stuarda* and Rossini's *La scala di seta,* the Nydahl collection of music manuscripts in Stockholm, which houses the autographs of these works, has become better known to the operatic world. The collection, brought together by Rudolf Nydahl, who had studied at the Conservatoire de Musique in Paris in the early part of this century, is now housed in the Stiftelsen Musikkulturens Främjande (Foundation for Promotion of Musical Culture). In addition to autograph manuscripts, the collection contains printed music from the eighteenth and nineteenth centuries, many of which are first editions. Vocal scores of opera are the predominant material in this part of the collection. There is also a vast iconographic collection as well as some five thousand letters. The author imparts the story of how the autograph of *Maria Stuarda* came to reside in Stockholm and outlines the other Donizetti manuscripts in the collection (songs, sketches for operas, and sacred music). Of the collection of letters, five are in Donizetti's hand, one of which gives instructions for cuts and changes in *Lucrezia Borgia*. A guide to the collection has been published by Bonnie Lomnäs: *Stiftelsen Musikkulturens främjande (Nydahl Collection): Catalogue of Music Manuscripts*. Stockholm: Musikaliska akademiens bibliotek, 1995. Music in Sweden, 9.

192. Zanolini, Bruno. "L'armonia come espressione drammaturgica in Gaetano Donizetti." In *Atti del 1° Convegno Internazionale di Studi Donizettiani*, 775–834. Bergamo: Azienda Autonoma di Turismo, 1983.

Presents several general aspects of the formal structure of aria forms and then proceeds to look at harmony from a dramaturgical point of view. Donizetti's use of tonality as an organizing device, and of modulation as a means to move the drama forward, is examined. In addition, the function of cadences to delineate form and dramatic structure, and the role chromaticism plays, is assessed.

193. Zedda, Alberto. "La strumentazione nell'opera teatrale." In *Atti del 1° Convegno Internazionale di Studi Donizettiani*, 453–542. Bergamo: Azienda Autonoma di Turismo, 1983.

The author assesses the conditions under which musicians of Donizetti's time worked and operated, especially in relation to the assignment of these individuals to various instrumental bodies: orchestras, choruses, instrumental groupings, and off-stage bands. As such, the instruments included in the typical Donizettian orchestra are outlined, as well as the basis for the composer's orchestration technique. The orchestration of various formal structures in the operas (aria, scena, ensembles, finales), and how the individual instruments have been employed in the stage works and to what effect, is surveyed.

194. Zoppelli, Luca. "Elementi narrativi nella drammaturgia donizettiana: Alcune osservazioni." In *L'Opera teatrale di Gaetano Donizetti: Atti del Convegno Internazionale di Studio,* 171–180. Bergamo: Comune di Bergamo, 1993.

In operatic works, there is a clear difference between mimesis and diegesis, between staging events taking place in real time and staging narratives that manipulate time and place seemingly at will. The opera composer as narrator, virtually unexplored in the seventeenth and eighteenth centuries, is an important aspect of the nineteenth century, and Donizetti is one of its chief proponents. This study focuses predominantly on the operas *Parisina* and *Lucrezia Borgia* but uses other stage works by Donizetti (*Anna Bolena* and *Lucia di Lammermoor*) to illustrate the evolution of the composer's dramaturgical style. The aspects of *musica di scena,* music sung or played as music, not as a mode of portraying a character's expression, offstage music, and reoccuring motives as vehicles for narrative treatment are explored. In Italian, with English summary. An English translation of this article by William Ashbrook appears under the title "Narrative Elements in Donizetti's Operas" in *Opera Quarterly* 10/1 (Autumn 1993): 23–32.

Production/Review Sources

Here are listed production-related sources such as staging manuals and discussions of singers and performing venues as they relate to the works of Donizetti; guides to biographical and historical information on singers who created roles or theaters in which premieres took place may be found in Chapter 8.

195. Ardoin, John. *Callas at Juilliard: The Master Classes,* 99–126. New York: Knopf, 1987. ISBN: 0-394-56367-0. LC: MT 820.C17 1987.

Gives the singer's remarks on the interpretation of several selections from *Lucia di Lammermoor, Anna Bolena,* and *Don Pasquale.*

196. Barblan, Guglielmo. "Donizetti alla Fenice." In *Gaetano Donizetti,* 33–38. Milan: Nuove Edizioni, 1983.

For a budding composer like Donizetti, the road leading to Venice's Teatro La Fenice was a long and uncertain one. After composing three one-act operas in 1818, all unperformed, Donizetti exploded onto the Italian opera scene with the Venetian premiere of his *Enrico di Borgogna.* This success at the Teatro San Luca led to premieres at other Venetian theaters. It was not until 1836, with the premiere of *Belisario,* that Donizetti completed his journey to La Fenice. This article, which also appears in expanded form in *La Fenice* (Milano: Nuove Edizioni, 1972. I Teatri nel mondo:

99–111), provides an overview of *Belisario*, as well as of *Pia de' Tolomei* and *Maria de Rudenz*.

197. Bini, Annalisa, and Jeremy Commons. *Le prime rappresentazioni delle opere di Donizetti nella stampa coeva*. L'arte armonica. Serie III, Studi e Testi, 3. Milan: Skira; Accademia Nazionale di Santa Cecilia, 1997.

Discusses the operas and their reception and includes excerpts from various review sources. Iconographical evidence is presented, including sketches and engravings of sets and costumes as well as caricatures in the contemporary press. The appendices include a list of the various review sources included in the book, complete with citations (pp. 1555–1573), biographical information on the critics (pp. 1575–1594), and a bibliography (pp. 1609–1611).

198. Black, John. "Code of Instructions for the Censorship of Theatrical Works, Naples 1849." *Donizetti Society Journal* 5 (1984): 147–150.

Reproduces a document found in the Gran Archivio di Stato (Sezione teatri, fascia 44) that governed the content and texts of theatrical works in mid-nineteenth century Naples. Although this document dates from after Donizetti's death, the guidelines presented here were probably in force in the preceding decades. In Italian with English translation in parallel columns.

199. Brindicci, Monica. "Donizetti e i teatri napoletani: Un caso giornalistico (1822–1848)." In *Donizetti e i teatri napoletani nell'ottocento*, 103–121. Naples: Electa, 1997.

Discusses the state of journalism in Naples and the papers that were most important in covering musical events. In addition, the author enumerates the various theaters in Naples and the particular kinds of musical entertainment they supported. From this background, the operas of Donizetti, their coverage in the local press, and their reception in the theaters is examined.

200. Crivelli, Filippo. "Problemi ed esperienze nelle regie delle opere donizettiane." In *L'Opera teatrale di Gaetano Doni-*

zetti: *Atti del Convegno Internazionale di Studio*, 395–405.
Bergamo: Comune di Bergamo, 1993.

Donizetti's operatic works can be presented in a simple manner.
The appropriate approach to staging these works is to realize that
the direction must serve the music; that is, support the musical dramaturgy. Above all, the wise stage director must realize that there
are moments in Donizetti's stage works, usually ensembles, in
which the dramatic action stops. This was a common procedure in
the nineteenth century. However, the directors of modern productions often try to fill these moments with gimmicks. This does not
serve the music and is to be avoided. Any variance from the original
intention for stage action must logically correspond to the music.
Donizetti's great sense of theater will never be compromised if the
director simply follows the music as it develops the emotional and
comical aspects of the work. In Italian; summary in English.

201. Croccolo, Enrico. *Donizetti a Lucca: Storia delle opere di
Donizetti rappresentate a Lucca dal 1827 al 1858.* Lucca:
Edizioni G. Biagini, 1985. ISBN: 3-011-85100-0.

An overview of the presentation of Donizetti's operas in Lucca during the composer's lifetime and in the decade immediately following
his death. Includes transcriptions of numerous contemporary press
notices.

202. Gencer, Leyla. "Notes on the Interpretation of Donizetti's
Queens." *Donizetti Society Journal* 5 (1984): 208–215.

The well-known Donizetti soprano, Leyla Gencer, presents her interpretation of roles in *Anna Bolena, Roberto Devereux,* and *Maria
Stuarda.* Using scenes that present the first and final appearances of
three queens in these works, Gencer outlines the pyschological
identity of the individual characters, and also outlines the need to
understand the linguistic conventions of the period and the vocal
style of the composer to create a convincing performance. These remarks were given at a series of seminars on the interpretation of
Donizetti's operas (Trieste, Spring 1982) and are here translated
into English by Stephen Hastings.

203. Hartmann, Rudolf, ed. *Les grands opéras: Decor et mise en scène*. Paris: Office du Livre-Vilo, 1977.

French translation by Michel R. Flechtner, Marie-Claire Gerard-Zai, and Antoine Golea of the collection of essays that appeared in Fribourg (Switzerland) under the title *Oper. Regie und Buhnenbild heute*. After a general introduction on theatrical decoration and its techniques, Hartmann presents eleven illustrated sequences of the scenery, essentially in productions in Germany and Austria, for *Don Giovanni, Zauberflöte, Fidelio, Barbiere di Siviglia, Don Pasquale, Don Carlos, Meistersinger, Götterdämmerung, Contes d'Hoffmann, Pelléas et Mélisande*, and *Frau ohne Schatten*, for productions from the period 1962–1976.

204. Maione, Paologiovanni, and Francesca Seller. "L'ultima stagione napoletana di Domenico Barbaja (1836–1840)." *Rivista italiana di musicologia* 27/1–2 (1992): 257–325.

The impresario Domenico Barbaja signed his final four-year contract in Naples on 1 June 1836. In order to understand the evolution of the partnership between Barbaja and the theatrical institutions he served, it is necessary to compare this document with his earlier contracts of 1815 and 1822. In general, this article looks at the responsibilities of an impresario, the organization of the royal Neapolitan theaters, and the programming choices for individual seasons. Further, a comparison of the rosters of singers and dancers that Barbaja represented is made, and the effects of the censors examined. An appendix provides a chronology of performances at the Teatro San Carlo for the 1838–1839 season.

205. Mancini, Franco. "La scenografia sancarliana all'epoca di Donizetti." In *Donizetti e i teatri napoletani nell'ottocento*, 89–102. Naples: Electa, 1997.

Unfortunately, there are few extant documents that provide concrete evidence on the visual aspects of Donizetti's Neapolitan operas. However, by examining the scenic requirements of other works given at the Teatro San Carlo during this time, the author hypothesizes about the look of the Donizetti works and the artisans who brought the dramas to life. A list of the operas mounted and the surviving scenic design sources appears at the end of the article.

206. McCorquodale, Charles P. "Operatic Stage Design, 1800–1840." *Donizetti Society Journal* 1 (1974): 121–128.

Profound changes in designs for the operatic stage during the period 1800 to 1840 paralleled those in other visual arts. The sparse settings typical of mid-eighteenth-century opera gave way to a more luxurious approach. The author discusses the major differences between eighteenth-and nineteenth-century stage design, as well as the various designers who were important to the changes accomplished during this period.

207. Morini, Enrica, and Rosanna Pavoni. "Gli scenografi di Donizetti." In *Gaetano Donizetti,* 107–115. Milan: Nuove Edizioni, 1983.

An overview of the reform of Italian scenic design, led by Antonio Niccolini in 1839, is provided. The professional training of scenic designers is also discussed, as well as the specific visual elements that constituted the staging requirements for Donizetti's operas. Short synopses are given for the careers of various artisans employed by the theaters in which Donizetti's works were performed, and the designs used in premiere performances of his operas are examined.

208. *One Hundred Years of Operatic Staging in France*. Musical Life in 19th-century France, 2. Stuyvesant, N.Y.: Pendragon, 1986. ISBN: 0-918-72869-X. LC: ML 128.O4 C63 1986.

A descriptive catalog compiled by H. Robert Cohen and Marie-Odile Gigou of staging manuals, annotated librettos, and full scores in the Bibliothèque de l'Association de la Régie Théâtrale in Paris. Included are entries for Donizetti's *Dom Sébastien, Don Pasquale, La favorite, La fille du régiment, Linda di Chamounix, Lucie de Lammermoor, Les martyrs, Nizza de Grenade, Rita,* and *Robert d'Evereux.*

209. *The Original Staging Manuals for Ten Parisian Operatic Premières, 1824–1843*. Musical Life in 19th-century France, 6. Stuyvesant, N.Y.: Pendragon, 1998. ISBN: 0-945-19361-0. LC: ML 1727.8.P2 D58 1998.

Introduction by H. Robert Cohen. Includes facsimiles of the stage directions for the first production of *Dom Sébastien* at the Opéra on 13 November 1843, for the first performance of *Lucie de Lammermoor* at the Théâtre de la Renaissance on 6 August 1839, and for the first performance of *Les martyrs* at the Opéra on 10 April 1840.

210. *The Original Staging Manuals for Twelve Parisian Operatic Premières*. Musical Life in 19th-century France, 3. Stuyvesant, N.Y.: Pendragon, 1991. ISBN: 0-918-72870-3. LC: ML 1727.8.P2 O7 1991.

Introduction by H. Robert Cohen, and preface by Marie-Odile Gigou. Includes facsimiles of the stage directions for the first performance of *La favorite* at the Opéra on 2 December 1840 and for the first performance of *La fille du régiment* at the Opéra-Comique on 11 February 1840. The stage directions for *La fille du régiment* are by M. Génot. The staging for *La favorite* was originally published as a supplement to the 17 January 1840 issue of *Revue et gazette des théâtres*.

211. Shulman, Laurie. *Music Criticism of the Paris Opéra in the 1830s*. Ph.D. diss.: Cornell University, 1985.

Traces developments in French grand opera between 1831 and 1840, through the music criticism in the contemporary Parisian press. The eleven operas discussed are representative of the great successes and failures of a brilliant decade for the Paris Opéra. The composers represented are Daniel François Auber, Berlioz, Donizetti, Halévy, Marco Aurelio Marliani, Meyerbeer, and Mozart. The origins of opéra-lyrique, which emerged in the 1840s and came to fruition in the 1850s and 1860s, are in part to be found in the grand operas of the 1830s and in part constitute a reaction to those works.

212. Smith, Marian. "The *livrets de mise en scène* of Donizetti's Parisian operas." In *L'Opera teatrale di Gaetano Donizetti: Atti del Convegno Internazionale di Studio*, 371–391. Bergamo: Comune di Bergamo, 1993.

Staging manuals, or *livrets de mise en scène,* were compiled beginning in the 1830s to help provincial French theaters mount productions that resembled those on the stages of large urban musical centers. After 1855, similar manuals began to be published in Italy as well. One of the most prolific publishers of livrets de mise en scène was Louis Palianti, a singer and assistant regisseur at the Opéra-Comique. Of the over two hundred such manuals published by Palianti, eleven are devoted to Donizetti's operas written in or translated into French. General observations pertaining to the structure and content of staging manuals are given, followed by a close study of the staging requirements for the three finales of *Les martyrs.*

213. Wild, Nicole. *Décors et costumes du XIXe siècle.* Catalogues de la Bibliothèque de l'Opéra, 3. Paris: Bibliothèque Nationale, 1987. ISBN: 2-717-71753-6.

A catalog arranged alphabetically by title of the opera. Part 1 covers set and costume designs for productions which took place at the Paris Opéra and includes entries for Donizetti's *Dom Sébastien, La favorite, Lucie de Lammermoor,* and *Les martyrs.* Part 2 provides biographical information on the designers and history of various theaters in Paris and in the provinces.

Singers and Theaters

A. General Works

214. Farkas, Andrew. *Opera and Concert Singers: An Annotated International Bibliography of Books and Pamphlets*. New York: Garland, 1985. ISBN: 08-2409-001-2. LC: ML 128.S295 F37 1985.

An exhaustive annotated bibliography of singer biographies in the form of books or pamphlets. No biographical information found in periodical literature is cited. Coverage is limited to those publications with imprint dates of 1983 or earlier, although a few 1984 citations do appear. The arrangement is in three parts: 1) those items that focus on a single performer, 2) those that contain information on multiple performers, and 3) books and translations into English that are in manuscript form. Includes entries on 796 singers written in 28 languages.

215. Kaufman, Thomas G. "A Bibliography of Opera House Annals." *Donizetti Society Journal* 5 (1984): 317–381.

An annotated bibliography of books devoted to various opera houses throughout the world. Corrections and additions to the list appear in the *Donizetti Society Journal* 6 (1988): 193–215.

216. Wild, Nicole. *Dictionnaire des théâtres parisiens au XIXe siècle: Les théâtres et la musique*. Domaine musicolo-

gique, 4. Paris: Aux Amateurs de Livres, 1989. LC: PN 2636.P3 W54 1989.

Includes bibliographical references (pp. 457–480) and index.

B. Singers

217. Appolonia, Giorgio. "I primi interpreti di Donizetti." In *Donizetti e i teatri napoletani nell'ottocento,* 65–70. Naples: Electa, 1997.

The author looks at the differences in assigning vocal types to the various roles in the operas of Rossini and Donizetti. At the center of Donizetti's stage works is the prima donna soprano, whose vocal characteristics are a combination of feminine energy in a continual struggle with fate. This particular voice is partnered with the tenor, who exudes a youthful spirit as a heroic lover. In opposition to these voice types, one often finds a lyric soprano and a baritone or bass. This article also examines the early interpreters of Donizetti's operas and their vocal abilities.

218. _____. "Vite, vezzi e virtù di cantanti donizettiani." In *Donizetti e i teatri napoletani nell'ottocento,* 202–235. Naples: Electa, 1997.

A biographical essay on the various singers that created roles in Donizetti's operas. This article provides information on the vocal qualities of the individuals and tables of performances of the composer's operas throughout the singer's career. The list is arranged alphabetically and contains bibliographical footnotes which point the reader to additional sources of information.

219. Ashbrook, William. "The Evolution of the Donizettian Tenor-persona." *Opera Quarterly* 14/3 (Spring 1998): 25–32.

Essential reading for an understanding of the development of the tenor voice and the differing vocal categories that individual roles demand. Terms such as *tenori contraltini* and *tenore di forza* are thoroughly explained, and the inclusion of excerpts from Donizetti's correspondence gives a clear indication of the composer's feelings about various singers and how he assigned or modified roles to suit the strengths of a particular voice. Donizetti's treatment of the tenor-persona was far more varied than that of Rossini, Bellini, and Verdi, mainly because he introduced greater flexibility of approach and subject matter into his operatic works. An earlier version of this paper was read in absentia at the 1997 Convegno Internazionale di Studi "Vocalità e Cantanti Donizettiani" in Bergamo.

220. Brewer, Bruce. "Il cigno di Romano: Giovan Battista Rubini: A Performance Study." *Donizetti Society Journal* 4 (1980): 117–165.

A short biography of the tenor; includes a chronology of performances (pp. 125–159) and a repertoire list (pp. 160–164).

221. Chorley, Henry F. "Giambattista Rubini." *Donizetti Society Journal* 4 (1980): 167–171.

A personal memoir of the tenor Giambattista Rubini, known as the "king of tenors," that originally appeared in the author's *Thirty-Years Musical Recollections* (London: Hurst and Blackett, 1862). Chorley assesses the tenor's career in England, gives a fairly detailed physical description of the man, and outlines his use of vocal ornamentation.

222. Ciarlantini, Paola. *Giuseppe Persiani e Fanny Tacchinardi: Due protagonisti del melodramma romantico.* Ancona: Lavoro Editoriale, 1988. ISBN: 88-7663-176-3.

The "minor" composer and impresario Giuseppe Persiani (1799–1869), known especially for his *Ines de Castro,* played a significant part in the period of transition from the operas of Rossini and that of Verdi. His wife, Fanny Tacchinardi (1812?–1867), one of the highest-paid singers of her era and now critically regarded as the model of the *lirico-leggero* soprano, is especially known as the creator of the title roles of Donizetti's *Rosmonda d'Inghilterra, Lucia di Lammermoor,* and *Pia de' Tolomei.* She was also an important interpreter of the major operas of the bel canto repertoire, in particular those of Rossini. Through archival documents, mostly previously unpublished, and analysis of the original scores, their closely linked careers are described.

223. Conati, Marcello. "L'avvento del 'baritono': profilo di Giorgio Ronconi." In *L'Opera teatrale di Gaetano Donizetti: Atti*

del Convegno Internazionale di Studio, 281–299. Bergamo: Comune di Bergamo, 1993.

Giorgio Ronconi is the singer who in the nineteenth century exemplified the vocal and dramatic characteristics that we associate today as common to the baritone voice. His combination of technical artistry and dramatic intelligence was a particularly effective fusion of actor and singer. However, contemporary descriptions of Ronconi demonstrate that the baritone who created several roles in Donizetti premieres possessed a voice that was anything but beautiful and not particularly robust or powerful. It was his acting abilities, perfect enunciation, and sure sense of portraying the musical expression that brought him success. His extended upper register was probably the most distinctive aspect of his vocal technique, and one that was thoroughly exploited by Donizetti and others. By looking at the parts that were written for him by Donizetti, a clearer impression of his vocal gifts may be identified. In Italian with a summary in English.

224. Corti, Sandro. "Gilbert Louis-Duprez: Le lettere (1833–1850) nell'Archivio dell'Impresario Alessandro Lanari." In *Ottocento e oltre: Scritti in onore di Raoul Meloncelli,* 277–318. Itinerari Musicale, 2. Rome: Editoriale Pantheon, 1993. ISBN: 88-78001-203-4.

Briefly chronicles the life and career of Duprez, the singer who specialized in *tenore leggero* roles, and who was famous for singing a high "C" in chest voice (*in petto*) rather than in the more traditional falsetto. Duprez created several roles for Donizetti, including Percy in *Anna Bolena* and Edgardo in *Lucia di Lammermoor*. This article, a condensed version of the author's tesi di laurea (Facoltà di Lettere, Università degli Studi di Pisa, 1990–1991), includes the texts of selected letters from the tenor to the impresario Alessandro Lanari.

225. Cox, John E. "Gian Battista Rubini." *Donizetti Society Journal* 4 (1980): 172–179.

A more fully worked out and documented biography of the tenor than the one by Chorley cited previously in item 221. The article is reprinted from the author's *Musical Recollections of the Last Half-Century* (London: Tinsley Brothers, 1872) and supplies a description of Rubini's vocal technique and quality of his instrument.

226. Duprez, Gilbert. *Souvenirs d'un chanteur*. Paris: Calman Lévy, 1880.

Memoirs of the tenor Gilbert Duprez, famous for his high "C" sung in chest voice and creator of several Donizettian operatic roles.

227. Forbes, Elizabeth. *Mario and Grisi: A Biography*. London: Gollancz, 1985. ISBN: 05-7503-606-0.

Documents the lives of the opera singers Giovanni Matteo Mario (1810–1883) and Giulia Grisi (1811–1869).

228. Gualerzi, Giorgio. "Tipologia del tenore serio donizettiano: Indagine nei teatri di Torino dell'ottocento." In *L'Opera teatrale di Gaetano Donizetti: Atti del Convegno Internazionale di Studio*, 353–360. Bergamo: Comune di Bergamo, 1993.

Surveys a variety of tenor voices associated with Donizetti's operas given in Turin from 1833 to 1837, comparing traits such as timbre and dramatic characterization. Several singers are discussed, including Antonio Poggi who, like Rubini before him, falls into the *tenore di grazia* category; Giambattista Genero, a light lyric tenor by today's standards; Giovanni Basadonna, who created the role of Roberto Devereux; and Domenico Donzelli, Gilbert Duprez, and Gaetano Fraschini. These last two singers also distinguished themselves in several works by Verdi, and the author argues that the imposition of a Verdian approach to singing was the cause of the gradual distortion that was to adversely affect the true Donizettian tenor. In Italian; includes a summary in English.

229. Kaufman, Thomas G. "Giorgio Ronconi." *Donizetti Society Journal* 5 (1984): 169–206.

A reprint of an article on the baritone that was originally published in the 21 August and 11 September 1847 issues of *The Musical World*, which deals with his career. Annotations to this biography are given by Kaufman, as well as a chronology of Ronconi's operatic performances from 1830–1878.

230. _____. "Giulia Grisi: A Re-evaluation." *Donizetti Society Journal* 4 (1980): 181–225.

A short biography of the soprano; includes a chronology of performances (pp. 197–223) and a repertoire list (pp. 224–225).

231. _____. "Giuseppe and Fanny Persiani." *Donizetti Society Journal* 6 (1988): 123–151.

A short biography of the composer, Giuseppe Persiani and his singer wife, Fanny, who created several roles in operas by Donizetti, including Adina in *L'elisir d'amore* and the title role in *Rosmonda d'Inghilterra*. Includes a reprint of an article on the soprano that appeared in the 27 November 1847 issue of *The Musical World*, a list of Giuseppe's operas with cast lists and premiere information, as well as a list of Fanny's operatic appearances from 1832 to 1859.

232. *Maria Callas alla Scala: Mostra documentaria a vent'anni dalla scomparsa : Teatro alla Scala, Ridotto dei Palchi, 16 settembre–16 novembre 1997*. Milan: Teatro alla Scala, 1997. LC: ML 141.M5 C356 1997.

Exhibition catalog. Contains several essays on Callas, her voice, and her art, as well as reminiscences of the soprano by conductors and other singers. An essay on Callas's performances at the Teatro alla Scala includes illustrations of the original posters advertising the production and pictures of the soprano in the various roles she played. For Donizetti, these include performances in *Lucia di Lammermoor, Anna Bolena*, and *Poliuto*. A chronology of the singer's life and career, a bibliography (pp. 172–173), and a discography (pp. 174–183) also appear.

233. Modugno, Maurizio. "Domenico Donzelli e il suo tempo." *Nuova rivista musicale italiana* 18/2 (April–June 1984): 200–216.

A biographical portrait of the tenor Donzelli (1790–1852) who was born in Bergamo, with a discussion of his vocal ability, style, and interpretation.

234. Pendle, Karin. "A Night at the Opera: The Parisian Prima Donna, 1830–1850." *Opera Quarterly* 4/1 (Spring 1986): 77–89.

The careers of French primadonnas Laure Cinti-Damoreau, Jenny Colon, Cornelie Falcon, Julie Dorus-Gras, Rosine Stolz, Marie-Julie Boulanger, and others are examined. The premature retirements of many singers are discussed. Repertoire lists and a list of women singers active in Paris from about 1830 to 1850 are included.

235. Pleasants, Henry. "Giovanni Battista Rubini (1794–1854)." *Opera Quarterly* 10/2 (Winter 1993–1994): 100–104.

Sketches the tenor's life and career.

236. _____. "A Tenor Tragedy: The Last Days of Adolphe Nourrit." *Opera Quarterly* 10/2 (Winter 1993–1994): 87–99.

Nourrit (1802–1839) was the principal tenor at the Paris Opèra from 1821 to 1837. Knowing that Gilbert-Louis Duprez would assume his position, Nourrit left for Italy to study Italian singing with Donizetti. Drawn from the biography by Quicherat, *Adolphe Nourrit: Sa vie, son caractère, sa correspondance,* Nourrit's experiences in Italy leading to his suicide are chronicled.

237. Smart, Mary Ann. "The Lost Voice of Rosine Stolz." In *En Travesti: Women, Gender Subversion, Opera,* ed. by Corinne Blackmer and Patricia Juliana Smith, 169–189. Between men—Between women. New York: Columbia University Press, 1995. ISBN: 0-231-10269-0. LC: ML 2100.E6 1995.

There has been no convergence of the practice of feminist interpretations of texts and the biographies of women. The amount of documentation needed to produce a biographical study overwhelms an author's attempts at critical interpretation, resulting in a genre that is conservative and anti-theoretical. This dichotomy occurs within recent opera criticism as well, but new explorations of synthesizing the two have been made. Here, the author takes Rosine Stolz, reigning prima donna of the Paris Opéra, and attempts to strip away the false veneer to find the real person beneath. As such, the blurring of art and life takes on a particular significance and helps to separate Stolz, the voice from Stolz, the woman. Also appears in the *Cambridge Opera Journal* 6/1 (March 1994): 31–50.

238. Tamvaco, Jean-Louis. "Paul-Bernard Barroilhet." *Donizetti Society Journal* 2 (1975): 131–142.

First appeared in *Connaissance de Paris et de la France* 17 (1973); this version translated by John Standen and edited by John Watts. Includes further excerpts on the singer's life and career found in other publications (pp. 139–142).

239. Walsh, Basil F. "Catherine Hayes: An Early Donizetti Prima Donna." *Opera Quarterly* 14/3 (Spring 1998): 46–54.

The Irish soprano Catherine Hayes studied with Manuel García in Paris from 1842 to 1844. In late 1844 she went to Milan to coach with Felice Ronconi, brother of the baritone Giorgio Ronconi. Her earliest exposure to the music of Donizetti was in 1841 in Dublin where she heard Franz Liszt perform his piano arrangement of *Lucia di Lammermoor*. From 1845 on, Hayes was a leading singer of the role of Lucia in all the major Italian opera houses. Her repertoire included several other works by Donizetti, among them *Linda di Chamounix, Anna Bolena, Don Pasquale,* and *Lucrezia Borgia*. Descriptions of her vocal abilities in this article demonstrate the evolution of the soprano's technique and artistry. Excerpted from the author's forthcoming book *Catherine Hayes (1818–1861), Global Prima Donna: Her Contemporaries and Times* (Dublin: Irish Academic Press).

C. Theaters

240. Cametti, Alberto. *Il Teatro di Tordinona poi di Apollo*. Atti e memorie della R. Accademia di S. Cecilia. Tivoli: A. Chicca, 1938.

A history of the Teatro Apollo in Rome.

241. Comuzio, Ermanno. *Il Teatro Donizetti*. Bergamo: Lucchetti, 1990. ISBN: 88-85839-65-8. LC: ML 1733.8.B47 C65 1990.

In two parts. Part 1 is a thorough, well-documented history of the theater up to 1989. For Donizetti, the most useful information can be found on pp. 111–118. Part 2 is a chronology of performances at the theater covering the period 1786–1989 and includes indexes for composers and performers (both vocal and instrumental).

242. Gossett, Philip. "Music at the Théâtre-Italien." In *Music in Paris in the Eighteen-Thirties*, ed. by Peter Bloom, 327–364. Stuyvesant, N.Y.: Pendragon, 1987. ISBN: 09-1872-871-1. LC: ML 270.8.P2 M76 1987.

An analysis of the repertoire of the Théâtre-Italien during the 1830s. Leading Italian opera composers did not merely leave their mark on Paris; rather, Bellini, Donizetti, and Mercadante emerged from their contact with the Théâtre-Italien and other Parisian musical institutions with an awareness of French operatic style that prompted them to rethink the standard procedures and forms of Italian opera, and the works resulting from this reconsideration helped to prepare the way for Verdi.

243. Mancini, Franco. "I teatri dei Borbone: due storie in cento immagini." In *Donizetti e i teatri napoletani nell'ottocento*, 149–186. Naples: Electa, 1997.

An exhaustive study, lavishly illustrated, of the two major Neapolitan theaters of the period, the Teatro San Carlo and the Teatro Fondo. Includes bibliographical citations of available primary and secondary resources on the construction, modifications, acoustics, orchestra, and seating arrangements of each theater.

244. _____. "I teatri minori." In *Donizetti e i teatri napoletani nell'ottocento*, 187–199. Naples: Electa, 1997.

A shorter, but no less exhaustive, study of the smaller Neapolitan theaters of the period, including the Teatro dei Fiorentini, the Teatro Nuovo, the Teatro San Ferdinando, the Teatro San Carlino, the Teatro Fenice, the Teatro Partenope, and the Teatro Sebeto, among others. Engravings of the facades and interior plans of the theaters are shown, and the bibliography cites historical sources that informed the study.

245. Pendle, Karin, and Stephen Wilkins. "Paradise Found: The Salle le Peletier and French Grand Opera." In Radice, Mark, ed. *Opera in Context: Essays on Historical Stagings from*

the Late Renaissance to the Time of Puccini, 171–207. Portland, OR: Amadeus, 1998. ISBN: 1-57467-032-8. LC: MT 955.O54 1998.

Although Donizetti's operas for the Paris Opéra are not covered, this article is essential for an understanding of how the Salle le Peletier was constructed and the facilities available therein to create the spectacle inherent in the genre of French grand opera.

246. Pinetti, Gian Battista. *Teatro Donizetti (già Riccardi): La stagione d'opera alla fiera di agosto. Cronistoria illustrata dal 1784 al 1936.* Bergamo: S.E.S.A. [i.e., Società Editrice S. Alessandro], 1937. LC: ML 1733.P54.

Provides a complete list of the operas presented at the Teatro Donizetti (once the Teatro Riccardi) from 1784 to 1936, with dates of premieres and names of the principal artists, the conductors, and the impresarios (pp. 153–174). A history of the theater precedes this list.

247. Tiby, Ottavio. *Il Real Teatro Carolino e l'ottocento musicale palermitano.* Historiae Musicae Cultores. Biblioteca, 9. Florence: Olschki, 1957. LC: ML 1733.P25 T5.

About the Teatro Bellini. The name of the theater changed in 1860 from the Teatro Carolino to the Teatro Bellini. This house saw the premiere of Donizetti's *Alahor in Granata* in 1826.

248. Tintori, Giampiero. *Cronologia: Opere, balletti, concerti 1778–1977.* Duecento anni di Teatro alla Scala, 2. Gorle, Italy: Grafica Gutenberg, 1979. LC: ML 1733.8.M5 T45.

Introduction in English and Italian; includes indexes.

249. Tirincanti, Giulio. *Il Teatro Argentina.* Rome: Palombi, 1979. LC: ML 1733.8.R62 A7.

A documented history of the Teatro Argentina in Rome, from the time of its construction in the eighteenth century. Among the more important personalities who figure in the story are Goldoni, Paisiello, Cimarosa, Cherubini, Rossini, Verdi, Donizetti, and Puccini.

The Operas

Here are listed individual works in chronological order. Each entry includes the following information, if applicable:

- Title (Date of Composition)
- Premiere (Date/Place/Venue)
- Autograph MS
- Other Contemporary Sources
- Critical Edition
- Libretti
- Articles/Dissertations/Critical Studies
- Discography
- Videography

A. 1816–1829

Il Pigmalione (1816)

> **Premiere:** Bergamo, Teatro Donizetti, 13 October 1960
>
> **Autograph:** *F-Pc*
>
> **Discography:**

250. *Il Pigmalione*. Susanna Rigacci, soprano; Paolo Pellegrini, tenor; Orchestra da camera dell'Associazione In Canto, Fabio Maestri, conductor. Bongiovanni, 1992. GB 2109/10-2.

Recorded live, September 1990, Teatro Verdi, Terni, in conjunction with Opera In Canto 1990.

Enrico di Borgogna (1818)

Premiere: Venice, Teatro San Luca, 14 November 1818

Autograph: *F-Pc* (copy)

Articles/Dissertations/Critical Studies:

251. Pilon, Luigi. "Gli esordi operistici di Donizetti." In *Atti del 1° Convegno Internazionale di Studi Donizettiani*, 1045–1053. Bergamo: Azienda Autonomo di Turismo, 1983.

The Venetian premiere of Donizetti's *Enrico di Borgogna* at the Teatro San Luca on 14 November1818 marked the real beginning of the composer's operatic career. This article offers an overview of the opera company in Venice that was formed by Paolo Zancla (singers, repertoire, and reception), and with the aid of various pieces of correspondence, examines the genesis of *Enrico di Borgogna*.

Discography:

252. *A Hundred Years of Italian Opera, 1810–1820*. Philharmonia Orchestra, David Parry, conductor. Opera Rara, 1989. ORCH 103.

Includes the recitative and aria "Elisa! Elisa! oh! me infelice! . . . Care aurette che spiegate" for Enrico (Della Jones, mezzo-soprano). Also included on the 1998 anthology entitled *Della Jones Sings Donizetti* (ORR 203).

Le nozze in villa (1819)

Premiere: Mantua, Vecchio, carn. 1820–1821

Autograph: copy *F-Pc*; composed Bergamo, 1819; also performed as *I provinciali, ossia, Le nozze in villa*, Genoa, 1822

Libretti:

253. *I provinciali, ossia, Le nozze in villa: Dramma buffo*. Genova: Stamperia Pagano, piazza nuova No. 43 [1822?]. LC: ML 48.S2764.

Discography:

254. *A Hundred Years of Italian Opera, 1820–1830*. Philharmonia Orchestra, David Parry, conductor. Opera Rara, 1994. ORCH 104.

Includes the trio "In lei vegg'io l'oggetto," for Sabina (Diana Montague, mezzo-soprano), Claudio (Paul Nilon, tenor), and Don Petronio (Jonathan Viera, baritone).

Il falegname di Livonia, o Pietro il grande, czar delle Russie (1819)

Premiere: Venice, Teatro San Samuele, 26 December 1819

Autograph: *I-Mr*

Discography:

255. *A Hundred Years of Italian Opera, 1810–1820*. Philharmonia Orchestra, David Parry, conductor. Opera Rara, 1989. ORCH 103.

Includes the sextet from Act II, "Ah qual colpo, oh ciel, qual fremito" for Madama Fritz (Marilyn Hill Smith, soprano), Caterina (Susan Bickley, mezzo-soprano), Annetta Mazeppa (Myrna Moreno, mezzo-soprano), Carlo Scavronski (Kevin John, tenor), Ser Cuccupis (Jonathan Best, baritone), and Pietro il Grande (Russell Smythe, baritone).

Zoraide di Granata (1822)

Premiere: Rome, Argentina, 28 January 1822

Autograph: *I-Mr*; rev. (J. Ferretti), Rome, 1824

Libretti:

256. *Zoraida de Granada: Drama heroico*. Lisbon: Na typografia de Bulhoes, 1825. LC: ML 48.S2759.

In Portuguese and Italian.

Discography:

257. *A Donizetti Festival*. MRF Records, 1978. MRF-149-S. LP.

Includes the aria, "Rose que un dì spiegasti" (Janet Price, soprano; The Raglan Players, Nicholas Kraemer, conductor). Recorded at the Hintlesham Festival, Suffolk, England, 1973.

La zingara (1822)

Premiere: Naples, Nuovo, 12 May 1822

Autograph: copy *I-Nc*

Other Contemporary Sources:

258. *La zingara: Opera semi-seria in due atti* / musica di G. Donizetti. Paris: Schonenberger, 1856. Plate no. S. 2170.

Vocal score.

Libretti:

259. *La zingara: dramma per musica.* Naples: Dalla Tipografia Orsiniana, 1822. LC: ML48.S2752.

Articles/Dissertations/Critical Studies:

260. Gazzaniga, Arrigo. "Donizetti a Napoli: Da *La zingara* a *L'esule.*" In *Atti del 1° Convegno Internazionale di Studi Donizettiani*, 351–399. Bergamo: Azienda Autonomo di Turismo, 1983.

Surveys the operatic productions of Donizetti during his first Neapolitan period. These works are notable mostly for their relationship to stage works of Giovanni Simone Mayr, a figure who insistently returns in the handling of these works.

Discography:

261. *A Hundred Years of Italian Opera, 1820–1830.* Royal Philharmonic Orchestra, David Parry, conductor. Opera Rara, 1994. ORCH 104.

Includes the cavatina, "A te nell'appressarmi," for Fernando (Bruce Ford, tenor).

La lettera anonima (1822)

Premiere: Naples, Fondo, 29 June 1822

Autograph: *I-Mr*

Other Contemporary Sources:

262. *La lettera anonima: Opera buffa in un atto.* Paris: Schonenbergeris, 1856. Plate no.: S.2178.

Vocal score.

Discography:

263. *La lettera anonima*. Benedetta Pecchioli, soprano; Pietro Bottazzo, tenor; Rolando Panerai, baritone; Orchestra Alessandro Scarlatti, Naples, Franco Caracciolo, conductor. On Stage!, [1990?]. 4702.

Recorded live, 12 December 1972, Naples.

Chiara e Serafina, o I pirati (1822)

Premiere: Milan, La Scala, 26 October 1822

Autograph: *I-Mr*

Libretti:

264. *Chiara e Serafina, ossia, Il pirata: Melodramma*. Milan: Dalle Stampe di Giacomo Pirola dirincontro al Detto I.R. teatro, [1822?]. LC: ML 48.S2766.

Discography:

265. *A Hundred Years of Italian Opera, 1820–1830*. Philharmonia Orchestra, David Parry, conductor. Opera Rara, 1994. ORCH 104.

Includes the trio, "Tremante, smarrito," for Serafina (Yvonne Kenny, soprano), Chiara (Lynn Davies, soprano), and Lisetta (Della Jones, mezzo-soprano).

Alfredo il grande (1823)

Premiere: Naples, San Carlo, 2 July 1823

Autograph: *I-Nc; F-Pc* (non-autograph manuscript)

Discography:

266. *Bruce Ford: Romantic Heroes*. Bruce Ford, tenor; Philharmonia Orchestra, David Parry, conductor. Opera Rara, 1997. ORR 202.

Includes the aria of Alfredo, "No! non m'ingannai."

267. *A Hundred Years of Italian Opera, 1820–1830*. Royal Philharmonic Orchestra, David Parry, conductor. Opera Rara, 1994. ORCH 104.

Includes the aria finale, "Che potrei dirti, o caro?" for Margherita (Linda Kitchen, soprano), Amalia (Della Jones, mezzo-soprano), Enrichetta (Theresa Goble, mezzo-soprano), Alfredo (Brendan McBride, tenor), Guglielmo (David Ashman, baritone), and Eduardo (Ian Platt, baritone). Also included on the 1998 anthology entitled *Della Jones Sings Donizetti* (ORR 203).

Il fortunato inganno (1823)

> **Premiere:** Naples, Nuovo, 3 September 1823
>
> **Autograph:** *I-Nc*
>
> **Libretti:**

268. *Il fortunato inganno: Dramma giocoso per musica.* Naples: Nella stamperia del giornale delle Due Sicilie, 1823. LC: ML 48.S2756.

L'ajo nell'imbarazzo, o Don Gregorio (1824)

> **Premiere:** Rome, Valle, 4 February 1824
>
> **Autograph:** rev. as *Don Gregorio,* Naples, 1826; as *Il governo della casa,* Dresden, 1828; *I-Nc* (partly autograph)
>
> **Other Contemporary Sources:**

269. *L'ajo nell'imbarrazzo: Opera buffa in due atti.* Paris: Schonenberger, 1856. Plate no.: S. 2152.

Vocal score.

270. *L'ajo nell'imbarazzo: Melodramma giocoso in due atti* / di Jacopo Ferretti. Milan: G. Ricordi, 1878. Plate no.: 45735

Vocal score.

> **Libretti:**

271. *L'ajo nell'imbarazzo: Melodramma giocoso.* Milan: Per Antonio Fontana, 1826. LC: ML 48.S2631.

272. *L'ajo nell'imbarazzo: Melodramma giocoso.* Genoa: Tipografia de' fratelli Pagano, [1839?]. LC ML 48.S11810.

273. *Der Hofmeister in Verlegenheit: Komische Oper in zwei Akten.* Berlin: [s.n.], 1841. LC: ML 48.S2632.

In German and Italian.

274. *Das Hausregiment: Heiteres Melodram in zwei Akten.* Dresden: [s.n.], 1828. LC: ML 48.S2633.

Libretto to *Il governo della casa*; in German.

Articles/Dissertations/Critical Studies

275. Watts, John. "*L'ajo nell'imbarazzo.*" *Donizetti Society Journal* 1 (1974): 41–50.

In 1822, Donizetti signed a contract with the impresario Giovanni Paterni to write an opera buffa for the Teatro Valle in Rome, as well as to revise the successful *Zoraide di Granata.* For the revisions to *Zoraide,* and for the new opera buffa, Donizetti chose Jacopo Ferretti as his librettist. The new work produced by this collaboration was *L'ajo nell'imbarazzo.* It is no coincidence that this work resembles Rossini's *La cenerentola:* Ferretti composed the libretto for that work as well. The author works out the compositional history of the opera and its reception with audiences in and out of Italy, as well as documenting the alterations made to the work for a performance in Naples at the Teatro Nuovo.

Discography:

276. *L'ajo nell'imbarazzo.* Luciana Serra, soprano; Aracelly Haengel, mezzo-soprano; Paolo Barbacini, tenor; Vito Gobbi, tenor; Alessandro Corbelli, baritone; Enzo Dara, bass; Teatro Reggio Orchestra, Turin, Bruno Campanella, conductor. Fonit Cetra, 1994. CDC 81.

Emilia di Liverpool (1824)

Premiere: Naples, Nuovo, 28 July 1824

Autograph: rev. (G. Checcherini), Naples 1828; also perf. as *L'ermitaggio di Liwerpool; I-Nc,* copy *F-Pc*

Libretti:

277. *L'eremitaggio di Liwerpool: Melo-dramma semi-serio.* Naples: Dalla stamperia dell'amministrazione provinciale e comunale di Napoli, [1828?]. LC: ML 48.S2755.

Articles/Dissertations/Critical Studies:

278. Commons, Jeremy. "*Emilia di Liverpool.*" *Music and Letters* 40/3 (July 1959): 207–228.

Donizetti's sixteenth opera, *Emilia di Liverpool,* attained only moderate success during its initial run. During the celebration of the City of Liverpool's 750th anniversary in 1957, the opera was revived and performed in a concert version. This event allows for a reinvestigation of the work. The opera has a complicated textual background, including more than one extant version and a libretto composed by an anonymous poet. The author outlines the stage history of the work in its various versions, documents that the libretto was based on a play by Scatizzi, and discusses the revised version of 1828 to a libretto by Giuseppe Checcherini. At the end, the author outlines the contents of the various extant manuscripts and printed score of the work.

Discography:

279. *Emilia di Liverpool.* Yvonne Kenny, soprano; Chris Merritt, tenor; Sesto Bruscantini, baritone; Geoffrey Mitchell Choir, Philharmonia Orchestra, David Parry, conductor. Opera Rara, 1987. ORC 8.

No spoken dialogue included. Recorded November–December 1986, Conway Hall, London.Includes a performance of *L'ermitaggio di Liwerpool* (sides 5–8).

Alahor in Granata (1826)

   Premiere: Palermo, Carolino, 7 January 1826

   Autograph: *US-Bm* (copy)

   Libretti:

280. *Alahor in Granata: Dramma per musica.* Naples: Dalla Tipografia Flautina, 1826. LC: ML 48.S2753.

   Articles/Dissertations/Critical Studies:

281. Freeman, James. "Donizetti in Palermo and *Alahor in Granata.*" *Journal of the American Musicological Society* 25/2 (Summer 1972): 240–250.

Donizetti put on his new serious opera *Alahor* in January 1826 during his year as musical director at the Teatro Carolino in Palermo. The only known score (of a production at the Carolino in 1830) was recently discovered in Boston. *Alahor* was heavily influenced by Rossini. Its anonymous libretto, possibly written with Donizetti's collaboration, seems derived from Romani's libretto for Meyerbeer's *L'esule di Granata* (1822) and is not especially powerful. Abstract from *RILM Abstracts Online*.

Discography:

282. *Alahor in Granata*. Patrizia Pace, soprano; Vivica Genaux, mezzo-soprano; Juan Diego Flórez, tenor; Orquesta Ciudad de Granada, Josep Pons, conductor. Almaviva DS 0125.

Live recording of the opera's first performance in the twentieth century during the 1998–1999 season at Seville's Teatro de la Maestranza.

283. *19th Century Heroines*. Yvonne Kenny, soprano; Philharmonia Orchestra, David Parry, conductor. Opera Rara, 1994. ORR 201.

Includes the rondò finale for Zobeida, "Zobeida, il mira . . . Confusa è l'alma mia."

Gabriella di Vergy (1826)

Premiere: Naples, San Carlo, 29 November 1869

Autograph: originally composed in two acts, 1826; rev. by others for 1869 performance; *I-BGi*

Libretti:

284. *Gabriella di Vergy: Tragedia lirica in tre atti*. Milan: Coi Tipi di Francesco Lucca, [18—]. LC: ML 48.S2696.

Articles/Dissertations/Critical Studies:

285. White, Don. "Donizetti and the Three 'Gabriellas'." *Opera* 29/10 (October 1978): 962–970.

Donizetti wrote *Gabriella di Vergy* in 1826 without having a contract for mounting a production, an unusual undertaking for the time. The tragic work was to form the chrysalis from which the mature style of the composer, as exemplified by *Anna Bolena,* would emerge. Until the appearance of this article, it had been thought that the opera existed in two versions, the original of 1826 and a 1869 reworking of the score by Giuseppe Puzone and Paolo Serrao.

Another version in manuscript by the composer dating from 1838 was discovered by the author in the Sterling Library at the University of London. This article presents the various versions as they are now known and provides a detailed analysis of the 1838 version.

Discography:

286. *Gabriella di Vergy.* Della Jones, Eiddwen Harrhy, sopranos; Royal Philharmonic Orchestra, Alun Francis, conductor. Opera Rara, 1978. ORC 3.

Recorded September–October 1979 at Henry Wood Hall, London. Includes the scena ed aria for Raoul, "Respiro alfin/A te sola/Ah, che fra palpiti," the scena e duetto for Gabriella and Raoul, "Minacciosa perchè me sgridi/Un padre severo," and the recitativo ed aria for Gabriella, "Ah fermate!...Perchè non chiusi al dì."

Second version (1838)

> **Premiere:** Belfast, White Hall, 9 November 1978
>
> **Autograph:** *GB-Lu* (partly autograph)
>
> **Discography:**

287. *Gabriella di Vergy.* Milla Andrew, soprano; Maurice Arthur, John Winfield, tenors; Christian du Plessis, baritone; John Tomlinson, bass; Geoffrey Mitchell Choir, Royal Philharmonic Orchestra, Alun Francis, conductor. Opera Rara, 1978. ORC 3.

Recorded September–October 1979 at Henry Wood Hall, London. Includes two arias and a duet from the 1826 version featuring Della Jones and Eiddwen Harrhy, sopranos. The aria "A te sola, ognor serbai" and the duet "Oh istante felice!" are also included on the 1998 anthology entitled *Della Jones Sings Donizetti* (ORR 203).

Olivo e Pasquale (1827)

> **Premiere:** Rome, Valle, 7 January 1827
>
> **Autograph:** *I-Nc*
>
> **Other Contemporary Sources:**

288. *Olivo e Pasquale: Opera buffa in due atti.* Paris: Schonenberger, 1856. Plate no.: S. 2147.

Vocal score.

Libretti:

289. *Olivo e Pasquale: Burletta in musica.* Prato: Presso i Fratelli Giachetti, [1831?]. LC: ML 48.S2738.

290. *Olivo und Pasqual: Komische Oper in zwei Akten.* Berlin: [s.n.], 1845. LC: ML 48.S2739.

In German and Italian.

Articles/Dissertations/Critical Studies:

291. Waidelich, Gerrit. "'In dem Vaterlande der Haydn, der Mozarte und so vieler andern berühmten Componisten': Ein unbekannter Brief Gaetano Donizettis betreffend den Vertrieb seiner Opera buffa *Olivo e Pasquale* in Deutschland." In *Semantische Inseln-Musikalisches Festland, 57–62.* Zwische/ Töne, Bd. 7. Hamburg: Bockel Verlag, 1997.

Identifies an unknown letter of Donizetti dated 1827 and written in German, which was originally published in the *Berliner Conversations-Blatt*. This letter outlines the background and plan to produce a German version of the composer's *Olivo e Pasquale* in Berlin.

Discography:

292. *Olivo e Pasquale.* Estelle Maria Gibbs, soprano; John Del Carlo, bass; Gastone Sarti, bass, Orchestra giovanile internazionale di Opera Barga, Bruno Rigacci, conductor. Bongiovanni, [1990?]. GB 2005/6-2.

Recorded live 27 July 1980, Teatro dei Differenti, Barga (Lucca).

Otto mesi in due ore, ossia Gli esiliati in Siberia (1827)

Premiere: Naples, Nuovo, 13 May 1827

Autograph: rev. (A. Alcozer), Naples, 1833; *I-Nc,* rev. by U. Fontana as *Elisabeth, ou La fille du proscrit* (De Leuven and Brunswick), Paris, 1853

Other Contemporary Sources:

293. *Elisabeth, ou, La fille du proscrit: Drame lyrique en trois actes* / poeme de MM. de Leuven et Brunswick; musique de

G. Donizetti mise en ordre par Mr. Fontana. Paris: L. Escudier, 1853. Plate no.: L.E. 1418.

Vocal score in French.

Libretti:

294. *Gli esiliati in Siberia, ossia, Otto mesi in due ore.* Genoa: Tipografia dei Fratelli Pagano con permissione, [1835?]. LC: ML 48.S2663.

Articles/Dissertations/Critical Studies:

295. Bini, Annalisa. "*Otto mesi in due ore, ossia Gli esiliati in Siberia:* Vicende di un'opera donizettiana." *Rivista italiana di musicologia* 22 (1987): 183–260.

Discusses the evolution of Donizetti's melodramma romantico *Gli esiliati in Siberia,* as reconstructed by an analysis of the libretto by Domenico Gilardoni, its literary sources, and the changes added by the composer to the score on the occasion of performances in Naples, Palermo, Livorno, Florence, Milan, Rome, Venice, Turin, Genoa, Bologna, and Modena. The Sezione Accademica of the Biblioteca di Santa Cecilia, Rome holds a manuscript of *Gli esiliati in Siberia* containing two fragments in autograph, which corroborates the revision for Rome.

296. Crutchfield, Will. "A Donizetti Discovery." *Musical Times* 125 (September 1984): 487–490.

Discusses the significance of the author's discovery of materials in the archives of Covent Garden and the Paris Opéra relating to *Elisabeth,* and their relationship to the earlier and later versions *Otto mesi* and *Elisabetta.*

297. Porter, Andrew. "A Double Century, One to Come: Andrew Porter on Donizetti and His *Elisabetta.*" *Opera* 48/12 (December 1997): 1411–1419.

By the end of the nineteenth century, all but a handful of operas by Rossini, Bellini, and Donizetti were forgotten, and Donizetti's serious works in particular were held in low esteem. The author first summarizes the accomplishments of the Donizetti Renaissance and then outlines the compositional history of *Elisabetta,* a reworking of the earlier *Otto mesi in due ore*. Various revisions to the work are also covered.

Discography:

298. *Secrets*. Christine Weidinger, soprano; Polish Radio Symphony Orchestra, Cracow, Richard Bonynge, conductor. Newport Classic, 1994. NPD 85560.

Includes the aria, "Rinata l'alma," from *Elisabetta di Siberia* as reconstructed by the conductor. Recorded December 15–21, 1992, Cracow, Poland.

Il borgomastro di Saardam (1827)

Premiere: Naples, Nuovo, 19 August 1827

Autograph: *I-Mr*

Other Contemporary Sources:

299. *Il borgomastro di Saardam: Opera buffa in due atti*. Paris: Schonenberger, 1856. Plate no.: S. 2147.

Vocal score in French.

Libretti:

300. *Il borgomastro di Saardam: Melodramma giocoso*. Turin: Presso Onorato Derossi stampatore e librajo de' teatri, [1833?]. LC: ML 48.S2645.

301. *Gesänge aus Der Bürgermeister von Saardam*. Berlin: [s.n., 18—]. LC: ML 48.S2646.

In German.

Articles/Dissertations/Critical Studies:

302. Schaap, Jan. "Donizetti and his *Il borgomastro di Saardam*." *Donizetti Society Journal* 1 (1974): 51–57.

In 1827, Donizetti obtained a three-year contract from the Neapolitan impresario, Domenico Barbaja, for a total of twelve new operas. The first of these works was *Otto mesi in due ore,* in which the lead character was the Russian Czar, Peter the Great. Later that year, the second opera premiered, also featuring Peter the Great as a character. This was Donizetti's *Il borgomastro di Saardam*. The character of Peter the Great fascinated authors and composers alike, the stories, often apocryphal, providing the catalyst for a series of operas by other composers during this period. The author discusses the libretto for the work by Domenico Gilardoni and its French antecedents, as well as the primary and secondary sources he used to reconstruct the score for modern performance. A short discussion of changes made to the libretto by the composer is included.

Discography:

303. *Il borgomastro di Saardam*. Peter van den Berg, Renato Capecchi, baritones; Philipp Langridge, tenor; Operastichtung Zaanstad, Jan Schaap, conductor. Pantheon, 1995. PHE 6630. Rarità dell'opera italiana.

Recorded in Zaanstad, The Netherlands in 1973.

Le convenienze ed inconvenienze teatrali (1827)

Premiere: Naples, Nuovo, 21 November 1827

Autograph: rev. (two acts), Milan, 1831, Vienna, 1840; *F-Pc* (partly autograph)

Other Contemporary Sources:

304. *Le convenienze ed inconvenienze teatrale: Opera in un atto*. Paris: Schonenberger, 1856. Plate no.: S. 2148.

Vocal score.

305. *Le convenienze teatrali: Opera giocosa in 2 atti*: Canto e piano / G. Donizetti; revisione, Eva Riccioli. Florence: Edizioni musicali OTOS, 1971. Plate no. 2056.

Vocal score.

Articles/Dissertations/Critical Studies:

306. Fiorentini, Rossella. *Le convenienze e le inconvenzienze teatrali di Gaetano Donizetti: Un'opera settecentesca nell'Ottocento*. Tesi di laurea, Storia del teatro: U. degli Studi di Trieste, 1985–1986.

Not examined.

Discography:

307. *Le convenienze ed inconvenienze teatrali.* Maria Costanza Nocentini, soprano; Bruno Lazzaretti, tenor; Alberto Noli, baritone; Bruno De Simone, bass; Orchestra dei Pomeriggi Musicali, Fabrizio Maria Carminati, conductor. Dischi Ricordi, 1996. 74321405872.

Recorded live October 1995, Teatro Donizetti, Bergamo during the XII Festival "Donizetti e il suo tempo." A recording of the critical edition prepared by Roger Parker and Anders Wiklund.

L'esule di Roma, ossia Il proscritto (1828)

Premiere: Naples, San Carlo, 1 January 1828

Autograph: also performed as *Settimio il proscritto; I-Mr*

Other Contemporary Sources:

308. *L'esule di Roma: Melodramma eroico* / del D. Gilardoni. Naples: B. Girard; Milan: G. Ricordi, 1840? Plate no.: 682/885.

Vocal score.

Libretti:

309. *Settimio, ossia, L'esule di Roma: tragedia lirica.* Ragusa: Pietro-Francesco Martecchini Tipografo e Librajo, [1838?]. LC: ML 48.S2676.

310. *L'esule di Roma: Melodramma eroico.* Milan: Per Antonio Fontana, 1828. LC: ML 48.S2675.

311. *Eustorgia da Romano: Azione tragica in due atti.* [S.l.]: Impresso a spese dell'impresa, 1838. LC: ML 48.S2767.

Articles/Dissertations/Critical Studies:

312. Kaufman, Thomas G. "*L'esule di Roma*: A Performance History." *Donizetti Society Journal* 4 (1980): 104–109.

A large number of Donizetti's opere serie have been revived since the end of World War II. Unfortunately, *L'esule di Roma* has not been among them. Of all of the earlier operas, this one in particular has a real performance history, numbering over sixty productions in the nineteenth century alone. The process of compiling a performance history for these works is complicated by the lack of annals for a large number of opera houses, as well as the errors found in printed general sources. The author bypasses the secondary sources and consults primary sources instead to produce a performance history for the work from 1828 to 1869. The performances cited not only took place in Italy, but in Spain, Eastern Europe, and Latin America.

313. Sarnaker, Benedict. "Chi cantò *L'esule di Roma?* ovvero, Parti in cerca di cantanti." In *Il melodramma italiano dell'ottocento,* 413–424. Saggi, 575. Turin: G. Einaudi, 1977. LC: ML 1733.4.M5.

L'esule di Roma was the fourth opera that Donizetti produced for Domenico Barbaja in Naples and had its premiere at the Teatro San Carlo on 1 January 1828. The author provides a plot summary for the work and describes two editions of the opera's libretto in which different singers are named for the roles of Settimio and Publio. The question of who actually sang these roles in the premiere performance is answered, documenting that Bernardo Winter and Salvadori respectively created these roles, while Rubini and Campagnoli sang in the following season's revival of the opera. Further, the author describes the differences in the two productions by what appears in the two editions of the libretto.

Discography:

314. *L'esule di Roma.* Cecilia Gasdia, soprano; Ernesto Palacio, tenor; Simone Alaimo, baritone; Armando Ariostini, baritone; Orchestra sinfonica di Piacenza, Massimo de Bernart, conductor. Bongiovanni, 1986. GB 2045/46/2.

Recorded in performance, 14 October 1986, Teatro Chiabrera di Savona.

Alina, regina di Golconda (1828)

> **Premiere:** Genoa, Carlo Felice, 12 May 1828

> **Autograph:** called opera buffa on libretto; rev. Rome, 1833; *I-Nc*

Other Contemporary Sources:

315. *La regina di Golconda: Opera buffa in due atti*. Milan: Ricordi, 1842.

Vocal score.

Libretti:

316. *La regina di Golconda: Melodramma in due atti*. Genoa: Dalla Tipografia dei Fratelli Pagano, piazza Nuova N.o 43, [1828?]. LC: ML 48.S2745.

317. *La regina di Golconda: Melodramma in due atti*. Modena: Tipografia Vincenzi e Rossi, [1842?]. LC: ML 48.S11813.

Articles/Dissertations/Critical Studies:

318. Mioli, Piero. "Da *Alina, regina di Golconda* a *Don Pasquale*: La 'prima buffa' nel vocalismo donizettiano." *Studi donizettiani* 4 (1988): 127–161.

This article looks at the construction of, and changes in, the way Donizetti composed vocal lines in the operas from *Alina, regina di Golconda* to *Don Pasquale*. Numerous musical examples illustrate the author's theories.

319. Rosso, Federica. *Gaetano Donizetti e il genere semiserio: Alina, regina di Golconda*. Tesi di laurea: U. degli Studi di Pavia, Scuola di Paleografia e Filologia Musicale, 1990–1991.

Not examined.

Discography:

320. *Alina, regina di Golconda*. Daniela Dessì, soprano; Rockwell Blake, tenor; Paolo Coni, bass; Orchestra giovanile dell'Emilia Romagna "Arturo Toscanini", Antonello Allemandi, conductor. Nuova Era, 1988. 033.6701.

Recorded 15–17 July 1987, Teatro Alighieri, at the Ravenna Festival.

Gianni di Calais (1828)

Premiere: Naples, Fondo, 2 August 1828

Autograph: *I-Nc*

Libretti:

321. *Gianni da Calais: Melodramma semiserio in tre atti.* Milan: Per Antonio Fontana, 1830. LC: ML 48.S2699.

Articles/Dissertations/Critical Studies:

322. Johnson, Janet. "Donizetti's First 'Affare di Parigi': An Unknown Rondò-Finale for *Gianni da Calais*." In *L'Opera teatrale di Gaetano Donizetti: Atti del Convegno Internazionale di Studio*, 329–352. Bergamo: Comune di Bergamo, 1993.

Marino Faliero is the opera that has until now been credited with launching Donizetti's Parisian career. However, the discovery of new manuscript and printed musical sources demonstrate that the composer's ties to the city date back to 1833. Plans to mount productions of two earlier works, *Gianni di Parigi* (1831) and *Gianni di Calais* (1828), helped Donizetti to adapt his style to Parisian taste. The former work was never mounted, but the latter was. As such, Donizetti created a new third-act rondò-finale, "Addio nembi," for the tenor Rubini who created the title role. The sources central to this study may be found in the Bibliothèque nationale. Reprinted with minor changes in the *Cambridge Opera Journal* 10/2 (1998): 157–177.

Il giovedì grasso, o Il nuovo Pourceaugnac (1828)

Premiere: Naples, Fondo, Autumn 1828

Autograph: *I-Nc*

Other Contemporary Sources:

323. *Il giovedì grasso: Opera buffa in un atto.* Paris: Schonenberger, 1856. Plate no.: S. 2169.

Vocal score; without recitatives.

Articles/Dissertations/Critical Studies:

324. Barblan, Guglielmo. "*Il giovedì grasso* e gli svaghi *Farsaioli* di Donizetti." In *Musicisti piemontesi e liguri*, 109–114. Siena: Accademia Musicale Chigiana, 1959. LC: ML 390.D29.

After providing a general overview of Donizetti's early operatic work in the genre of farce, this article takes a closer look at *Il giovedì grasso,* raising several important issues. Among them are the identity of the work's librettist and the opera's relationship to *Monsieur de Pourceaugnac,* Lully and Molière's seventeenth-century collaboration based on the same theme. In addition, a brief harmonic and structural analysis of the opera is provided.

Discography:

325. *Il giovedì grasso.* Jill Gomez, soprano; Malcolm Williams, tenor; Ugo Benelli, bass; Radio Telefis Eireann Symphony Orchestra, David Atherton, conductor. Foyer, 1990. 1-CF 2036.

Recorded live at the 1970 Wexford Festival.

Il paria (1829)

Premiere: Naples, San Carlo, 12 January 1829

Autograph: *I-Nc*

Other Contemporary Sources:

326. *Il paria: Opera seria in due atti.* Paris: Schonenberger, 1856. Plate no.: S. 2151.

Vocal score.

Discography:

327. *A Hundred Years of Italian Opera, 1820–1830.* Royal Philharmonic Orchestra, David Parry, conductor. Opera Rara, 1994. ORCH 104.

Includes the aria, "Qui per figlio una madre gridava," for Zarete (John Rawnsley, baritone).

Elisabetta, o Il castello di Kenilworth (1829)

Premiere: Naples, S. Carlo, 6 July 1829

Autograph: *I-Nc*

Other Contemporary Sources:

328. *Il castello di Kenilworth: Opera in tre atti.* Paris: Schonenberger, 1856. Plate no.: S. 2150.

Vocal score.

Libretti:

329. *Elisabetta: Dramma lirico in tre atti.* Milan: Dall'I.R. Stabilimento Nazionale Privilegiato di Tito di Gio. Ricordi, cont. degli Omenoni N. 1720 e sotto il Portico a Fianco dell'I.R. Teatro alla Scala, 18—]. LC: ML 48.S2665.

330. *Gesänge aus Die Macht der kindlichen Liebe.* Berlin: [s.n., 18—]. LC: ML 48.S2664.

In German.

Articles/Dissertations/Critical Studies:

331. Mitchell, Jerome. "Kenilworth." In *The Walter Scott Operas: An Analysis of Operas Based on the Works of Sir Walter Scott,* 210–259. University: University of Alabama Press, 1977. ISBN: 0-8173-6401-3. LC: ML 2100.M59 1977.

Mitchell's work presents the first serious attempt to identify the many operas based on the works of Walter Scott, and discuss these operas in relation to the originals. The stage works are approached from the point of view of the literary historian rather than the musicologist or music critic. As such, the works are discussed in terms of what the composer and librettist did to the literary original in order to reshape it into a stage drama. Besides Donizetti's *Il castello di Kenilworth,* the following operas are examined: Auber's *Leicester, ou, Le château de Kenilworth,* Christoph Weyse's *Festen paa Kenilworth,* Eugen Seidelmann's *Das Fest zu Kenilworth,* Luigi Badia's *Il Conte di Leicester,* Isidore de Lara's *Amy Robsart,* and Bruno Klein's *Kenilworth.*

Discography:

332. *Elisabetta al castello di Kenilworth.* Mariella Devia, Denia Mazzola, sopranos; Clara Foti, mezzo-soprano; Barry Anderson, tenor; Jozsef Kundiak, tenor; Milan RAI Symphony Orchestra, Jan Latham-König, conductor. Fonit Cetra, 1990. RFCD 2005.

Recorded live in October 1989 at the Teatro Donizetti, Bergamo, during the VIII Festival "Donizetti e il suo tempo."

B. 1830–1835

I pazzì per progetto (1830)

> **Premiere:** Naples, Fondo, 7 February 1830
>
> **Autograph:** *I-Nc*
>
> **Other Contemporary Sources:**

333. *Pazzi per progetto: Opéra in un atto*. Paris: Schonenberger, 1856. Plate no.: S. 2168.

Vocal score.

> **Libretti:**

334. *I pazzi per progetto: Operetta in un atto*. Florence: Tipografia Papini, 1863. LC: ML 48.S2743.

> **Articles/Dissertations/Critical Studies:**

335. Smart, Mary Ann. "Bedlam Romanticized: Donizetti's *I pazzi per progetto* and the Tradition of Comic Madness." In *L'Opera teatrale di Gaetano Donizetti: Atti del Convegno Internazionale di Studio*, 197–217. Bergamo: Comune di Bergamo, 1993.

A more sympathetic and moral perception of madness evolved in the first part of the nineteenth century. Indeed, innovations in the treatment of the insane evoked a change in the affliction's representation in the artistic and cultural world. The *comédies larmoyantes,* sentimental plays that used madness as a central subject, provided a simple and emotionally direct vehicle for such a portrayal. As such, these plays were well suited to operatic adaptations, and were designed to bring the audience to tears. This differed from the eighteenth-century treatment of the subject, which portrayed madness as a comic element, rather than a sympathetic one. In this sense, Donizetti's *I pazzi per progetto* retains a relationship with a past aesthetic. However, our appreciation of the work increases when it is considered in the context of the nineteenth-century shift in attitude toward insanity and the changes in the relationship between comedy and tragedy.

Discography:

336. *I pazzi per progetto*. Susanna Rigacci, soprano; Adriana Cicogna, mezzo-soprano; Leonardo Monreale and Graziano Polidori, basses; Orchestra sinfonica dell' Emilia Romagna "Arturo Toscanini," Bruno Rigacci, conductor. Bongiovanni, 1988. GB 2070-2.

Recorded live, December 1988, Teatro Rossini, Lugo.

Il diluvio universale (1830)

Premiere: Naples, San Carlo, 28 February 1830

Autograph: *I-Nc*

Other Contemporary Sources:

337. *Il diluvio universale: opéra in tre atti*. Paris: Schonenberger, 1856. Plate no.: S. 2183.

Vocal score.

Libretti:

338. *Il diluvio universale: Azione tragico-sacra in tre atti*. Genoa: Dalla Tipografia dei Fratelli Pagano, piazza Nuova N.o 43, [1834?]. LC: ML 48.S2652.

Articles/Dissertations/Critical Studies:

339. Zanolini, Bruno. "L'azione tragico-sacra in Rossini e Donizetti dal *Mosè in Egitto* al *Diluvio Universale*." In *L'Opera teatrale di Gaetano Donizetti: Atti del Convegno Internazionale di Studio*, 149–169. Bergamo: Comune di Bergamo, 1993.

An analysis of Rossini's *Mosè in Egitto* (1818) and Donizetti's *Il diluvio universale* (1830), two very similar works, can help us to understand the important artistic links between these composers. Theater works based on biblical themes, usually taken from Old Testament subjects, were typically given during the Lenten season. Characteristic of these works was the figure of a prophet as a main character, increased involvement of a chorus that represented the voice of the people, and a *preghiera*, or prayer, for solo voice. The extended range of the bass voice, often referred to as a *basso cantante*, lent a certain nobility of tone to the central figure of these operas. The two works discussed here share several characteristics, including dramatic structure, characters, psychological situations, expressive techniques, and even a shared source for their texts. However, Donizetti's opera should not be quickly dismissed as merely an imitation of Rossini's earlier setting. *Il diluvio universale* is thoroughly original, displaying Donizetti's sensitivity to newly emerging Romantic sensibilities and his obvious skills in compositional technique and dramaturgical functions. In Italian; with summary in English.

Discography:

340. *Rare Donizetti*. Margreta Elkins, soprano; Philharmonia Orchestra, James Judd, conductor. Opera Rara, 1979. OR 4.

Recorded January 1979, London. Includes the recitative and aria, "Non mi tradir speranza/Ah non tacermi in core."

Imelda de' Lambertazzi (1830)

Premiere: Naples, San Carlo, 23 August 1830

Autograph: *I-Nc*

Libretti:

341. *Imelda de' Lambertazzi: Melo-dramma tragico*. Naples: Dalla Tipografia Flautina, 1830. LC: ML 48.S2763.

Discography:

342. *Rare Donizetti*. Margreta Elkins, soprano; Philharmonia Orchestra, James Judd, conductor. Opera Rara, 1979. OR 4.

Recorded January 1979, London. Includes the recitative and aria, "Vincesti alfin/Amarti nel martiro."

Anna Bolena (1830)

Premiere: Milan, Carcano, 26 December 1830

Autograph: *I-Mr*

Other Contemporary Sources:

343. *Anna Bolena: Tragedia lirica* / di Felice Romani, rappresentata al Teatro Carcano; ridotta con accompag[namen]to di

piano forte dal Mo. [Luigi]. Florence; Milan: Ricordi e Co., 1830 or 1831. Plate nos.: 4241, 5130/T. 5241 B.

Vocal score. A second edition of this score was issued in 1876.

Libretti:

344. *Anna Bolena* / by Gaetano Donizetti; English version by Donald Pippin. San Francisco, CA: Pocket Opera, 1993. LC: ML 50.D683 A62 1993.

Libretto in English.

345. *Anna Bolena: Tragedia lirica in due atti.* Milan: Per Gaspare Truffi, 1840. LC: ML 48.S2634.

Libretto in Italian.

346. *Anna Boulen: Grosse Oper in zwei Akten.* Berlin: [s.n., 18—]. LC: ML 48.S2637.

In German.

347. *Anna Boleyn: Grosse tragische Oper in zwei Aufzügen.* Stuttgart: in C. Eichele's Musikverlag, 1835. LC: ML 48.S2638.

In German.

348. *Anna Boleyn: Lyrische Tragödie in 2 Akten.* Dresden: [s.n.], 1833. LC: ML 48.S2636.

In German and Italian.

349. *Anna Boulen: Tragische Oper in zwei Akten.* Berlin: [s.n.], 1841. LC: ML 48.S2635.

In German and Italian.

Articles/Dissertations/Critical Studies:

350. Cagli, Bruni. "Donde tal pianto." *Donizetti Society Journal* 4 (1980): 110–114.

Critics and scholars alike have identified *Anna Bolena* as the work in which Donizetti reaches artistic maturity. This work, therefore, divides the composer's operatic output into two categories: 1) those of his apprenticeship, which precede this work; and 2) those of his artistic genius, which follow this work. In this article, the author looks at this work in comparison to other operatic works produced in the same time period, especially Bellini's *La sonnambula* and *Il pirata*.

351. Gattey, Charles N. "Donizetti's *Anna Bolena*: Historical Accuracy Considered." *About the House* 7/11 (1988): 11–14.

With the success of *Anna Bolena*, Donizetti finally attained the international recognition that he so ardently sought. In an extended plot summary, the author investigates whether this particular opera seria is true to history or not. As such, he outlines the main inventions of the libretto as opposed to historical fact. This article was written on the occasion of a new production of the opera given by the Royal Opera, London on 30 May 1988 starring Joan Sutherland as Anna.

352. Gossett, Philip. *Anna Bolena and the Artistic Maturity of Gaetano Donizetti*. Studies in Musical Genesis and Structure. Oxford: Clarendon Press, 1985. ISBN: 01-9313-205-2. LC: ML 410.D7 G67 1985.

An exhaustive history and critical evaluation of the opera and of Donizetti's role as an operatic reformer which uses the autograph score as a basis for study. As such, it examines the compositional decisions made by Donizetti that affected *Anna Bolena*'s structure, continuity, and proportion. It is demonstrated that the composer's instincts in these decisions return to Rossinian models, but also that he forces the boundaries of the established conventions.

353. _____. "Un nuovo duetto per *Anna Bolena*: 'Sì, son io che a te ritorno'." In *Atti del 1° Convegno Internazionale di Studi Donizettiani*, 311–332. Bergamo: Azienda Autonomo di Turismo, 1983.

In February 1831, the Milanese newspaper *L'eco* reported that Donizetti had made several changes to his new opera *Anna Bolena*. This report did not explicitly name the changes made, but a direct examination of the autograph score allows for several suppositions: the abbreviation of the introductory chorus and the substitution of a new cabaletta for the trio "Ambo morrete, o perfidi." However,

an additional change is more important than these other two: that
of a new duet for Anna and Percy in the Act I finale. Gossett provides the new text and analyzes the effect of the new duet on the
formal and dramatic structure of the opera.

354. Hauser, Richard. *Felice Romani — Gaetano Donizetti —
     Anna Bolena. Zur Asthetik politischer Oper in Italien zwi-
     schen 1826 und 1831.* Ph.D. diss., Theology — Philosophy:
     Albert Ludwigs U., Freiburg, 1980.

Romani revolutionized the Italian libretto, creating a clearly con-
toured *melodramma romantico* that was suitable for a through-
composed setting. First Bellini, in *Il pirata* and succeeding works,
then Donizetti, in *Anna Bolena,* appropriated the reform libretto
and produced virtually through-composed operas in keeping
with Romani's aim, avoiding the usual negligence in setting the
words and making the meter conform to the dramatic situation
and mood. In Act I, all the characters enter immediately after the
prima donna, so that in place of the usual introductory aria there is
now an ensemble. The entry of the seconda donna now leads as a
rule to a concerted piece, the stretta of the pezzo concertato un-
leashing all the passions of the protagonists. Act II proceeds simi-
larly, except that its final scene is treated as a composition in its own
right: out of a stretta finale there emerges the finale largo concertato
(structured as a concert piece). Without Romani's reform libretto,
Verdi's three operas on state themes would not have been possible.

355. Pipes, Charlotte F. *A Study of Six Selected Coloratura So-
     prano Mad Scenes in Ninteenth-Century Opera.* D.M.A. the-
     sis, Louisiana State University, 1990.

The coloratura "mad scene" was an outstanding feature found in
several nineteenth-century operas. Significant in its display of the
performer's talent, it requires the ultimate combination of vocal virtuosity and dramatic expression. This study seeks to define and illustrate some of these characteristics as found in Donizetti: "Al
dolce guidami" from *Anna Bolena,* and "Argon gl'incensi" from
Lucia di Lammermoor, as well as in works by other composers of
the time. After an introductory chapter that surveys the musical, literary, and social influences that affected the development of the Romantic era mad scene, each individual scene is examined. The
libretto, the dramatic action in the scene, and certain elements of

musical style are explored for their contribution to the effectiveness of the scene. A final chapter offers a comparative analysis of all the mad scenes covered in this work to evaluate their relative effectiveness. This author concludes that the heroines of *Anna Bolena* and *Lucia di Lammermoor* seem the most believable in their madness. Abstract abridged from *Dissertation Abstracts Online*.

Discography:

356. *Anna Bolena.* Elena Souliotis, soprano; Marilyn Horne, mezzo-soprano; Nicolai Ghiaurov, bass; Vienna State Opera Chorus, Vienna Opera Orchestra, Silvio Varviso, conductor. London Records, [1997], p1970. 455 069-2.

Recorded at Sofiensaal, Vienna, September 1968 and August–September 1969.

357. *Anna Bolena.* Edita Gruberova, soprano; Delores Ziegler, mezzo-soprano; Stefano Palatchi, tenor; José Bros, bass; Hungarian Radio Symphony Orchestra, Elio Boncompagni, conductor. Nightingale Classics, 1995. NC 070565-2.

358. *Anna Bolena.* Maria Callas, soprano; Giulietta Simionato, mezzo-soprano; Gabriella Carturan, contralto; Gianni Raimondi, Luigi Rumbo, tenors; Nicola Rossi Lemeni, Plinio Clabassi, basses; Orchestra e Coro del Teatro alla Scala, Gianandrea Gavazzeni, conductor. EMI Classics, 1993. 0777 7 64941 2 8.

Recorded live at La Scala, Milan, 14 April 1957.

359. *Anna Bolena.* Joan Sutherland, soprano; Susanne Mentzer, mezzo-soprano; Jerry Hadley, tenor; Samuel Ramey, bass; Orchestra and Chorus of the Welsh National Opera, Richard Bonynge, conductor. London, 1988. 421 096-2.

Recorded February 1987 at Walthamstow Assembly Hall, Walthamstow, Essex.

360. *Anna Bolena.* Beverly Sills, soprano; Shirley Verrett, mezzosoprano, Stuart Burrows, tenor; Paul Plishka, bass; John Alldis Chorus, London Symphony Orchestra, Julius Rudel, conductor. Angel, 1985. Angel Voices. Angel: AVC-34031 LPs.

Complete recording; no cuts. Recorded at EMI Studios, London, August 1972. Previously released in 1973 by ABC Records (ATS-20015).

Gianni di Parigi (1831)

Premiere: Milan, La Scala, 10 September 1839

Autograph: *I-Nc*

Other Contemporary Sources:

361. *Gianni di Parigi: Melodramma comico* / di Felice Romani. Milan: G. Ricordi, 1843. Plate nos.: 14806–14831.

Vocal score.

362. *Gianni di Parigi: Melodramma comico* / di Felice Romani. Paris: S. Richault, 1842? Plate no.: 7651.R.

Vocal score.

Libretti:

363. *Gianni di Parigi: Melodramma in due atti.* Milan: Per Gaspare Truffi, 1839. LC: ML 48.S2700.

Discography:

364. *Gianni di Parigi.* Luciana Serra, soprano; Giuseppe Morino, tenor; Angelo Romero, bass-baritone; Orchestra sinfonica and Coro di Milano della RAI, Carlo Felice Cillario, conductor. Nuova Era, 1988. 6752–6753.

Recorded 18–25 September 1988, at Bergamo.

365. *Rare Donizetti.* Margreta Elkins, soprano; Philharmonia Orchestra, James Judd, conductor. Opera Rara, 1979. OR 4.

Recorded January 1979, London. Includes the Canzon d'Oliviero, "Mira o bella il trovatore."

Francesca di Foix (1831)

Premiere: Naples, San Carlo, 30 May 1831

Autograph: *I-Nc*

Libretti:

366. *Francesca di Foix: Melo-dramma in un atto*. Naples: Dalla Tipografia Flautina, 1831. LC: ML 48.S2762.

Discography:

367. *Della Jones Sings Donizetti*. Della Jones, mezzo-soprano; Philharmonia Orchestra, Royal Philharmonic Orchestra, London Symphony Orchestra, Alun Francis, David Parry, conductors. Opera Rara, 1998. ORR 203.

Includes the aria for the Page "È la giovane straniera." With the Geoffrey Mitchell Choir. Recorded June 1990 in Conway Hall, London.

La romanziera e l'uomo nero (1831)

> **Premiere:** Naples, Fondo, 18 June 1831
>
> **Autograph:** *I-Nc*
>
> **Other Contemporary Sources:**

368. *La romanziera: Opera buffa in un atto*. Paris: Schonenberger, 1856. Plate no.: S. 2172

Vocal score; without recitatives.

Fausta (1832)

> **Premiere:** Naples, San Carlo, 12 January 1832
>
> **Autograph:** overture added, Milan, 1832; rev. Venice, 1834; *I-Nc*
>
> **Other Contemporary Sources:**

369. *Fausta: Melodramma in due atti* / ridotta di L. Truzzi. Milan: G. Ricordi, 1832 or 1833. Plate nos.: 6675/6740.

Vocal score.

> **Libretti:**

370. *Fausta: Melodramma in due atti*. Milan: Per Luigi di Giacomo Pirola, 1832. LC: ML 48.S2677.

371. *Fausta: Oper in 2 Akten.* Berlin: [s.n., 18—]. LC: ML 48.S2678.

In German.

Discography:

372. *Fausta.* Rajna Kabaiwanska, soprano; Giuseppe Giacomini, tenor; Renato Bruson, baritone; Orchestra and Coro del Teatro dell'Opera di Roma, Daniel Oren, conductor. Italian Opera Rarities, 1993. LO 7701/03.

Ugo, conte di Parigi (1832)

Premiere: Milan, La Scala, 13 March 1832

Autograph: *I-Nc*

Other Contemporary Sources:

373. *Ugo conte di Parigi* / musica del Cave. Gaetano Donizetti; ridotta per piano-forte solo [dal Maestro Luigi Truzzi]. Milan: Ricordi, 1832. Plate nos.: 5961, 5963–5964, 5968–5970, 5974, 6025.

Vocal score; each number has separate title page and pagination.

Libretti:

374. *Ugo, conte di Parigi: Tragedia lirica in quattro parti.* Milan: Per G. Truffi e Comp., cont. del Cappuccio N. 5433, [1832?]. LC: ML 48.S2751.

Articles/Dissertations/Critical Studies:

375. Ashbrook, William. "An Air of Competition (Climate of *Norma*'s Early Years)." *Opera News* 43 (March 17 1979): 16–17, 35.

The concept of an established repertory of operas was foreign to the audience of nineteenth-century Italian opera, who were interested mostly in new works. In 1831–1832, the Carnival season of opera at Milan's La Scala included the premieres of Bellini's *Norma* and Donizetti's *Ugo, conte di Parigi*. Also included was the local premiere of Donizetti's *Anna Bolena* that convinced the Milanese audience that this "Neapolitan" composer had much to offer. Bellini in contrast was a respected member of

Milanese society. Comparing these two premiere performances by outlining the problems of bringing a new work to the stage, several distinctions between the reception of Bellini and Donizetti can be made.

Discography:

376. *Ugo conte di Parigi*. Janet Price, Yvonne Kenny, Eiddwen Harrhy, sopranos; Della Jones, mezzo-soprano; Maurice Arthur, tenor; Christian du Plessis, baritone; Geoffrey Mitchell Choir; New Philharmonia Orchestra, Alun Francis, conductor. Opera Rara, [199-?]. ORC 1.

Recorded July 1977, Henry Wood Hall, London. The scene and aria of Luigi, "Provo mi dai, lo sento" is also included on the 1998 anthology entitled *Della Jones Sings Donizetti* (ORR 203).

L'elisir d'amore (1832)

Premiere: Milan, Canobbiana, 12 May 1832

Autograph: *I-Nc* (Act I), *I-BGi* (Act II)

Other Contemporary Sources:

377. *L'elisire d'amore: Opéra buffa in due atti* / del maestro Donizetti. Paris: chez Pacini, ca. 1832? Plate no.: 3591.

Vocal score.

378. *L'elisir d'amore: Melodramma in due atti* / di Felice Romani; musica di Gaetano Donizetti. Milan: G. Ricordi, [1869?]. Plate no.: 41688.

Vocal score; second edition of score originally published in 1832.

Libretti:

379. *Donizetti, L'elixir d'amour*. L'Avant scène opéra, 95. Paris: L'Avant Scène, 1987.

Libretto in Italian with French translation in parallel columns (pp. 19–77); includes a discography (pp. 90–97) and bibliography (pp. 110–111).

380. *L'elisir d'amore* / libretto di Felice Romani ; musica di Gaetano Donizetti; traduction mot à mot accent tonique par Marie-

Thérèse Paquin. Montréal, Québec: Presses de l'Université de Montréal, 1981. ISBN: 2760605558. LC: ML 50.D683 E457 1981.

Opera libretto in Italian with word-for-word and line-by-line renderings in English and French (in the middle column) and English and French translations (in the outer columns); prefatory material and synopsis in English and French.

381. *L'elisir d'amore: Melodramma giocoso in due atti.* Florence: Presso David Passigli e Socj, 1838. LC: ML 48.S2666.

382. *Donizetti's opera L'elisire d'amore.* Boston: Oliver Ditson & Co., 277 Washington Street, [18—]. LC: ML 48.S2670.

In English and Italian.

383. *Der Liebestrank: Komische Oper in 2 Akten.* Munich: [s.n.], 1839. LC: ML 48.S2674.

In German.

384. *Der Liebestrank: Komische Oper in zwei Aufzügen.* Stuttgart: Carl Eichele's Musikalienhandlung, (Eberhardstrasse Nro. 59.), [18—]. LC: ML 48.S2673.

In German.

385. *Der Liebestrank: Komische Oper in 2 Akten.* Leipzig: Druck und Verlag von J. F. Fischer, [18—]. LC: ML 48.S2672.

In German.

386. *Textbuch zu Der Liebestrank: Komische Oper in zwei Akten.* Breslau: Druck und Verlag von Gratz, Barth und Comp, [n.d.]. LC: ML 48.S2671.

In German.

387. *Das Liebestränkchen: Scherzhaftes Melodrama in zwei Akten.* [S.l.: s.n., 18—]. LC: ML 48.S2669.

In German and Italian.

388. *Der Liebestrank: Komische Oper in zwei Akten.* Berlin: [s.n.], 1846. LC: ML 48.S2668.

In German and Italian.

389. *Der Liebestrank: Komische Oper in zwei Akten.* [S.l.: s.n., 18—]. LC: ML 48.S2667.

In German and Italian.

Articles/Dissertations/Critical Studies:

390. Allitt, John S. "Donizetti, the Last of the Troubadours (Notes on the *L'elisir d'amore*)." *Studi donizettiani* 2 (1972): 69–80.

Donizetti's spiritual nature is an element of the more sensitive studies of the composer. This article examines *L'elisir d'amore* in the context of traditional thought, focusing on the musical inspiration Donizetti found in a libretto that could have an infinite number of hidden meanings. Donizetti insisted on a close relationship between words and music, but also connected the meaning of a character's name with the creation of its psychological profile and hence the music which is sung by a character. The author covers these issues for this work in an extended plot synopsis that combines dramatic action with an exegesis of traditional thought and symbolism. A summary in Italian follows the article (p. 81).

391. Gavazzeni, Gianandrea. "Donizetti e *L'elisir d'amore.*" *Rassegna musicale* 7 (1934): 44–50.

This article examines how Donizetti portrays the pastoral setting, as well as the characters and their emotions, in his music for the opera.

392. Kirsch, Winfried. "Zur musikalischen Konzeption und dramaturgischen Stellung des Opernquartetts im 18. und 19. Jahrhundert." *Musikforschung* 27/2 (April–June 1974): 186–199.

Looks at the dramaturgical function of the operatic quartet in several operas of the eighteenth and nineteenth centuries, including "Dell'elisir mirabile" from Donizetti's *L'elisir d'amore*. Concludes that the quartet marks a turning point in the dramatic action, while maintaining a certain sonorous beauty.

393. Merkling, Frank. "The Furtive Tear: The Most Famous Aria in *L'elisir d'amore.*" *Opera News* 53 (April 15, 1989): 28–29.

Donizetti's *L'elisir d'amore* has been characterized as in either the Rossinian vein or the sentimental vein exemplified by the French *comédie larmoyante*. The aria "Una furtiva lagrima" is often cited as central to this latter view. How can one single aria color the view of an entire opera? The answer to this question is based on the placement of this aria in the dramatic action, but also on the distinctions we make between art that exists in time and art that exists in space. The theories of Gotthold Ephraim Lessing and those of Christoph Willibald Gluck are used to explore this aria in the context of the whole work.

394. Peschel, Enid R., and Richard E. Peschel. "Medicine and Opera: The Quack in History and Donizetti's Dr. Dulcamara." *Medical Problems of Performing Artists* 2/4 (December 1987): 145–151.

Quacks and charlatans have existed in medicine from the earliest times to the present day. Many people are vulnerable to the miracles promised by these unlicensed practitioners, including singers, dancers, actors, and instrumentalists. Perhaps these "doctors" are best known in recent history as purveyors of love potions or elixirs, the ingredients of which have varied from natural sources to unsavory substances. The characteristics of Doctor Dulcamara (which roughly translates into "bittersweet") as quack can be easily demonstrated within the context of the plot of *L'elisir d'amore*.

395. Petrobelli, Pierluigi. "Dulcamara e Berta: Storia di una canzone." In *Liedstudien: Wolfgang Osthoff zum 60. Geburtstag*, 307–312. Tutzing: Schneider, 1989.

The canzonetta sung by Dulcamara and Adina at the beginning of the second act of *L'elisir d'amore* bears the title "Barcarola." The musical setting, however, does not reflect the peculiarities (especially metrical) of the *barcarola* genre. In fact, Donizetti chose his model—Berta's aria "Il vecchietto cerca moglie", from the second act of Rossini's *Il barbiere di Siviglia*—not because of its form, but for its textual content (reflecting a parallel dramatic situation). Yet the flexibility of Rossini's setting is no longer felt in Donizetti's rigid and flat imitation. Abstract from *RILM Abstracts Online*.

396. Rosenthal, Harold. *"L'elisir d'amore."* In *Opera on Record:* 173–183. London: Hutchinson, 1979.

Discography.

397. Smith, Patrick J. "Sunlight and Shadow: Examining 'Una furtiva lagrima'." *Opera News* 56/9 (January 1992): 16.

Argues that the aria "Una furtiva lagrima" from Donizetti's *L'elisir d'amore* expresses Nemorino's combined joy and sadness. The aria also demonstrates Donizetti's underrated skill as a composer.

398. Wynne, Peter. "Zanies, Lovers, Scoundrels, Fools." *Opera News* 57/6 (December 5, 1992): 18–20+.

The *commedia dell'arte*, a partially rehearsed and partially improvised mixture of comedy, slapstick, and satire, was the dominant form of theater in Renaissance Italy. Several of its stock characters—for example, Pedrolino (better known as Pierrot) or Colombina—are the epitome of the unrequited lover and the comic maidservant. The characters in Donizetti's *L'elisir d'amore* find their roots in these commedia dell'arte figures. Belcore is a variation on the figure known as "Il Capitano," and Dulcamara is patterned after "Il Dottore." Adina codifies the *innamorata*, a romantic character who wishes to find a husband, but who retains the acerbic tongue of Colombina. Donizetti's work is not peculiar in using stock characters. The method can be traced in operatic works up to the present day.

Discography:

399. *L'elisir d'amore.* Ileana Cotrubas, soprano; Placido Domingo, tenor; Ingvar Wixell, baritone; Sir Geraint Evans, bass; Royal Opera Covent Garden, John Pritchard, conductor. CBS Records, 1977. M2K 79210/M2K 34585 (US/Canada).

Recorded 1977, EMI Studios, London.

Videography:

400. *L'elisir d'amore.* Alda Noni (Adina), Ferruccio Tagliavini (Nemorino), Arturo LaPorta (Belcore), Paolo Montarsolo (Dulcamara); Chorus and Orchestra of Lirica Italiana, Tokyo, Alberto Erede, conductor. Legato Classics, 1959. VHS.

In black and white; Japanese subtitles.

401. *L'elisir d'amore*. Judith Blegen (Adina), Luciano Pavarotti (Nemorino), Brent Ellis (Belcore), Sesto Bruscantini (Dulcamara); Metropolitan Opera, Nicola Rescigno, conductor. Paramount/Pioneer, 1981. Paramount 12608 (VHS). Pioneer Artists 87169 (Laserdisc).

402. *L'elisir d'amore*. Kathleen Battle (Adina), Luciano Pavarotti (Nemorino), Juan Pons (Belcore), Enzo Dara (Dulcamara); Metropolitan Opera, James Levine, conductor. Deutsche Grammophon, 1992. VHS/Laserdisc.

Sancia di Castiglia (1832)

Premiere: Naples, San Carlo, 4 November 1832

Autograph: *I-Nc*

Other Contemporary Sources:

403. *Sancia di Castiglia: Tragedia lirica* / ridotta di L. Truzzi. Milan: G. Ricordi, [1832?]. Plate nos.: 6706–6720.

Vocal score.

Libretti:

404. *Sancia di Castiglia: Tragedia lirica in due atti*. Naples: Dalla Tipografia Flautina, 1832. LC: ML 48.S2757.

405. *Sancha de Castella: Tragedia lyrica em dous actos*. Lisbon: Typografia Lisbonense, Largo do Conde Bario N.o 21, 1839. LC: ML 48.S2758.

In Portuguese and Italian.

Discography:

406. *Sancia di Castiglia*. Antonella Bandelli, soprano; Adriana Cicogna, contralto; Guiseppe Costanzo, tenor; Franco De Grandis, bass; Orchestra and Chorus RAI Milan, Roberto Abbado, conductor. Voce, [1985?]. VOCE 103. LP.

Recorded at Teatro Donizetti, Milan, 4 October 1984.

Il furioso all'isola di San Domingo (1833)

Premiere: Rome, Valle, 2 January 1833

Autograph: rev. Milan, 1833; *I-Mr*

Other Contemporary Sources:

407. *Il furioso all'isola San Domingo* / poesia di G. Feretti. Naples?: B. Girard?, 1833? Plate nos.: 752–857.

Vocal score; a vocal score in two acts was published in Paris, ca. 1845.

Libretti:

408. *Il furioso nell'isola di S. Domingo: Melo-dramma in due atti.* Verona: Tipi di Pietro Bisesti, 1835. LC: ML 48.S2694.

409. *Der Wahnsinnige auf der Insel San Domingo: Oper in zwey Akten.* Wien: Anton Mausberger's Druck und Verlag, 1835. LC: ML 48.S2695.

In German.

Discography:

410. *Il furioso all'isola di San Domingo.* Luciana Serra, Elisabetta Tandura, sopranos; Luca Canonici, tenor; Stefano Antonucci, Maurizio Picconi, Roberto Coviello, baritones; Coro Francesco Cilea, Orchestra sinfonica di Piacenza, Carlo Rizzi, conductor. Bongiovanni, [1989?]. GB 2056-2/GB 2058-2. Novità del Passato.

Recorded live at Teatro Chiabrera di Savona, November 10, 1987.

Parisina (1833)

Premiere: Florence, Pergola, 17 March 1833

Autograph: *I-BGi*

411. *Parisina: Melodramma in three acts* / libretto by Felice Romani; music by Gaetano Donizetti. Early Romantic Opera, 25. New York: Garland, 1981. ISBN: 0-8240-2924-0. LC: M 1500.D68 P3.

A facsimile of the composer's autograph manuscript now housed in the Museo Donizettiano in Bergamo. The introduction by Philip Gossett provides the genesis of the opera and gives insight into the manuscript source.

Other Contemporary Sources:

412. *Parisina: Melodramma* / di Felice Romani; posto in musica dal maestro Gaetano Donizetti. Milan: Presso Gio. Ricordi, [1833?]. Plate nos.: 7000–7017.

Vocal score; second edition published in 1911.

413. *La Parisina: Tragedia lirica in tre atti* / di Felice Romani; posta in musica dal Maestro G. Donizetti; riduzione completa con accompagnamento di pianoforte. Naples: Girard, [183-?]. Plate no.: 2338.

Vocal score.

Libretti:

414. *Parisina: Melodramma in tre atti*. Vienna: Tipografia Ferd. Ullrich, [18—]. LC: ML 48.S2740.

415. *Parisina: Oper in drei Akten*. Berlin: [s.n.], 1841. LC: ML 48.S2742.

In German and Italian.

416. *Parisina: Melodram in 3 Akten*. Dresden: [s.n.], 1839. LC: ML 48.S2741.

In German and Italian.

Articles/Dissertations/Critical Studies:

417. Barblan, Guglielmo. "Alla ribalta un'ottocentesca tragedia lirica: *Parisina d'Este* di Donizetti." *Chigiana* 21(1964): 207–238.

In this article, the author works out the genesis and reception of this opera. He provides an analysis of the melodic and harmonic conventions employed in the work and includes a discussion of recurring themes within the opera.

Discography:

418. *Parisina d'Este*. Montserrat Caballé, soprano; Jérome Pruett, tenor; Louis Quilico, baritone; James Morris, bass; Opera Orchestra of New York and Chorus, Eve Queler, conductor. Pantheon, 1995. PHE 6638/PHE 6639 Capolavori di Donizetti, vol. 3.

Recorded in New York, 1974.

Torquato Tasso (1833)

> **Premiere:** Rome, Valle, 9 September 1833
>
> **Autograph:** *I-Mr*; also performed as *Sordello il trovatore*
>
> **Other Contemporary Sources:**

419. *Torquato Tasso: melodramma in tre atti* / di Giacopo Ferretti; musica del Gaetano Donizetti; ridotta con accomp. di pianoforte dall'abate G. Moro. Milan: Ricordi, 1833.

Vocal score.

420. *Torquato Tasso: Opera*. Paris: Pacini, [183-?]. Plate nos.: 3830–3850.

Vocal score.

> **Libretti:**

421. *Torquato Tasso: Melo-dramma in tre atti*. Florence: Nella stamperia di F. Giachetti presso il teatro Nuovo, [1836?]. LC: ML 48.S2749.

422. *Torquato Tasso: Grosse Oper in drei Akten*. Cologne: Langen'sche Buchdruckerei, 1852. LC: ML 48.S11814.

In German.

423. *Torquato Tasso: Oper in drei Akten*. Berlin: [s.n.], 1841. LC: ML 48.S2750.

In German and Italian.

> **Articles/Dissertations/Critical Studies:**

424. Ballola, Giovanni Carli. "Lettura del *Torquato Tasso*." In *Atti del 1° Convegno Internazionale di Studi Donizettiani*, 201–213. Bergamo: Azienda Autonomo di Turismo, 1983.

Looks at the elements of Donizetti's *Torquato Tasso* that were informed by Carlo Goldoni's 1755 tragi-comedy *Il Tasso*, as well as the writings of the poet himself. These elements find their way into Jacopo Ferretti's libretto and the composer's setting of the text.

Discography:

425. *Torquato Tasso*. Luciana Serra, soprano; Nicoletta Ciliento, mezzo-soprano; Ernesto Palacio, Diego D'Auria, tenors; Roberto Coviello, baritone; Simone Alaimo, Ambrogio Riva, basses; Coro e Orchestra del Teatro comunale di Genova, Massimo de Bernart, conductor. Bongiovanni, [1986?]. GB 2028-2/GB 2030–2. Novità del Passato.

Recorded live, 16 October 1985, Teatro Chiabrera, Savona.

Lucrezia Borgia (1833)

> **Premiere:** Milan, La Scala, 26 December 1833
>
> **Autograph:** rev. Milan, 1840; *I-Mr*
>
> **Other Contemporary Sources:**

426. *Lucrezia Borgia: Melodramma in un prologo e due atti: Opera completa per canto e pianoforte* / G. Donizetti. Milan: G. Ricordi, 1834. Plate no.: k 41690 k.

Vocal score; the second edition of 1859 or 1860 is reprinted in *Gaetano Donizetti: Collected Works. Series 1: Operas. No. 3*. London: Egret House, 1974.

> **Libretti:**

427. *Lucrezia Borgia: Opéra en deux actes et un prologue* / di Gaetano Donizetti; livret de Felice Romani d'après Victor Hugo; traduction et présentation d'André Segond. Marseille: Actes Sud; Opéra de Marseille, 1992. ISBN: 2-8686-9877-8.

Libretto in French and Italian. Includes chronology of world, social, and cultural events that occurred in 1833, the year of the opera's premiere. Essays by Segond and others provide information on the genesis of the opera, the characters involved, and a synopsis.

428. *Lucrezia Borgia: Melodramma*. Milan: Per Luigi di Giacomo Pirola, 1833. LC: ML 48.S2714.

429. *Donizetti's Opera Lucrezia Borgia*. Boston: Oliver Ditson & Co., 277 Washington Street, [18—]. LC: ML 48.S2718.

In English and Italian.

430. *Arien und Gesänge aus Lucretia Borgia: Grosse Oper.*
[Berlin: Gedruckt in der königlichen Geheimen Ober-Hof-
buchdruckerei (R. v. Decker), 18—]. LC: ML 48.S2721.

In German.

431. *Lucrezia Borgia: Grosse Oper in zwei Aufzügen.* Munich:
Gedruckt bei Georg Franz, [18—]. LC: ML 48.S2719.

In German.

432. *Arien und Gesänge aus Lucrezia Borgia: Grosse Oper.* Stral-
sund: Gedruckt in der Regierungs-Buchdruckerei, [18—]. LC:
ML 48.S2720.

In German.

433. *Lucretia Borgia: Oper in drei Akten.* Berlin: [s.n.], 1860. LC:
ML 48.S2717.

In German and Italian.

434. *Lucrezia Borgia: Melodram in zwei Akten.* [S.l.: s.n., 18—.]
LC: ML 48.S2715.

In German and Italian.

435. *Lucretia Borgia, M.D., or, La grande doctresse: An Original
Extravaganza, Founded on a Famous Opera.* London:
T. Lacy, 1868.

The libretto to a parody of Donizetti's opera created by Henry J.
Byron. Includes titles of airs (popular and borrowed) to be sung, indications for incidental music, and a cast list for the original production.

Articles/Dissertations/Critical Studies:

436. Allitt, John. "*Lucrezia Borgia.*" *Donizetti Society Journal* 2
(1975): 179–187.

Choosing Victor Hugo's play *Lucrèce Borgia* as the basis for an
opera solidifies Donizetti's relationship to the Romantic movement.
The resulting opera, *Lucrezia Borgia*, was an important step in the

development of his style. Here the composer considers new aspects of his art, exemplified by the use of an orchestration that moves away from that of Italy and looks toward France, as well as a new approach to the image of women. The author looks at this opera from the viewpoint of traditional thought. Of great interest is the author's inclusion in English translation of two letters from Donizetti to his brother-in-law Antonio Vasselli in which he extensively shares his thoughts on the work's performance.

437. Commons, Jeremy. "*Lucrezia Borgia.*" *About the House* 5/10 (1979): 28–37.

An article written for a 26 March 1980 performance of the opera at the Royal Opera House. It includes a discussion of the work's disappearance from the nineteenth-century stage and its reappraisal by modern audiences. The libretto, by Felice Romani based on Victor Hugo's *Lucrèce Borgia,* gave Donizetti the opportunity to imbue his score with new emotional effects, especially in the final scene. In Italy, the opera posed a difficult problem with the censors, and was often performed in a disguised form and under different titles. The author looks at problems of genre (is the work a tragedy or semiseria?) and at the relationship of the work to Verdi's *Rigoletto,* also based on Hugo.

438. Crutchfield, Will. "Dark Shadows." *Opera News* 63/1 (July 1998): 32–35.

Discusses the Verdian aspects of *Lucrezia Borgia*. Historians generally discuss Verdi in terms of his predecessors, but the reverse can also be rewarding to investigate. The influence of Donizetti on Verdi was indeed great, and deserves the respect that a Verdi-oriented study of his operas can help attain.

439. Edwards, Geoffrey C. *Grand et vrai: Portrayals of Victor Hugo's Dramatic Characters in 19th-Century Italian Opera.* Ph.D. diss., Northwestern University, 1991.

Discusses five operatic adaptations of plays by Hugo, among them Donizetti's *Lucrezia Borgia*. Examines the treatment of the characters in the libretto, the role of the music in the development of the characters, and the importance of staging in characterization. Concludes that the libretto, rather than the musical setting, is of utmost importance in establishing characters and their psychological complexities.

440. Gazzaniga, Arrigo. "La geminazione nel linguaggio di Donizetti." *Nuova rivista musicale italiana* 18/3 (August–September 1984): 420–433.

Discusses the "Romanza" from Act I of *Lucrezia Borgia* and the "Preghiera" from Act III of *Maria Stuarda* as a method of understanding "gemination," or the repetition of the same sound as a hallmark of Donizetti's compositional style. This procedure in Donizetti, common in contemporary linguistic usage, may be traced back to the composer's teacher, Giovanni Simone Mayr.

441. Guaricci, Joseph. "*Lucrezia Borgia.*" *Donizetti Society Journal* 2 (1975): 161–177.

Lucrezia Borgia is portrayed by the author as one of Donizetti's greatest achievements, one that concretely foreshadows Verdi's style. As supporting evidence for this statement, the author cites the brassier aspects of the orchestration and the lack of embellishments as providing a stronger sense of dramatic unity. From this standpoint, the author provides an extended plot synopsis of the work combined with an analysis of the opera's formal and harmonic structure.

442. Kaufman, Thomas G. "*Lucrezia Borgia*: Various Versions and Performance History." *Donizetti Society Journal* 5 (1984): 37–81.

Lucrezia Borgia was a tremendously popular work on many operatic stages after its premiere at the Teatro alla Scala on 26 December 1833. The author provides commentary on the principal changes made to the work for subsequent performances, often under a title different from the original. A performance history covering the years 1833 to 1902 is appended and divided into three sections: 1) a list of early performances in chronological order; 2) the premiere dates and casts of the opera as given in a large number of countries, cities, and theaters; and 3) the runs of the opera in a number of important cities and theaters. Each of the lists, culled mostly from theatrical journals, is nonetheless incomplete.

443. Loppert, Max. "*Lucrezia Borgia* and *La favorite*." In *Opera on Record 3*, 68–90. Dover, NH: Longwood, 1984. ISBN: 0-89341-531-6. LC: ML 156.4.O64 O553 1984.

Following a discussion of the history of these operas, an extended critical discographical essay is provided. At the end, bibliographical citations and cast lists for recordings of these works released between 1910 and 1978 are given.

444. Richards, John B. "Lucrezia Borgia: The Brindisi, Il segreto per esser felice (Orsini's ballata)." *Record Collector* 20/11–12 (December 1972): 270–275.

Discography. Not examined.

Discography:

445. *Lucrezia Borgia*. Montserrat Caballé, soprano; Shirley Verrett, mezzo-soprano; Alfredo Kraus, tenor; Ezio Flagello, bass; RCA Italiana Opera Orchestra and Chorus, Jonel Perlea, conductor. RCA Victor Gold Seal, 1989. 6642-2-RG.

Recorded May 1966 at RCA Italiana Studios, Rome.

446. *Lucrezia Borgia*. Joan Sutherland, soprano; Marilyn Horne, mezzo-soprano; Giacomo Aragall, tenor; Ingvar Wixell, baritone; London Opera Chorus, National Philharmonic Orchestra, Richard Bonynge, conductor. London, [1989], p1978. 421 497-2 (421 498-2/421 499-2).

Recorded August 1977 in Walthamstow Town Hall, London.

Videography:

447. *Lucrezia Borgia*. Joan Sutherland (Lucrezia), Anne Howells (Maffio Orsini), Alfredo Kraus (Gennaro), Stafford Dean (Don Alfonso d'Este); Royal Opera Covent Garden, Richard Bonynge, conductor. Pioneer Classics. PC-97-093. Laserdisc.

With English subtitles.

448. *Lucrezia Borgia*. Joan Sutherland (Lucrezia), Margreta Elkins (Maffio Orsini), Ronald Stevens (Gennaro), Robert Allman (Don Alfonso d'Este); Australian Opera, Richard Bonynge, conductor. Kultur, 1977. VHS.

No subtitles.

Rosmonda d'Inghilterra (1834)

Premiere: Florence, Teatro Pergola, 27 February 1834

Autograph: *I-Nc*; rev. as *Eleonora di Gujenna*, Naples, 1837, *I-Nc*

Other Contemporary Sources:

449. *Elénora di Guienna: Opera seria* / del maestro G. Donizetti. Paris: B. Latte, 1840?

Vocal score.

Libretti:

450. *Rosmonda d'Inghilterra: Melodramma serio*. Florence: Nella stamperia Fantosini, 1834. LC: ML 48.S2748.

451. *Rosmonda d'Inghilterra*. [S.l.: s.n.], c1976.

Italian and English in parallel columns; English translation by Thomas G. Kaufman.

Articles/Dissertations/Critical Studies:

452. Thornton, Brian. "History, Legend, and Romani's *Rosmonda d'Inghilterra*." *Donizetti Society Journal* 4 (1980): 73–87.

There have been many versions of the Rosamond tale. The author recounts the few facts upon which her legend is based and, with this background, takes a closer look at Romani's libretto for Donizetti's opera. Essentially, this article is an extended plot synopsis that intertwines the dramatic action of the opera with actual historical facts and known fictions of Rosamond's story. The author also summarizes the relationships between the characters.

453. Weatherson, Alexander. "English Legend, French Play, Two Italian Composers." *Donizetti Society Journal* 6 (1988): 107–121.

On occasion, Donizetti wrote an opera to a libretto already set by another composer. This is the case with *Rosmonda d'Inghilterra*, which was previously composed by Carlo Coccia. For both works, Felice Romani supplied the text. For Donizetti's setting, the librettist made significant changes to the text. By comparing the changes made to the libretto, the author is able to summarize the compositional style of the two composers, as well as the requirements for stage works of the Italian Romantic movement.

Discography:

454. *Bruce Ford: Romantic Heroes.* Bruce Ford, tenor; Philharmonia Orchestra, David Parry, conductor. Opera Rara, 1997. ORR 202.

Includes the duet for Enrico (Ford) and Rosmonda (Renée Fleming, soprano), "Giurasti un di."

455. *Rosmonda d'Inghilterra.* Nelly Miricioiu, Renée Fleming, sopranos; Diana Montague, mezzo-soprano; Bruce Ford, tenor; Alastair Miles, bass; Geoffrey Mitchell Choir, Philharmonia Orchestra, David Parry, conductor. Opera Rara, 1996. ORC 13.

Recorded July 1994, Henry Wood Hall, London.

Maria Stuarda (1835)

   Premiere: Milan, La Scala, 30 December 1835

   Autograph: composed for Naples, 1834, banned by censor; *S-Smf*

   Other Contemporary Sources:

456. *Maria Stuarda: Dramma in tre atti* / poesia di Giuseppe Bardari; musica di G. Donizetti. Riduzione per canto e pianoforte dell'autore. Paris: Ancienne maison Meissonnier; E. Gérard et Cie, 1855. Plate no.: C.M. 10,320.

Vocal score; reprinted in *Gaetano Donizetti: Collected Works. Series 1: Operas. No. 1.* London: Egret House, 1973.

   Critical Edition:

457. *Maria Stuarda: Tragedia lirica in due atti* / di Giuseppe Bardari [e] Gaetano Donizetti. Edizione critica delle opere di Gaetano Donizetti. Milan: Ricordi, 1991. ISBN: 88-7592-077-X.

Edited by Anders Wiklund. Includes four appendices that present alternative readings or vocal variations to several set numbers in the opera.

Libretti:

458. *Maria Stuarda. Donizetti Society Journal* 3 (1977): 108–149.

In Italian, with English translation by William Ashbrook.

459. *Maria Stuarda: Tragedia lirica in quattro parti.* Florence: Presso Gius. Galletti, via Porta-Roma, 1840. LC: ML 48.S2729.

Articles/Dissertations/Critical Studies:

460. Allitt, John S. "*Maria Stuarda*: Notes on Aspects of Platonic and Traditional Thought." *Donizetti Society Journal* 1 (1974): 17–29.

Substantially taken from the author's book on *Donizetti and the Tradition of Romantic Love,* this essay illustrates the economy and dramatic sense that Donizetti brought to the stage with this particular work. Bardari's libretto remains faithful to Schiller's play, but the work's inner themes and ideas are solely Donizetti's. From the standpoint of platonic and traditional thought, the author examines what each character represents and the effect this has on the composer's break with convention in this opera. Also covered is Mayr's influence on Donizetti's orchestration for this work and how certain words in the text are underscored by the use of a particular instrument or instrumental color.

461. Antonini, Giacomo, and John Carter. "*Maria Stuarda* on Record." *Donizetti Society Journal* 3 (1977): 259–263.

A discographical essay that focuses on two long-playing album recordings of the opera. The first, issued by ABC/EMI (SLS 848), features Beverly Sills and Eileen Farrell, and the second, issued by Decca/London (13117), features Joan Sutherland and Huguette Tourangeau. Also includes a discography of twentieth-century recordings of the work up to 1977.

462. Ashbrook, William. "*Maria Stuarda,* the Libretto: Its Source, the Historical Background, and Variants." *Donizetti Society Journal* 3 (1977): 97–105.

The source that Giuseppe Bardari used for the libretto to *Maria Stuarda* was obviously Schiller's play, *Maria Stuart,* but in an Italian versification by Andrea Maffei. Ashbrook outlines the changes

Bardari makes in the number of characters in the opera as opposed to the play, and how the dramatic action in Schiller's five-act original is pared down into the three acts of the opera. Also discussed is the relationship between the events in the opera to the actual historical events, as well as a comparison of nine different nineteenth-century libretti for the work.

463. _____. "*Maria Stuarda*: The Opera and Its Music." *Donizetti Society Journal* 3 (1977): 73–83.

After briefly outlining the four principal phases of Donizetti's career, the author delves deeply into the problems that surrounded the composition and premiere of the work. The historical genesis of the opera is given first, followed by a discussion of problems with the censors concerning the subject and the language of the text. At the end, Ashbrook explains Donizetti's self-borrowings which appear in *Maria Stuarda*, as well as in the construction of the melodies, many of which anticipate Verdi. Donizetti's mastery is revealed by his avoidance of frequent rote repetitions in the conventional aria forms used in the work.

464. Baker, Janet. "Mary Stuart." *Who's Who in Opera: A Guide to Opera Characters*, 392–394. Oxford: Oxford University Press, 1998.

The mezzo-soprano examines her thoughts and ideas about Maria Stuarda and how she created the character onstage.

465. Brookens, Karen. *A Comparative Study of Thea Musgrave's Mary, Queen of Scots, and Gaetano Donizetti's Maria Stuarda*. D.M.A. thesis, Arizona State University, 1997.

Examines the historical figure of Mary, Queen of Scots from a literary and musical perspective. Beginning with a biographical sketch of each composer, the study continues with an overview of the genesis of each opera and its premiere, provides a brief plot synopsis, and details the available performing editions of the two works. The dissertation concludes with a musical analysis that identifies the distinct musical characteristics that contribute to each opera's structure and unity. Donizetti unifies his work through key structures, while Musgrave employs thematic and motivic material as well as important pitch centers to create structural unity. At the end, the study compares the orchestral and vocal similarities between the two settings. Annotation adapted from the author's abstract as found in *Dissertation Abstracts Online.*

466. Cecchi, Paolo. "Per rendere Il soggetto musicabile: Il percorso fonte-libretto-partitura in *Maria Stuarda* e *Marin Faliero.*" In *L'Opera teatrale di Gaetano Donizetti: Atti del Convegno Internazionale di Studio,* 229–277. Bergamo: Comune di Bergamo, 1993.

In the 1830s, the choice of a subject suitable for operatic treatment was a complex procedure. Various constituents, not just the composer, had a voice in the deliberations: librettist, censors, theater management, and in some instances, singers. By using *Maria Stuarda* and *Marin Faliero* as examples, the path from literary source to libretto may be analyzed. Donizetti, in an effort to gain control over all aspects of production, including those that traditionally were the domain of the poet, found his relationship with librettists like Felice Romani often to be difficult. In *Maria Stuarda,* the relationship of composer to the librettist, Giuseppe Bardari, was more collaborative in nature. Bardari drastically reduced the complicated plot of Schiller's original drama, entirely changing the focus of the work. The action simplifies the complexities of the conflicts between characters. As such, the distribution of numbers within the opera can be made more flexible, allowing expansion of the traditional aria form. In *Marin Faliero,* the technique is somewhat different, emphasizing the spectacular elements of the original source for the text by creating new dramatic narrative forms. In Italian; summary in English.

467. Commons, Jeremy. "*Maria Stuarda* and the Neapolitan Censorship." *Donizetti Society Journal* 3 (1977): 151–167.

Looks at the facts and fictions that surround the censoring of *Maria Stuarda.* Through the use of contemporary documents and the careful re-reading of the correspondence, the author reconstructs the events that led up to this censorship.

468. Commons, Jeremy, Patric Schmid, and Don White. "19th Century Performances of *Maria Stuarda.*" *Donizetti Society Journal* 3 (1977): 217–242.

Documents the performances of *Maria Stuarda* in various European opera houses between 1835 and 1865. Also discusses the changes made in the score for several of these performances, as well as indicating cast changes.

469. Fraser, Antonia. "Mary, Queen of Scots in Fact and Fiction." *Donizetti Society Journal* 3 (1977): 17–20.

Looks at the main elements in the story of Mary, Queen of Scots, evaluating the aspects of various adaptations and fictionalizations of Mary's life in nineteenth- and twentieth-century literature.

470. "G. Donizetti, *Maria Stuarda,* Teatro alla Scala, 30-12-1835." *Donizetti Society Journal* 3 (1977): 210–216.

Iconographical article consisting of illustrations of the interior and exterior of the Teatro alla Scala, an English translation of the contract between Donizetti and Duke Carlo Visconti di Modrone for the production of the work, a facsimile of the libretto's title page (Milan: Per Luigi di Giacomo Pirola, 1835), as well as portraits of the singers who created the various roles: Maria Mailbran (Maria), Giancinta Puzzitoso (Elizabeth I), Pietro Novelli (Cecil), Domenico Reina (Leicester), and Ignazio Marini (Talbot).

471. Hudson, Elizabeth. "*Maria Stuarda*: Introduzione storica." In *Maria Stuarda: Tragedia lirica in due atti / di Giuseppe Bardari [e] Gaetano Donizetti,* XI–XXII. Milan: Ricordi, 1991.

A history of the genesis and performance of *Maria Stuarda* and of its transformation into *Buondelmonte*. A discussion of the opera's reception after its premiere culminates in an outline of the work's performance history up to 1865.

472. Inasaridse, Ethery. *Schiller und die italienische Oper: Das Schillerdrama als Libretto des Belcanto.* Europäische Hochschulschriften, 1–1130. Frankfurt am Main: Lang, 1989.

Schiller is the poet most often set by composers of the bel canto tradition. Although the differences between spoken and sung drama are well documented, the widespread use of Schiller as a source for opera librettos can be attributed to the poet's predilection for structures in his plays that are analogous to those of opera. This phenomenon is looked at in terms of Donizetti's *Maria Stuarda,* as well as in operas by Rossini and Verdi. An expansion of the author's Ph.D. dissertation (Universität München, 1985). In German.

473. Lo Presti, Fulvio. "Maria Stuarda regna felicemente sulla renaissance donizettiana." *Donizetti Society Journal 5* (1984): 217–230.

The reappearance of *Maria Stuarda* onstage after World War II heralds in the twentieth century's first Donizetti Renaissance. This article looks at the genesis and history of the opera, as well as character development and text changes made to the work.

474. Paulson, Michael G. *The Queens' Encounter: The Mary Stuart Anachronism in Dramas by Diamante, Boursault, Schiller, and Donizetti*. Currents in Comparative Romance Languages and Literatures, 1. New York: P. Lang, 1987. ISBN: 0-8204-0604-X. LC: PN 1879.M37 P37 1987.

This comparative literature study combines two types of investigations: a historical account of Mary, Queen of Scots and her role in the politics of the day, and literary interpretations by several authors of Mary's story. The author offers interpretations of Juan Bautista Diamante's *La reina María Estuarda* (1660), which recreates Mary as a martyr, Edme Boursault's *Marie Stuard* (1683), which elaborates on the elements of romance in the story, Schiller's play *Maria Stuart* (1801), which stresses the moral and pyschological transformations of the characters involved, and Donizetti's opera *Maria Stuarda* (1835). Includes a bibliography (pp. 219–235).

475. Schmidgall, Gary. "Maria Stuarda and Lucia di Lammermoor." In *Literature as Opera*, 111–147. New York: Oxford University Press, 1977. ISBN: 01-950-2213-0. LC: ML 3858.S37.

A look at how Donizetti (among others) has addressed the process of turning literary works into musical drama. As such, the author looks at how the literary model undermines or supports the musical setting, how the taste of contemporary society affects the choice of literary work to be transformed into opera, and what attributes, both literary and musical, indicate a particular work's success or failure.

476. Watts, John. "Maria Stuarda in Performance." *Donizetti Society Journal 1* (1974): 31-40.

Documents performances of *Maria Stuarda* in various European opera houses between 1958 and 1973. Casts and date and place of performance are given. The author updates the list to 1977 in the *Donizetti Society Journal* 3 (1977): pp. 244–258.

477. _____. "Other Operas about Mary Stuart." *Donizetti Society Journal* 3 (1977): 265–267.

Lists fifteen operas written between 1813 and 1977 that are about the character of Mary Stuart. Genre types, names of librettists, and date and place of first performance are cited.

478. Witte, William. "Schiller: *Maria Stuart.*" *Donizetti Society Journal* 3 (1977): 23–66.

A reprint of the author's introduction to his edition of Schiller's play (London: Macmillan, 1965. Macmillan's Modern Language Texts) which exhaustively covers the genesis of the play and the actual historical events, as well as hypothesizing whether the play presents a truthful picture of these events. Briefly describes *Maria Stuart* in conjunction with Schiller's formulated theory of tragedy. At the end, a bibliography lists the important resources on Schiller's life and works.

Discography:

479. *Maria Stuarda.* Joan Sutherland, soprano; Huguette Touran-geau, mezzo-soprano; Luciano Pavarotti, tenor, Orchestra e coro del Teatro Comunale, Bologna, Richard Bonynge, con-ductor. London, 1990. 425 410–2 (425 411–2/425 412–2).

Donizetti's manuscript of *Maria Stuarda* was once thought lost. There are at least four nonautograph manuscript scores, as well as several versions of *Buondelmonte,* a new opera with a libretto by Pietro Saladino and Donizetti's music for *Maria Stuarda,* performed in Naples on 18 October 1834. There are a large number of variants. This recording offers a composite text. While omitting the 1835 overture, it uses the orchestration of the 1835 version and intro-duces a number of the Malibran variants from that year. Recorded at the Teatro Comunale, Bologna, September 1974 and July 1975.

480. *Maria Stuarda.* Montserrat Caballé, soprano; Jane Berbié, mezzo-soprano; Alain Vanzo, tenor; Jonel Perlea, conductor. Standing Room Only, ? SRO 801–2.

Recorded live, 20 April 1965, New York.

Videography:

481. *Mary Stuart* (Maria Stuarda). Janet Baker (Mary Stuart), Rosalind Plowright (Elizabeth I), David Rendall (Leicester), John Tomlinson (Talbot), Alan Opie (Cecil); English National Opera, Charles Mackerras, conductor. Thorn EMI/HBO Video, 1982. TVE 3396. VHS; also issued by Home Vision MAR01 (VHS) and Arts International 04AI005. Laserdisc.

Sung in English.

Second version: **Buondelmonte** (1834)

Premiere: Naples, San Carlo, 18 October 1834

Autograph: new libretto fitted to music for Naples perf., *I-Nc* (partly autograph)

Other Contemporary Sources:

482. *Buondelmonte*. Milan: G. Ricordi, 1834 or 1835. Plate nos.: 7860/8351.

Vocal score.

483. *Buondelmonte* / musica del Cave. Gaetano Donizetti; ridotta per piano-forte dal Mo. Neumane. Milan: Ricordi, 1833 or 1834. Plate nos.: 7714, 7717–7720, 7722, 8343.

Contains arias and ensembles from the opera, arranged for piano solo; each number has separate title page and pagination; some numbers have interlinear Italian words.

Libretti:

484. *Buondelmonte: Tragedia lirica in due atti*. Naples: Dalla Tipografia Flautina, 1834. *Donizetti Society Journal* 3 (1977): 177–209.

Facsimile of the Italian libretto used at the Teatro San Carlo in the autumn of 1834.

Articles/Dissertations/Critical Studies:

485. "*Buondelmonte*: Teatro di S. Carlo 18-10-1834." *Donizetti Society Journal* 3 (1977): 168–170.

Iconographical article consisting of illustrations of the interior and exterior of the Teatro San Carlo, as well as portraits of the singers who created the various roles: Anna Del Sere (Irene), Ronzi De Begnis (Bianca degl'Amidei), Carlo Porto (Tedaldo), Achille Balestracci (Oderigo Fifanti), and Francesco Pedrazzi (Buondelmonte).

486. Schmid, Patric. "*Buondelmonte* and *Maria Stuarda*." *Donizetti Society Journal* 3 (1977): 171–176.

Briefly spells out the changes that were made to *Maria Stuarda* in turning it into *Buondelmonte*. Still of concern is where the 1865 version of *Maria Stuarda* originated and whether it is the closest to Donizetti's original intention. Since the autograph to the score is lost, the answer remains only speculative. Originally appeared (with illustrations) under the title "*Maria Stuarda* and *Buondelmonte*," in *Opera* 24/12 (December 1973): 1060–1066.

Gemma di Vergy (1834)

Premiere: Milan, La Scala, 26 December 1834

Autograph: *I-Mr*

Other Contemporary Sources:

487. *Gemma di Vergy: Tragedia lirica* / posta in musica dal Gaetano Donizetti; riduz. per canto con acco. di piano. Milan: Gio. Ricordi, 1835. Plate nos.: 8303–8324, 8326.

Vocal score; second edition published by Ricordi in 1870 or 1871.

Libretti:

488. *Gemma di Vergy: Tragedia lirica in due atti*. Milan: Per Luigi di Giacomo Pirola, 1834. LC: ML 48.S2697.

489. *Gemma von Vergy: Tragische Oper in drei Akten*. Berlin: [s.n.], 1841. LC: ML 48.S2698.

In German and Italian.

Articles/Dissertations/Critical Studies:

490. Black, John. "The Revival of *Gemma di Vergy* at the S. Carlo of Naples in June 1838." *Donizetti Society Journal* 5 (1985): 82–87.

After the 1834 premiere of Donizetti's *Gemma di Vergy* in Milan and an 1837 performance in Naples, nothing more is heard about the opera until its revival at the Teatro San Carlo in Naples in 1838. The decision to mount this particular opera must have been a hasty one, as no scenery was available for the production. Through various documents, the author works out how the scenery for this revival was put together from other operas by Donizetti given at the San Carlo. The suitability of the substitute scenery is assessed by comparing the scenic requirements in Bidera's libretto to the scenery suggested for use by the architect of the theater, Antonio Niccolini.

Discography:

491. *Gemma di Vergy*. Montserrat Caballé, soprano, Anna Ringart, mezzo-soprano; Luis Lima, tenor; Vicente Sardinero, baritone; Juan Pons, François Loup, basses; Choeurs de Radio France, Nouvel Orchestre philharmonique, Armando Gatto, conductor. Rodolphe, 1987. RPC 32499.500 (RPC 32499/RPC 32500).

Recorded in the Salle Pleyel, Paris, 20 April 1976.

Marino Faliero (1835)

Premiere: Paris, Italien, 12 March 1835

Autograph: *I-Nc*

Other Contemporary Sources:

492. *Marino Faliero: Dramma in tre atti* / del Sigr. G. E. Bidera; posto in musica dal Cavaliere Donizetti; ridotta con accompto. di pianoforte dal Maestro Tadolini. Paris: Pacini, 1835? Plate no.: 3110.

Vocal score.

493. *Marino Faliero: Tragedia lirica* / del Sigr. Bidéra. Milan: G. Ricordi, 1835 or 1836. Plate nos.: 8676–8693, 9341–9350.

Vocal score.

Libretti:

494. *Marino Faliero: Azione tragica in tre atti*. Zara: Tipografia Demarchi, [1840?]. LC: ML 48.S2730.

495. *Marino Faliero: Oper in drei Akten*. Berlin: [s.n.], 1839. LC: ML 48.S2732.

In German.

496. *Marino Faliero: Oper in drei Akten.* Berlin: [s.n.], 1843. LC: ML 48.S2731.

In German and Italian.

Articles/Dissertations/Critical Studies:

497. Gossett, Philip. "Music at the Théâtre-Italien." In *Music in Paris in the Eighteen-Thirties,* 327–364. Musical Life in 19th-century France, 4. Stuyvesant, NY: Pendragon, 1987.

Discusses *Marino Faliero,* Donizetti's first commission for an operatic premiere in Paris. Essentially an Italian opera, the work underwent several revisions to make it more accessible to the aesthetics of the Parisian audience. Donizetti's experiences with this work led him to make a more concerted effort to capture the style and spirit of French opera in his next opera, *L'assedio di Calais.*

Discography:

498. *Marin Faliero.* Margherita Roberti, Lina Rossi, sopranos; Agostino Ferrin, tenor; Orchestra e Coro del Teatro Donizetti di Bergamo, Adolfo Camozzo, conductor. Melodram, 1988. MEL 27030.

Recorded live 15 October 1966, Teatro Donizetti di Bergamo.

Lucia di Lammermoor (1835)

Premiere: Naples, San Carlo, 26 September 1835

Autograph: owned by the Comune di Bergamo; rev., in French as *Lucie de Lammermoor* (Paris, 1839)

499. *Lucia di Lammermoor: Dramma tragico / di Gaetano Donizetti.* Milan: E. Bestetti, 1941.

Reproduction of composer's manuscript owned by Giovanni Treccani degli Alfieri, with bio-bibliographical notes by Guido Zavadini. A list of productions of the work may be found on pp. 15-17.

Other Contemporary Sources:

500. *Lucia di Lammermoor: Dramma tragico in due parti /* Gaetano Donizetti; libretto di Salvatore Cammarano. Milan: Ricordi, c1910.

Full score.

501. *Lucia di Lammermoor: Dramma tragico* / di Salvatore Cammarano; musica del Cave. G. Donizetti. Milan: G. Ricordi, [1837]. Plate nos.: 8988–8989, 8993, 8995–8996, 10076–10094.

Vocal score.

502. *Lucie de Lammermoor: Grand opéra en 4 actes* / musique de G. Donizetti; paroles de M.rs Alphonse Roger et Gustave Vaëz. Paris: B. Latte, 1839? Plate no.: B.L.3068.

Vocal score of the French version.

Libretti:

503. *Donizetti, Lucia di Lammermoor*. L'Avant-scène opera-operette-musique, 55. Paris: L'Avant-Scène, 1983.

Libretto in Italian with French translation in parallel columns. There are introductory essays by Charles Pitt (on Donizetti's life in the theater) and Mariel Dolfini (comparing the work to Scott's novel). A musical analysis by Joël-Marie Fauquet is included, as well as a discography, performance history, and biographical information on the singers of the work's premiere.

504. *Lucia di Lammermoor*. Translated and introduced by Ellen H. Bleiler. Dover Opera Guide and Libretto Series. New York: Dover, 1972.

Libretto in Italian with a modern English translation in parallel columns. Includes biographical information on the composer, a performance history in European and American opera houses, reception history, and an English translation of the French libretto to *Lucie de Lammermoor*. A new edition was published by the same press in 1986.

505. *Lucie de Lammermoor: Opéra en trois actes* / di Gaetano Donizetti; livret de Salvatore Cammarano d'aprés le roman de Sir Walter Scott: "The Bride of Lammermoor"; traduction et présentation d'André Segond. Arles (France): Actes Sud; Opéra de Marseille, 1994. ISBN: 2-742-7034-7-0.

French libretto for the 1839 version of *Lucia di Lammermoor*. Includes essays by Segond and others, as well as a synopsis in French.

506. *Lucia di Lammermoor: Dramma serio in due parti.* Bologna: Tipi delle Belle Arti, [1838?]. LC: ML 48.S2706.

507. *The Bride of Lammermoor: A Serious Opera, in Three Acts.* London: Printed and sold by George Stuart, 38 Rupert Street, Haymarket, [18—]. LC: ML 48.S2712.

In English.

508. *Lucia di Lammermoor: A Tragic Opera, in Three Acts.* London: Published and sold at Her Majesty's Theatre, [1851?]. LC: ML 48.S2771.

In English and Italian.

509. *Donizetti's opera Lucia di Lammermoor.* Boston: Published by Oliver Ditson & Co., 277 Washington Street, [18—]. LC: ML 48.S2710.

In English and Italian.

510. *Lucia di Lammermoor = Lucie of Lammermoor: A Serious Opera.* London: Printed and sold by G. Stuart, 38 Rupert Street, Haymarket, [18—]. LC: ML 48.S2709.

In English and Italian.

511. *Lucie de Lammermoor: Opéra en trois actes.* Paris: Chez l'éditeur, 13 Rue Grange-Batelière, 1862. LC: ML 48.S2713.

In French and Italian.

512. *Lucia von Lammermoor: Tragische Oper in 3 Akten.* Leipzig: Druck von Sturm und Koppe, [18—]. LC ML 48.S2711.

In German.

513. *Lucia von Lammermoor: Tragische Oper in drei Akten.* Berlin: [s.n.], 1842. LC: ML 48.S2708.

In German and Italian.

514. *Lucia von Lammermoor: Tragisches Melodram in 2 Akten.* [S.l.: s.n., 18—]. LC: ML 48.S2707.

In German and Italian.

515. *Lucia di Lammermoor, or, The Laird, the Lady, and the Lover: A New and Original Operatic Burlesque Extravaganza.* London; New York: Samuel French, 1865.

A libretto to a parody of Donizetti's opera created by Henry J. Byron and first performed at the Prince of Wales Theatre, 25 September 1865. Includes titles of airs (popular and borrowed) to be sung, indications for incidental music, and a cast list.

Articles/Dissertations/Critical Studies:

516. Allitt, John. "*Lucia di Lammermoor.*" *Donizetti Society Journal* 2 (1975): 209–228.

A discussion of the opera as the ideal vehicle for romantic love, an idea that waned after the work's premiere with the rapid transition of the image of womanhood. Offers an analysis of the opera in such terms.

517. Ashbrook, William. "Popular Success, the Critics and Fame: The Early Careers of *Lucia di Lammermoor* and *Belisario.*" *Cambridge Opera Journal* 2/1 (March 1990): 65–81.

Traces the early reception of these two operas, both of which share the same librettist, were commissioned by the same impresario, and were premiered within four months of each other. The reception history is based on archival documents and contemporary criticism of the two works.

518. Aspinall, Michael. "The Lucia Cadenza." In *Secondo Convegno Europeo di Analisi Musicale*, 15–20. Trento: U. degli Studi, Dipartimento di Storia della Civilta, 1992.

As realized by twentieth-century singers, the cadenza for flute and coloratura soprano from the Mad Scene (Act III, Scene 2) of Donizetti's *Lucia di Lammermoor* is traceable to the performances of Adelina Patti from 1859 to 1896. Variants of the music as performed by Luisa Tetrazzini (1907), Toti Dal Monte (1926), Maria Callas, Renata Scotto, and Joan Sutherland are compared in vocal-technical terms. The earliest and latest recordings—of the interpretations by Tetrazzini and Sutherland—are closest to the authentic bel canto style; Dal Monte, on the other hand, evinces neither understanding nor real technical proficiency.

519. Black, J. N. "Cammarano's Notes for the Staging of *Lucia di Lammermoor.*" *Donizetti Society Journal* 4 (1980): 29–44.

A facsimile of notes in Cammarano's hand, now in the library of the Conservatorio San Pietro a Majella in Naples, outlining his staging of *Lucia* for the possible mounting of the production in another Italian theater. Includes an English translation and gloss on several ambiguous passages in the original.

520. Bortolotto, Mario. "Sul sestetto nell'opera *Lucia di Lammermoor.*" In *Atti del 1° Convegno Internazionale di Studi Donizettiani,* 51–64. Bergamo: Azienda Autonomo di Turismo, 1983.

The second-act sextet in Lucia is generally believed to be one of the most compelling examples of Donizetti's mature compositional style, and for some the vital core to understanding his work. This article provides an analysis of the sextet and includes a discussion of its operatic precursors and successors.

521. Cagli, Bruno. "Il dolce suono di sua voce." *Donizetti Society Journal* 4 (1980): 46–51.

This article looks at Lucia's famous mad scene from several different perspectives: the composer's indication in his autograph of a glass harmonica, instead of a flute, to accompany this scene; the events in the opera that lead up to this scene and their effects on Lucia's mental state, and the vocal expressiveness needed to convincingly convey the emotions of the scene.

522. Gazzaniga, Arrigo. "Un intervallo nelle ultime scene di *Lucia.*" *Nuova rivista musicale italiana* 13/3 (July–September 1979): 620–633.

Discusses the use of large intervals (wider than an octave) in operatic music of the early nineteenth century, focusing in particular on the interval used by Donizetti in the final aria of *Lucia di Lammermoor* to convey deep emotion in a way that provokes uncertainty and tension.

523. Green, London. "Callas and *Lucia.*" *Opera Quarterly* 14/3 (Spring 1998): 65–71.

Maria Callas can be credited for transforming our understanding of bel canto opera in general and of Donizetti's *Lucia di Lammermoor* in particular. Until Callas's portrayal of the tragic heroine in the 1950s, Lucia had fallen into neglect, described pejoratively as either "decorative" or "touching." Callas's special vocal and acting talents were able to reveal the opera as profoundly expressive of the depths of human feelings.

524. Heilbrun, C. G. "Method in Madness: Why Lucia and Elektra Must Sacrifice Their Sanity to Preserve the Male Order." *Opera News* 58 (January 22, 1994): 18–19, 45.

Both Lucia and Richard Strauss's Elektra must go mad before they die. Lucia's madness is portrayed in a simple and direct way, reaffirming the patriarchy and denying her the right to control her own destiny. This characterization fits most closely the theories of Lévi-Strauss that hold that men exchange women as pawns in their search for power and wealth.

525. Izzo, Francesco. *Carafa e Donizetti: Due metamorfosi musicali di The bride of Lammermoor di Walter Scott.* Tesi di laurea, Stor. del' mus.: U. degli Studi di Roma, La Sapienza, 1991–1992.

After hearing Carafa's opera *Gabriella di Vergì,* Donizetti remarked in a letter to his mentor, Giovanni Simone Mayr, that the elder composer wrote such beautiful music that it made him weary. This dissertation chronicles the genesis of Carafa's and Donizetti's settings of Sir Walter Scott's *The Bride of Lammermoor,* concluding that Carafa's work is firmly in the conservative classical vein, while Donizetti's reworking of the story is a hallmark of the new Romantic movement in early nineteenth-century Italian opera. A revised version of this dissertation appears as an article entitled "Michele Carafa e *Le Nozze di Lammermoor:* Un oscuro precedente della Lucia." In *Ottocento e oltre: Scritti in onore di Raoul Meloncelli* (Roma: Pantheon, 1993: 161–193).

526. Kestner, Joseph. "Beyond Reason (the Violent Love Depicted in *The Bride of Lammermoor.*" *Opera News* 53 (February 18, 1989): 8–11+.

Walter Scott's novel *The Bride of Lammermoor* provided the perfect vehicle for Donizetti to depict violent love within his opera. Here the compositional history of *Lucia di Lammermoor* is juxtaposed with themes and characters found in the original novel. Other operatic settings of the same story, especially those by Michele Carafa and Alberto Mazzucato, are also assessed.

527. Markow, Robert. "Looney Tunes." *Opera News* 58/9 (January 22, 1994): 17.

Perhaps Lucia's attraction for most opera audiences is the beauty of its melodies. However, there is more to the work than just melody. The tenets of early nineteenth-century Romanticism can be found here, generated by the orchestral colors Donizetti used. The horns, used to convey the dark and tragic atmosphere of the Lammermoor castle, and the woodwinds, adding infinite coloring to the arias, play an especially important role. It is the flute, however, that underscores the listless and remote world of Lucia's madness.

528. McClary, Susan. "Excess and Frame: The Musical Representation of Madwomen." In *Feminine Endings: Music, Gender, and Sexuality*, 80–111. Minnesota: University of Minnesota Press, 1991. ISBN: 0-8166-1898-4. LC: ML 82.M38 1991.

Composers and opera audiences have always been fascinated by the dramatic subject of madwomen. The vocal expressions that reveal the mental state of a character like Lucia have become almost an essential ingredient of the interpretation of these roles by opera stars. However, musicologists and theorists have shunned these excesses as unworthy of critical or analytical investigation. The author demonstrates that the links between madness, women, and music are not trivial, and examines several portrayals of madwomen in music from both cultural and musical points of view. Theories formulated by Michel Foucault and Klaus Doerner inform this study. The discussion of *Lucia di Lammermoor* appears on pp. 90–99.

529. McDonald, Katherine. "Fatal Meeting." *Opera News* 30/16 (February 19, 1966): 24–25.

The first few decades in the performance history of *Lucia di Lammermoor* demonstrate the tremendous success of this work. However, changing fashions in the nineteenth century, especially the rise of Richard Wagner's declamatory style, have shed a different light on the opera as nothing more than a vehicle for the soprano. In the 1960s, a revival of interest in bel canto opera allowed Lucia to be seen in a new light. The Act II Sextet and the following Mad Scene become more meaningful to the audience if seen as a culmination of the personalties of the three main characters—Lucia, Edgardo, and Enrico—as established earlier in the work.

530. Mitchell, Jerome. "The Bride of Lammermoor." In *The Walter Scott Operas: An Analysis of Operas Based on the Works of Sir Walter Scott,* 105–144. University: University of Alabama Press, 1977. ISBN: 0-8173-6401-3. LC: ML 2100.M59 1977.

Mitchell's work presents the first serious attempt to identify the many operas based on the works of Walter Scott and discuss these operas in relation to the originals. The stage works are approached from the point of view of the literary historian rather than the musicologist or music critic. As such, the works are discussed in terms of what the composer and librettist did to the literary original in order to reshape it into a stage drama. Besides Donizetti's *Lucia di Lammermoor,* the following works are examined: Adolphe Adam's *Le caleb de Walter Scott,* Michele Carafa's *Le nozze di Lammermoor,* Luigi Rieschi's *La fidanzata di Lammermoor* and *Ida di Danimarca,* Ivar Frederik Bredal's *Bruden fra Lammermoor,* and Alberto Mazzucato's *La fidanzata di Lammermoor.*

531. Morelli, Giovanni. "La scena di follia nella *Lucia di Lammermoor:* Sintomi, fra mitologia della paura e mitologia della liberta." In *La drammaturgia musicale,* 411–434. Problemi e Prospettive. Serie di Musica e Spettacolo. Bologna: Mulino, 1986. ISBN: 8-815-01127-7.

A paper presented at the conference "Il melodramma da Bellini a Verdi" organized by the Istituto di Lettere, Musica e Teatro della Fondazione Cini, Venice, September 1977. Not examined.

532. Osborne, Charles. "*Lucia di Lammermoor.*" In *Opera on Record,* 184–191. London: Hutchinson, 1979. ISBN: 0-091-39980-7. LC: ML 156.4.O46 O55.

Discography.

533. Paduano, Guido. "*Lucia di Lammermoor:* Procedure di drammatizzazione." In *Il giro di vite: Percorsi dell'opera lirica,*

85–114. Discanto/Contrappunti, 30. Florence: La Nuova Italia, 1992. ISBN: 88-221-1090-0.

A point-by-point comparison of the opera with its original literary model, Sir Walter Scott's *The Bride of Lammermoor*. This comparison looks at the specific differences between the theatrical genre and the literary genre, and at the numerous transformations of the text that governed the opera's genesis. The aesthetic principles of Georg Wilhelm Friedrich Hegel, and their effect on Romantic discourse, is worked into this discussion of the opera.

534. Ringger, Kurt. "*Lucia di Lammermoor* ou les regrets d'Emma Bovary." In *Litterature et opera,* 69–79. Grenoble: Presses U. de Grenoble, 1987.

Flaubert's choice of Lucia as the opera Emma is seen attending in Madame Bovary is not arbitrary; its implications are considered.

535. Siegwart, Hervine, and Klaus R. Scherer. "Acoustic Concomitants of Emotional Expression in Operatic Singing: The Case of Lucia in *Ardi gli incensi.*" *Journal of Voice* 9/3 (1995): 249–260.

Little research in the psychology of music has been conducted on the communication of emotions on the operatic stage. The authors pose three major questions in this study: 1) how does an emotional state manifest itself within changes in the acoustic parameters of the voice? 2) Can listeners correctly infer the nature of the emotion based on cues in the singing voice? and 3) What are the acoustic cues in the singing voice that listeners use to infer the nature of the expressed emotion? By analyzing five recorded versions of the cadenza of *Ardi gli incensi* sung by Toti dal Monte, Maria Callas, Renata Scotto, Joan Sutherland, and Edita Gruberova, this article contributes to our knowledge of emotional expression in operatic singing and of how an audience evaluates such expression.

536. Smart, Mary Ann. "The Silencing of Lucia." *Cambridge Opera Journal* 4/2 (July 1992): 119–141.

Explores Lucia's mad scene in the context of recent feminist and psychoanalytical writings on the "male gaze." The frames created by the opera's plot and by contemporary visual representations of madness help to assess Lucia's resistance to the boundaries of her musical world and to portray the potential for madness to free women from societal constraints.

537. Tanguiane, Andranick S. "Analysing Three Interpretations of the Same Piece of Music." In *Secondo Convegno Europeo di Analisi Musicale,* 21–40. Trento: U. degli Studi, Dipartimento di Storia della Civilta, 1992.

Compares recorded interpretations by Toti Dal Monte, Maria Callas, and Renata Scotto of the Mad Scene (Act III, scene 2) of *Lucia di Lammermoor* by Donizetti. By means of an analytic technique called "performance interpretation" it is argued that, intuitively or consciously, each singer conceives of her vocal line as a succession of analytically derived segments that are then shaded or artistically nuanced. Each of the three performances is shown as a vocal line distributed among three or four staves of score notation. Each staff corresponds to a distinct performance quality, and the several qualities represented by the staves are options in a system of choices employed by the performer. The differing approaches of the three singers call for the representation of three different sets of performance options. Callas's interpretation is judged to be highly analytical, in that her segmentation follows the explicit formal subdivisions of the music, whereas that of Scotto is especially theatrical and thus appropriate to convey the general idea of madness.

538. Willier, Stephen. "Through Dooms of Love: Flaubert's Emma Bovary Found a Kindred Spirit in Donizetti's *Lucia*." *Opera News* 53 (February 18, 1989): 12–14+.

The viewing of a distant time through a nostalgic haze is the essence of nineteenth-century aesthetic. The fatal associations contained in *Lucia di Lammermoor* have had an impact on other heroines in the second half of the century, most notably Balzac's Emma Bovary and Tolstoy's Anna Karenina. Both of these characters committed suicide after seeing Donizetti's portrayal of romantic madness and unrequited love. The aspect of early nineteenth-century art acting as an intoxicant or escape from reality actually allows these characters to see themselves and their circumstances in a truer light.

Discography:

539. *Lucia di Lammermoor.* Anthony Michaels-Moore, Andrea Rost, Bruce Ford, Paul Charles Clarke, Alastair Miles, Louise

Winter, Ryland Davies; London Voices, The Hanover Band, Sir Charles Mackerras, conductor. Sony Music Entertainment, 1998. S2K 63174.

First recording of original 1835 version of the opera performed on period instruments. Recorded 2–13 August 1997 at Abbey Road Studio, London,

540. *Lucia di Lammermoor*. Montserrat Caballé, soprano; José Carreras, tenor; Samuel Ramey, bass; Ambrosian Opera Chorus, New Philharmonia Orchestra, Jesús López-Cobos, conductor. Philips 426 563-2.

541. *Lucia di Lammermoor*. Maria Callas, soprano; Giuseppe di Stefano, tenor; Rolando Panerai, baritone; La Scala Orchestra and Chorus, Herbert von Karajan, conductor. Standing Room Only SRO 831-2.

Recorded live, 18 January 1954, Milan.

542. *Lucia di Lammermoor*. Maria Callas, soprano; Giuseppe di Stefano, tenor; Tito Gobbi, bass; Maggio Musicale Fiorentino, Tullio Serafin, conductor. Angel CDMB 69980.

543. *Lucia di Lammermoor*. Anna Moffo, soprano; Carlo Bergonzi, tenor; Ezio Flagello, bass-baritone; RCA Italiana Opera, Georges Prêtre, conductor. RCA 6504-2 RG.

544. *Lucia di Lammermoor*. Beverly Sills, soprano; Alfredo Kraus, tenor; Buenos Aires Teatro Colón Orchestra and Chorus, J. E. Martini, conductor. Arkadia CDMP 474.2.

Recorded in 1968.

545. *Lucia di Lammermoor*. Cheryl Studer, soprano; Plácido Domingo, tenor; Samuel Ramey, bass; London Symphony Orchestra, Ion Marin, conductor. Deutsche Grammophon 435 309-2.

546. *Lucia di Lammermoor*. Joan Sutherland, soprano; Luciano Pavarotti, tenor; Sherrill Milnes, baritone; Royal Opera, Covent Garden, Richard Bonynge, conductor. London 410 193-2.

547. *Lucie de Lammermoor*. Patrizia Ciofi, soprano; Alexandru Badea, tenor; Nicolas Rivenq, baritone; Orchestra inter-

nazionale d'Italia, Maurizio Benini, conductor. Dynamic, 1998. CDS 204/1-2.

Recording of the 1839 French version. Recorded July 25–27, 1997, Martina Franca, Palazzo Ducale, Italy.

Videography:

548. *Lucia di Lammermoor*. Anna Moffo (Lucia); Lajos Kozma (Edgardo); Giulio Fioravanti (Enrico); RAI Chorus and Rome Symphony Orchestra, Carlo Felice Cillario, conductor. Video Artists International, 1984. VAI OP-1.

English subtitles; originally produced in 1971. A film version of the opera.

549. *Lucia di Lammermoor*. Joan Sutherland (Lucia); Alfredo Kraus (Edgardo); Pablo Elvira (Enrico); Metropolitan Opera Orchestra and Chorus, Richard Bonynge, conductor. Live from the Met. Paramount Home Video, 1983. Paramount 12508.

With English subtitles; tape of the stage production, recorded 13 November 1982.

C. 1836–1843

Belisario (1836)

> **Premiere:** Venice, La Fenice, 4 February 1836
>
> **Autograph:** *I-Mr*
>
> **Other Contemporary Sources:**

550. *Belisario: Tragedia lirica in tre parti: Opera completa per canto e pianoforte* / G. Donizetti. Milan: G. Ricordi, 1836. Plate no.: 42045.

Vocal score; second edition published in 1870.

551. *Bélisaire: Grand opéra en 4 actes: partition avec accompt. de piano* / paroles d'Hipe. Lucas; musique de Donizetti. Paris: Pacini, 1836? Plate nos.: 3710–3799.

Vocal score in French.

Libretti:

552. *Belisario: Tragedia lirica in tre parti.* Venice: Tipografia di Commercio, [1836?]. LC: ML 48.S2640.

553. *Belisario, oder, Mutterrache und Kindesliebe.* Groningen: Gedruckt in Groningen bei J. S. Oppenheim, 1855. LC: ML 48.S2644.

In German.

554. *Belisar: Oper in 3 Akten: Nach dem Italienischen.* Königsberg: [s.n.], 1843. LC: ML 48.S2643.

In German.

555. *Belisar: Tragische Oper in drei Akten.* Berlin: [s.n.], 1843. LC: ML 48.S2642.

In German and Italian.

556. *Belisar: Tragische Oper in drei Abtheilungen.* [S.l.: s.n., 18—]. LC: ML 48.S2641.

In German and Italian.

Discography:

557. *Belisario.* Leyla Gencer, soprano; Giuseppe Taddei, baritone; Teatro La Fenice, Gianandrea Gavazzeni, conductor. Melodram, 1989. MEL 27051.

Recorded live in 1969.

Il campanello di notte (1836)

Premiere: Naples, Nuovo, 1 June 1836

Autograph: *I-Nc*

Other Contemporary Sources:

558. *Il campanello: Melodramma giocoso in un atto /* parole e musica del Mo. G. Donizetti. Milan: G. Ricordi, 1839. Plate nos.: 9359/11270.

Vocal score.

Critical Edition:

559. *Il campanello: Farsa* / parole e musica di Gaetano Donizetti. Edizione critica delle opere di Gaetano Donizetti. Milan: Ricordi, 1994. ISBN: 88-7592-441-4.

Edited by Ilaria Narici. Both the 1836 and 1837 versions are presented in an integrated format.

Libretti:

560. *Il campanello: Farsa con prosa*. Milan: Dall'I.R. Stabilimento Nazionale Privileg.o di Giovanni Ricordi, cont. degli Omenoni N. 1720 e sotto il portico a fianco dell'I.R. Teatro alla Scala, 1851. LC: ML 48.S2649.

561. *Il campanello = The Bell: A Comic Operetta, in One Act*. London: W. Jeffs, 15 Burlington Arcade, foreign bookseller to the royal family, 1861. LC: ML 48.S2650.

In English and Italian.

Articles/Dissertations/Critical Studies:

562. Commons, Jeremy, and John Black. "*Il campanello di notte*: Further Evidence, Further Questions." *Donizetti Society Journal 5* (1984): 231–239.

Many myths and legends about the rapidity of Donizetti's compositional technique abound. Certainly the anecdote by Adolphe Adam concerning the genesis of *Il campanello di notte* has held force in the literature, even though scholars like Ashbrook have proved otherwise. The author reinforces the idea that this account is apocryphal, and outlines the aspects of the story that are documentable and those that are sheer bunk.

563. Narici, Ilaria. "*Il campanello*: Genesi e storia di una farsa napoletana." In *L'Opera teatrale di Gaetano Donizetti: Atti del Convegno Internazionale di Studio,* 93–110. Bergamo: Comune di Bergamo, 1993.

Upon the death of Queen Maria Christina in 1836, the state theaters of Naples were closed until the impresario Domenico Barbaja took control of them in May of that year. However, the independent theaters were functioning as usual during this time. An understanding of this situation helps to illuminate the genesis of Donizetti's one-act farce, *Il campanello di notte*. The opera contains only five numbers and borrows material from *Lucrezia Borgia* and *Marino Faliero*. It was most likely prepared in great haste. Donizetti constructed the libretto from the French text of *La Sonnette de nuit*, a vaudeville by Leon Lhérie that premiered in Paris in November 1835. The composer's adaptation closely follows the original, appropriating characters typical to farce in the eighteenth century. For the 1837 revival of the work, Donizetti made several changes to the piece, adding two new numbers and setting previously spoken dialogue as sung recitative. The surviving sources for this work present several problems to the scholar, including disagreements between autograph score, manuscript copies of the work, and the 1836 vocal score. In Italian; summary in English.

564. _____. "Il campanello: Introduzione storica." In *Il campanello*, XI–XIX. Milan: Ricordi, 1994.

Presents the historical background to the genesis and performance of *Il campanello di notte*. The first version of 1836 and second version of 1837 are compared and contrasted. A performance history is included that covers European productions from 1836 to 1860. In Italian.

Discography:

565. *Il campanello di notte*. Agnes Baltsa, soprano; Carlo Gaifa, tenor; Enzo Dara, bass; Wiener Symphoniker, Gary Bertini, conductor. CBS Records Masterworks, 1983. MK 38450.

Recorded June 1981, Studios Wien Film GmbH, Hamburg.

566. *Il campanello di notte*. Madeline Bender, soprano; Shon Sims, tenor; Samuel Helper, baritone; Chorus and Orchestra of the Manhattan School of Music, Christopher Larkin, conductor. Newport Classic, 1997. NPD 85608.

Betly, ossia La capanna svizzera (1836)

Premiere: Naples, Nuovo, 24 August 1836

Autograph: rev. (two acts), Palermo, 1837; *I-Nc*

Other Contemporary Sources:

567. *Betly: Opera giocosa* / parole e musica del Cavaliere G. Donizetti. Naples: B. Girard, 1836? Plate nos.: 3205/4208.

Vocal score.

568. *Betly: Melodramma giocoso in due atti* / parole e musica del mo. G. Donizetti. Milan: Ricordi, 1836 or 1837. Plate nos.: 9601–9608, 10163, 11271–11275.

Vocal score.

Libretti:

569. *Betly: Opera buffa di un'atto*. Florence: Presso Giuseppe Galletti in via Porta Rossa, [1838?]. LC: ML 48.S2647.

570. *Betly: Dramma giocoso in due atti*. Milan: Regio Stabilimento Ricordi, [18—]. LC: ML 48.S2648.

571. *Betly: Opera semiseria in tre parti*. Turin: Tipografia Teatrale di B. Som, via Carlo Alberto 22, 1883. LC: ML 48.S2761.

Discography:

572. *Betly*. Susanna Rigacci, soprano; Maurizio Comencini, tenor; Roberto Scaltriti, baritone; Orchestra Sinfonica dell'Emilia Romagna "Arturo Toscanini", Bruno Rigacci, conductor. Bongiovanni, [1990?]. GB 2091/92-2.

Recorded live in 1990.

L'assedio di Calais (1836)

Premiere: Naples, San Carlo, 19 November 1836

Autograph: *F-Pc*, *?I-Nc*

Other Contemporary Sources:

573. *L'assedio di Calais: Melodramma lirico in tre atti* / poesia di Salvatore Cammarano; riduzione del L. Gervasi. Milan: G. Ricordi, 1836. Plate nos.: 9678/9961.

Vocal score.

Libretti:

574. *L'assedio di Calais: Dramma lirico in tre atti.* Naples: Dalla Tipografia Flautina, 1836. LC: ML 48.S2754.

Articles/Dissertations/Critical Studies:

575. Cafiero, Rosa. "Musica per gli occhi, ovvero ballo teatrale e musica coreutica sulle scene napoletane." In *Donizetti e i teatri napoletani nell'ottocento,* 74–81. Naples: Electa, 1997.

Several of Donizetti's operas were preceded by ballets on the same subject. This article looks at the genre of theatrical dance known as "pantomime ballet." Salvatore Taglioni's choreography for a "Scottish dance" in Donizetti's *L'assedio di Calais* (1836) was based on *Edoardo III o sia L'assedio di Calais* (1828), a ballet pantomime by Louis Henry with music by Mozart, Meyerbeer, Rossini, and Pacini. The author tabulates the evolution of the two works, comparing their individual scenarios in parallel columns.

Discography:

576. *L'assedio di Calais.* Della Jones, soprano; Christian Du Plessis, baritone; Geoffrey Mitchell Choir, Philharmonia Orchestra, David Parry, conductor. Opera Rara, 1988. ORC 9.

Recorded at All Saints Church, London, 24 June–1 July 1988. The scene and aria of Aurelio, "Al mio core oggetti amati," is also included on the 1998 anthology entitled *Della Jones Sings Donizetti* (ORR 203).

Pia de' Tolomei (1837)

Premiere: Venice, Apollo, 18 February 1837

Autograph: rev. Sinigaglia, 1837; *I-Nc*

Other Contemporary Sources:

577. *Pia de' Tolomei* / musica del Cave. Gaetano Donizetti; ridotta per piano-forte solo. Milan: Ricordi, [1837]. Plate nos.: 963–967.

Comprises arias from the opera, arranged for piano solo; each number has separate caption title and pagination; some numbers have interlinear Italian words.

578. *Pia de' Tolomei: Dramma tragico* / di S. Cammarano. Naples: B. Girard, 1837? Plate nos.: 3386, 10026, 10028–10035.

Vocal score. Reissued from Ricordi plates.

Libretti:

579. *Pia de' Tolomei: Tragedia lirica in due parti*. Venice: Tipografia di Commercio, [1837?]. LC: ML 48.S2744.

Articles/Dissertations/Critical Studies:

580. Barblan, Gugliemo. "Lettura di un'opera dimenticata: *Pia de' Tolomei* di Donizetti (1836)." *Chigiana* 24 (1967): 221–243.

The fifty-sixth opera of Donizetti, based upon a libretto by Salvatore Cammarano, was mounted in Venice in February of 1837 at the Teatro Apollo. In spite of the fine performers (Tacchinardi-Persiani and Ronconi), the opera as a whole failed. It obtained a success, however, in 1838 in Rome. The principal performers on this occasion were the soprano Strepponi and the tenor Moriani. For the Rome performance, Donizetti composed a new finale for the first act. The autograph of the revised score, conserved at Naples, reveals that Donizetti strove toward a dramatic rather than a lyric end. There are surprising anticipations of the master's final style as well as some typically Verdian melodic inflections. In one of the tenor arias there is a quotation of the future *La Traviata*. The chorus serves to provide dramatic relief.

581. Donizetti, Gaetano, and Salvatore Cammarano. "Il nuovo finale atto primo della *Pia de' Tolomei* con scritti di Donizetti e Cammarano." *Studi donizettiani* 1 (1962): 143–151.

Two letters concerning the Act I finale of *Pia de' Tolomei* are transcribed. The entire text of the new finale, one that proved unpleasing, is provided.

Discography:

582. *Pia de' Tolomei*. Jolanda Meneguzzer, soprano; Aldo Bottion, tenor; Franco Ventriglia, baritone; Orchestra and Chorus of the Teatro Comunale, Bologna, Bruno Rigacci, conductor. Melodram, 1988. CDM 37017.

Roberto Devereux, ossia Il conte di Essex (1837)

Premiere: Naples, San Carlo, 29 October 1837

Autograph: *I-Nc*

583. *Roberto Devereux: Tragedia lirica in three acts* / libretto by
     Salvatore Cammarano; music by Gaetano Donizetti. Early
     Romantic Opera, 26. New York: Garland, 1982. ISBN:
     0-8240-2925-9.

A facsimile of the composer's autograph now in the Biblioteca del
Conservatorio di Musica San Pietro a Maella in Naples. The introduction by Philip Gossett works out the genesis and discusses the
problems found in the manuscript source. A synopsis by Laura De-
Marco follows.

Other Contemporary Sources:

584. *Roberto Devereux: Tragedia lirica in tre atti* / di Salvatore
     Cammarano; posta in musica dal Cavaliere G. Donizetti.
     Naples: B. Girard, 1837. Plate nos.: 1750–1761.

Vocal score.

585. *Roberto Devereux: Tragedia lirica in tre atti* / di Salvadore
     Cammarano. Milan: Ricordi, 1838. Plate no.: 42047.

Vocal score; reprinted in *Gaetano Donizetti: Collected Works. Series 1: Operas. No. 5.* London: Egret House, 1975; a second edition
was published 1870 or 1871.

Libretti:

586. *Roberto Devereux: opéra en trois actes* / de Gaetano Doni-
     zetti; livret de Salvatore Cammarano; ouvrage publié sous la
     directoin d'André Segond. Marseille: Opéra de Marseille,
     1998. ISBN: 2-7427-1562-2.

A libretto in Italian and French which accompanied performances
of the opera in February 1998 in Marseille. Includes a listing of
world, social, and cultural events that occurred in 1837, the year of
the opera's first performance and several essays by André Segond,
Gabriel Vialle, and Pierre Échinard on the genesis of the work and
the historical characters involved in the drama. Synopsis in French.

587. *Roberto Devereux: Melodramma tragico in tre atti.* Milan: Per Gaspare Truffi, 1839. LC: ML 48.S2746.

588. *Robert Devereux: Tragische Oper in drei Akten.* Berlin: [s.n.], 1841. LC: ML 48.S2747.

In German and Italian.

Articles/Dissertations/Critical Studies:

589. Black, John. "Élisabeth d'Angleterre, Il Conte d'Essex, and *Roberto Devereux." Donizetti Society Journal 5* (1984): 135–146.

Identifying the literary source of an opera libretto can be a complex undertaking. Once the source has been identified, it is important to understand how the poet molded the basic material to make it suitable for the conventions that governed operatic works. The case of Donizetti's *Roberto Devereux,* to a libretto by Salvatore Cammarano, is particularly illuminating, due to its close relationship to the original source, *Elisabeth d'Angleterre* by Ancelot. However, even more instructive is that this original play was also used by Felice Romani as a basis for an opera by Saverio Mercadante (*Il conte d'Essex* [1833]). The author provides an outline of the contents of each scene in Ancelot's play and the corresponding numbers in both operas in an effort to compare the work habits of the two librettists.

590. Dean, Winton. "Donizetti and Queen Elizabeth." In *Essays on Opera,* 182–186. Oxford: Clarendon Press, 1990. ISBN: 0-19-315265-7. LC: ML 1700. D4 1990.

A critical assessment of *Roberto Devereux* that focuses on the popularity of English history as an inspiration for the plots of Romantic opera. An analysis in the form of an extended plot summary is provided. Originally appeared in *Opera* 4/6 (June 1953): 333–336.

591. Parente, Alfredo. "Un nuovo, grande acquisto donizettiano: La riscoperta del *Roberto Devereux." In L'opera italiana in musica: Scritti e saggi in onore di Eugenio Gara,* 75–79. Milan: Rizzoli, 1965. LC: ML 1733.O64.

On 2 May 1964, the author attended a performance of *Roberto Devereux* at the Teatro San Carlo in Naples, starring the soprano

Leyla Gencer. This was the catalyst for this reassessment of the work. He opines that this opera shows Donizetti at the height of his powers, artistically mature and absolutely secure in his compositional technique. The musical language employed in this work is extremely rich, a profound assimilation of all that had come before him into a unified language, one undeniably Donizettian.

592. Tatian, Carol W. *Structural Conventions in Roberto Devereux*. M.A. thesis, University of Pittsburgh, 1986.

Studies the facsimile of the composer's autograph manuscript published by Garland in 1982 to ascertain what evidence it might provide on Donizetti's use of structural units within *Roberto Devereux*. Four typical structural units were regularly used in early nineteenth-century opera: the *introduzione e cavatina,* the *scena ed aria*, the *scena e duetto,* and the *finale.* These units grew out of double aria form, and each contains a prescribed number and grouping of movements. After defining and discussing the individual units, it can be demonstrated that Donizetti did indeed use these structural units in composing *Roberto Devereux,* and that he uses a system of notation in his manuscript to indicate their presence. This system includes naming five out of the eight units, using markings for key, tempo, time signature, and instrumentation at the beginning of the unit, and marking the last bar of the unit with a special mark. An appendix divides the autograph manuscript into the eight units and enumerates the composer's reworking of the unit by folio number. A bibliography may be found on pp. 51–58.

Discography:

593. *Roberto Devereux.* Edita Gruberova, soprano; Delores Ziegler, mezzo-soprano; Don Bernardini, tenor; Ettore Kim, baritone; Philharmonic Orchestra of Strasbourg, Friedrich Haider, conductor. Nightingale Classics, 1994. NC 070563-2.

Recorded March 1994.

594. *Roberto Devereux.* Beverly Sills, soprano; Susanne Marsee, mezzo-soprano; Placido Domingo, John Lankston, tenors; Louis Quilico, baritone; David Rae Smith, bass; New York City Opera Orchestra and Chorus, Julius Rudel, conductor. Melodram, p1993. CDM 270107.

Recorded live 24 October 1970, in New York.

595. *Roberto Devereux*. Leyla Gencer, soprano; Anna Maria Rota, mezzo-soprano; Ruggero Bondino, tenor; Piero Cappuccilli, baritone, Orchestra e Coro del Teatro San Carlo di Napoli, Mario Rossi, conductor. Hunt, 1988. 2 HUNTCD 545.

Recorded during a performance in the Teatro San Carlo, Naples, 2 May 1964.

Videography:

596. *Roberto Devereux*. Beverly Sills (Queen Elizabeth), Susanne Marsee (Sara, Duchess of Nottingham), John Alexander (Roberto Devereux), Richard Fredricks (Duke of Nottingham); Wolf Trap Opera, Julius Rudel, conductor. Video Artists International, 1993. VAI-69080. VHS.

A 1975 production; with subtitles.

597. *Roberto Devereux*. Montserrat Caballé (Queen Elizabeth), José Carreras (Roberto Devereux); Aix-en-Provence, Julius Rudel, conductor. Lyric Distribution, 1977. Lyric Distribution 1809. VHS.

No subtitles.

Maria de Rudenz (1838)

Premiere: Venice, La Fenice, 30 January 1838

Autograph: *I-Vt*

Other Contemporary Sources:

598. *Maria de Rudenz: Dramma tragico* / di Salvatore Cammarano. Milan: F. Lucca, [1845?]. Plate nos.: 1875–1886, 1895.

Vocal score.

599. *Maria de Rudenz: Tragische Oper in drei Akten* / gedichtet von S. Cammarano; vollständiger Klavierauszug mit italienischem und deutschem Texte. Leipzig: F. Hofmeister, ca. 1845. Plate no.: 2387.

Vocal score in German and Italian.

Libretti:

600. *Maria de Rudenz: Dramma tragico in tre parti.* Venice: Tipografia Molinari edit., [1838?]. LC: ML 48.S2722.

Articles/Dissertations/Critical Studies:

601. Joly, Jacques. "La nonne sanglante tra Donizetti, Berlioz e Gounod." In *L'opera tra Venezia e Parigi,* Maria Teresa Muraro, ed., 193–252. Studi di Musica Veneta, 14. Florence: Olschki, 1988. ISBN: 88-222-3600-9 (v. 1). LC: ML 1720.O63 1988.

The enthusiasm for English Gothic literature waned at the beginning of the nineteenth century, paving the way for a new interest in Romanticism. In the 1820s, the genres of Romanticism and horror were often confused. This led to an amalgamation of the two genres into a more trivialized form of literary expression. Many of these resultant works inspired operatic treatment. One of the highly influential works in this genre was Bourgeois and Maillan's *La nonne sanglante.* This article provides a lengthy plot summary of this French melodrama and discusses how it influenced Donizetti's *Maria di Rudenz.*

Discography:

602. *Maria de Rudenz.* Katia Ricciarelli, soprano; Alberto Cupido, tenor; Leo Nucci, baritone; Teatro La Fenice, Eliahu Inbal, conductor. Fonit Cetra, 1994. CDC 91.

Recorded January 1981.

Poliuto (1838)

Premiere: Naples, San Carlo, 30 November 1848

Autograph: composed for San Carlo, 1838, banned by censor, *I-Nc*

Other Contemporary Sources:

603. *Poliuto: Tragedia lirica in tre atti* / G. Donizetti; opera completa, canto e pianoforte. Milan: G. Ricordi, ca. 1850.

Vocal score.

Critical Edition:

604. *Poliuto*. Edizione Critica delle Opere di Gaetano Donizetti. Milan: Ricordi, [forthcoming].

Edited by William Ashbrook and Roger Parker.

Articles/Dissertations/Critical Studies:

605. Bailbe, Joseph-Marc. "Polyeucte: De Donizetti a Gounod." *Revue d'histoire litteraire de la France* 85/5 (September–October 1985): 799–810.

The transformations wrought on Corneille's play in three different operas: Donizetti's *Poliuto* (1838), his *Les martyrs* (the 1840 reworking of the earlier opera), and Gounod's *Polyeucte* (1878).

606. _____. "Le sacré dans l'art lyrique: Autour de l'opéra français de XIXe siècle." In *Littérature et opéra*, 117–127. Grenoble: Presses U. de Grenoble, 1987. ISBN: 2-706-10277-2. LC: ML 1700.L58 1987.

A discussion of the use of biblical themes in Mehul's *Joseph*, Rossini's *Moise et Pharaon*, Donizetti's *Poliuto*, Meyerbeer's *Robert le diable* and *Les Huguenots*, Saint-Saëns's *Samson et Dalila*, and other works. Abstract taken from *RILM Abstracts Online*.

607. Black, J. N. "Cammarano's Self-Borrowings: The Libretto of *Poliuto*." *Donizetti Society Journal* 4 1980): 89–103.

The fate of Donizetti's original libretto to *Poliuto*, after its reworking into *Les martyrs*, is virtually undocumented. The opera's librettist, Salvatore Cammarano, used this libretto as a source of verses for other texts he was developing. Self-borrowing by composers is a well-established practice. However, this practice by librettists has not been extensively studied.

608. Schlitzer, Franco. "Dumas, Cammarano e le vicende del *Poliuto*." In *Mondo teatrale dell'ottocento*, 49–53. Naples: Fausto Fiorentino Libraio, 1954.

Alexandre Dumas the elder traveled to Naples for the first time in the autumn of 1835, a season that saw the premiere of Donizetti's *Lucia di Lammermoor* and the death of Vincenzo Bellini. The author describes a letter of 1840 or 1841 from the writer to Donizetti that hints at the preparation of a libretto for a work to be produced at the Théâtre-Italien in Paris. Dumas revealed he had three acts already sketched out. It cannot be ascertained to which projected work this letter refers, as no response from the composer is extant. Likewise, a letter from the librettist Cammarano to Donizetti provides information for the author's musings on the creation of *Poliuto* and its transformation into the French grand opera, *Les martyrs*.

Discography:

609. *Poliuto*. Denia Gavazzeni Mazzola, soprano; José Sempere, tenor; Simone Alaimo, baritone; Orchestra Sinfonica dell'Emilia Romagna "Arturo Toscanini", Gianandrea Gavazzeni, conductor. Dischi Ricordi, 1994. RFCD 2023.

Recorded live, September 1993, Teatro Donizetti, Bergamo at the XI Festival "Donizetti e il suo tempo." A recording of the critical edition by William Ashbrook and Roger Parker.

610. *Poliuto*. Katia Ricciarelli, soprano; José Carreras, tenor; Juan Pons, baritone; Wiener Symphoniker, Oleg Caetani, conductor. CBS Masterworks, 1989. M2K 44821.

Recorded live in 1986, Vienna Konzerthaus.

Second version: **Les martyrs** (1840)

    Premiere: Paris, Opéra, 10 April 1840

    Autograph: *I-Mr*

    Other Contemporary Sources:

611. *Les martyrs: Opéra en quatre actes* / paroles de E. Scribe. Paris: Schonenberger, 1840. Plate no.: S. 567.

Vocal score; reprinted in *Gaetano Donizetti: Collected Works. Series 1: Operas. No. 4*. London: Egret House, 1975.

612. *I martiri: Dramma in quattro atti* / traduzione italiana di F. Jannetti; ridotta da Wagner. Milan: F. Lucca, [1843?]. Plate nos.: 3323–3347.

Vocal score in French and Italian.

613. *Les martyrs: Opéra in four acts* / libretto by Eugène Scribe; music by Gaetano Donizetti. Early Romantic Opera, 27. New York: Garland, 1982. ISBN: 0-8240-2926-7. LC: M 1500.D68 M2 1982.

A facsimile of the printed orchestral score published in Paris by Schonenberger (1840?). The introduction by Philip Gossett works out the genesis of the opera and its relationship to *Poliuto*. A synopsis by Laura DeMarco follows.

Libretti:

614. *Les martyrs: Opéra en quatre actes.* [Paris?: s.n., 1840?] LC: ML 48.S2733.

615. *Donizetti's Opera I martiri, (Poliuto).* Boston: Oliver Ditson & Co., 277 Washington Street, [18—]. LC: ML 48.S2735.

In English and Italian.

616. *Polyeucte: Tragédie lyrique en trois actes.* Paris: Michel Levy frères, libraires-éditeurs, rue Vivienne, 2 bis, 1859. LC: ML 48.S2737.

In French and Italian.

617. *Die Märtyrer: Grosse Oper in vier Aufzügen.* Mainz: Grossh. Hess. Hofmusikhandlung von B. Schott's Söhnen, 1840. LC: ML 48.S2734.

In German.

618. *Poliuto: Tragedia lirica in tre atti.* Genoa: Tipografia dei Fratelli Pagano, piazza S. Giorgio, N.o 1383, [1850?]. LC: ML 48.S2736.

In Italian.

619. *Os martyres: Opera em 4 actos.* Lisbon: Typografia Do Gratis, rua dos Douradores N.o 43 B., 1843. LC: ML 48.S2760.

In Portuguese and Italian.

Articles/Dissertations/Critical Studies:

620. Allitt, John. "*Les martyrs* Revived." *Donizetti Society Journal* 2 (1975): 37–50.

The qualities of religious truth and human passion inspired Donizetti during the composition of *Les martyrs*. This article re-assesses this work in light of an early 1970s performance of the opera in London.

621. Cella, Franca. "Il libretto e sue vicende." In *Les martyrs*. Venice: La Fenice, 1978.

Notes in the program for a production of the work at La Fenice during the 1977–1978 season. Discusses the newly devised libretto by Scribe, the events surrounding the premiere of the work, and the transformation of the earlier *Poliuto* into this new work.

622. Girardi, Michele. "Donizetti e il grand opéra: Il caso de *Les martyrs*." In *L'Opera teatrale di Gaetano Donizetti: Atti del Convegno Internazionale di Studio*, 135–147. Bergamo: Comune di Bergamo, 1993.

Although the bulk of Donizetti's career focused on creating stage works for Italian theaters, conquering the operatic world in Paris, especially the Académie Royale de Musique, better known as the Opéra, was one of his primary goals. *Les martyrs*, Donizetti's French adaptation of his earlier *Poliuto*, follows in a long line of French grand opera, especially Meyerbeer's *Robert le diable* (1831) and *Les Huguenots* (1836), as well as Halévy's *La juive* (1835). Inspiration for Donizetti's adaptation can be traced to the tenor Alfred Nourrit, who had premiered the Meyerbeer and Halévy works. All four of these works share a common theme: the religious background of a character as the basis for conflict. Although Donizetti's original score remained largely the same, his adaptation focused more closely on details of orchestration, as well as melodic and harmonic embellish-ments. The force of *Les martyrs* was great enough that Verdi adapted two moments from the work for inclusion in *Il trovatore* and *La forza del destino*. In Italian; summary in English.

Discography:

623. *Les martyrs.* Leyla Gencer, soprano; Mario di Felici, tenor; Renato Bruson, baritone; Teatro Donizetti di Bergamo, Adolfo Camozzo, conductor. Myto, 1997. MCD 972.154.

Recorded live in performance, 8 September 1975.

624. *Les martyrs.* Leyla Gencer, soprano; Ottavio Garaventa, tenor; Ferruccio Furlanetto, Renato Bruson, baritones; Orchestra e Coro del Teatro La Fenice, Gianluigi Gelmetti, conductor. Italian Opera Rarities, p1994. LO 7716/LO 7718.

La fille du régiment (1840)

Premiere: Paris, Opéra-Comique, 11 February 1840

Autograph: *I-Nc*

Other Contemporary Sources:

625. *La fille du régiment: Opéra comique en deux actes* / paroles de MM. de Saint-Georges et Bayard; musique de G. Donizetti; partition, piano et chant, réduite par A. Bazille. Paris: Lemoine, [1840?]

Vocal score in French.

626. *La figlia del regimento: Opera buffa in due atti* / da G. Donizetti. Paris: Schonenberger, [1840?]. Plate no.: S.N. 1146.

Vocal score in Italian.

627. *La figlia del reggimento: Opera comica in due atti* / musica del Mo. ce. G. Donizetti; riduz. per canto con accto. di pianoforte del Mo. A. Bazzini. Milan: Ricordi, 1840 or 1841. Plate nos.: 12528–12550.

Vocal score in Italian; a second edition was published in 1879.

Libretti:

628. *La fille du régiment: Opéra-comique en deux actes.* [The Hague]: Imprimerie de H. S. J. de Groot, imprimeur-libraire en face de l'Hôtel-de-Ville, à La Haye, [18–?] LC: ML 48.S2688.

629. *Marie, oder, Die Regiments-Tochter: Komische Oper in 2 Akten.* [S.l.: s.n., 18–]. LC: ML 48.S2690.

In German.

630. *Die Tochter des Regiments: Oper in 2 Akten.* [Berlin]: Eduard Bloch, Theater-Buchhändler in Berlin, Brüderstrasse Nr. 2, [18—]. LC: ML 48.S2692.

In German.

631. *Die deutsche Regimentstochter* / Oper von Donizetti. Berlin: Druck von R. Bittner, Leipziger Str. 107, 1870. LC: ML 48.S2693.

In German.

632. *Marie, die Tochter des Regiments: Komische Oper in 2 Akten.* Berlin: [s.n.], 1860. LC: ML 48.S2691.

In German and Italian.

633. *La figlia del reggimento: Opera comica in due atti.* Genoa: Tipografia de' Fratelli Pagano, [1841?]. LC: ML 48.S2689.

In Italian.

634. *La vivandière, or, True to the Corps! An Original Operatic Extravaganza.* Liverpool: Montague, 1868.

The libretto to a parody of Donizetti's opera created by W. S. Gilbert, with music selected and arranged by Mr. Wallerstein. Includes titles of airs (popular or borrowed) to be sung.

Articles/Dissertations/Critical Studies:

635. Berlioz, Hector. "*La fille du régiment.*" *Journal des débats* (February 16, 1840); Reprint in *Les musiciens et la musique* (Paris, 1903: 145).

Berlioz's famous critique of Donizetti's opera may be regarded as a personal attack on the composer and his artistic principles. The elder composer claimed that this work was a direct imitation of Adolphe Adam's *Le chalet,* that it took no effort to produce such lightweight music, and that it was more of a *pasticcio*, unworthy of being presented onstage.

636. Loveland, Karl. *Reading Donizetti's 'La fille du régiment': Genesis, Transformations, and Interpretations.* Ph.D. diss., University of Rochester, 1996.

Throughout its history this opera has been subjected to a number of transformations involving both its textual and musical content. This dissertation attempts to reconstruct that history in order to restore the work to its original version and gains new depth of meaning through a reading illuminated by recent gender-related scholarship in musicology.

Discography:

637. *La fille du régiment.* Edita Gruberova, soprano; Deon van der Walt, tenor; Philippe Fourcade, bass; Münchner Rundfunk-orchester, Marcello Panni, conductor. Nightingale Classics, 1995. NC 070566-2.

Recorded 10 and 12 March 1995, Herkulessaal, Münchner Residenz.

Videography:

638. *The Daughter of the Regiment* (La fille du régiment). Beverly Sills (Marie), William McDonald (Tonio), Spiro Malas (Sul-1pice); Wolf Trap Opera, Charles Wendelken-Wilson, con-ductor. Video Artists International, 1992. VAI-69071. VHS.

Sung in English.

639. *La fille du régiment.* Joan Sutherland (Marie), Anson Austin (Tonio), Gregory Yurisch (Sulpice); Australian Opera, Richard Bonynge, conductor. Kultur, 1986. Kultur 1211. VHS.

With subtitles.

La favorite (1840)

Premiere: Paris, Opéra, 2 December 1840

Autograph: Malfieri Collection; rev. and expanded from *L'ange de Nisida*

Other Contemporary Sources:

640. *La favorita: Opéra en 4 actes* / Gaetano Donizetti; paroles de Mrs. Scribe, Alph. Royer et G. de Vaëz. Partition piano et chant arrangée par Richard Wagner. Paris: Brandus et Cie, [184-?].

Vocal score in French.

641. *La favorita: Opéra seria in quattro atti* / dei Sigri. Scribe, A. Royer & G. Vaëz; posta in musica dal maestro Donizetti. Partizione per canto con accompto. di piano. Paris: Brandus et Cie, [1851?]. Plate no.: B. et Cie. 5435.

Vocal score in Italian.

642. *La favorite: Opéra in four acts* / libretto by Eugène Scribe, Alphonse Royer, and Gustave Vaëz; music by Gaetano Donizetti. Early Romantic Opera, 28. New York: Garland, 1982. ISBN: 0-8240-2927-5. LC: M 1500.D68 F3 1842a.

A facsimile of the printed orchestral score published by M. Schlesinger in 1842. The introduction by Philip Gossett works out the genesis of the opera and its relationship to the aborted works *L'ange de Nisida* and *Adelaide*. A synopsis by Laura DeMarco follows.

Critical Edition:

643. *La favorite: Opéra en quatre actes* / di Alphonse Royer, Gustave Vaëz e Eugène Scribe. Edizione critica delle opere di Gaetano Donizetti. Milan: Ricordi, 1997. ISBN: 88-7592-506-2. ISMN: M-041-35544-3. LC: M 1500.D68 F3 1997 Case.

Edited by Rebecca Harris-Warrick.

Libretti:

644. *La favorite: Grand-opéra en 4 actes*. The Hague: Imprimerie de H. S. J. deGroot, [18—]. LC: ML 48.S2679.

645. *Arien und Gesänge aus Die Favorite: Oper in 4 Akten*. Berlin: [s.n., 18—]. LC: ML 48.S2686.

In German.

646. *Die Favoritin: Grosse Oper mit Tanz in 4 Akten.* Leipzig: Gedruckt bei J. F. Fischer, [18—]. LC: ML 48.S2687.

In German.

647. *Die Favoritin: Oper in vier Akten.* Karlsruhe: Druck und Verlag von C. Macklot, 1855. LC: ML 48.S2685.

In German.

648. *Leonore: Grosse Oper in 4 Akten.* Vienna: Gedruckt bei A. Pichler's Witwe & Sohn, 1853. LC: ML 48.S2684.

In German.

649. *Eleonore von Gusman, oder, Die Favoritin: Oper in vier Akten.* Berlin: [s.n.], 1842. LC: ML 48.S2680.

In German and Italian.

650. *Die Favoritin: Oper in vier Akten.* Berlin: [s.n., 18—]. LC: ML 48.S2682.

In German and Italian.

651. *La favorita: Opera in quattro atti.* Venice: Giuseppe Molinari tipografo-fonditore in rugagiuffa San Zaccaeria N. 4879, [1846?] LC: ML 48.S2681.

In Italian.

652. *Donizetti's Opera La favorita.* Boston: Oliver Ditson & Co., 277 Washington Street, [18—]. LC: ML 48.S2683.

In Italian.

Articles/Dissertations/Critical Studies:

653. Ashbrook, William. "La composizione de *La favorita.*" *Studi donizettiani* 2 (1972): 13–27.

No history of a Donizetti opera has been more insistently falsified than that of *La favorite*. Indeed, one of the more interesting "facts" is that the composer wrote the fourth act in only a few hours. The history of the genesis of this opera is complex, but the author reconstructs the events in his usual clear and authoritative way.

654. Glasow, E. Thomas. "Berlioz on the Premiere of *La favorite*."
Opera Quarterly 14/3 (Spring 1998): 33–43.

This new translation by E. Thomas Glasow of Hector Berlioz's
Journal des débats review of the premiere performance of *La favorite* at the Paris Opéra tempers the French composer's remarks
about Donizetti's abilities that appeared in an earlier unfavorable
review of *La fille du régiment*.

655. Harris-Warrick, Rebecca. "*La favorite*: Introduzione storica."
In *La favorite: opéra en quatre actes di Alphonse Royer, Gustave Vaëz e Eugène Scribe*, XI–XXXII. Milan: Ricordi, 1997.

A history of the genesis and performances of both the French and
Italian versions of the opera. The importance of the aborted and/or
incomplete works *Adelaide* and *L'ange di Nisida* to *La favorite* are
discussed.

656. _____. "The Parisian Sources of Donizetti's French Op-
eras: The Case of *La favorite*." In *L'opera teatrale di Gaetano
Donizetti: Atti del Convegno Internazionale di Studio*, 77–92.
Bergamo: Comune di Bergamo, 1993.

The French have always had a penchant for generating and saving
written documents. This phenomenon partially explains the abun-
dance of materials pertaining to Donizetti's French operas that are
available to support research. Two fundamental differences explain
the musical source situation in France as compared to that in Italy:
French musical life was centered in Paris and around the productions at one institution, the Opéra, and Paris had a large and active
publishing industry. The sources pertinent to a study of Donizetti's
La favorite are briefly described here, and help to illustrate what is
available to scholars studying the composer's French operas. The
Appendix (pp. 85–90) cites and describes the contents of the most
important sources for the opera, as well as for the aborted *L'ange di
Nisida,* found in Parisian libraries.

657. Leavis, Ralph. "*La favorita* and *La favorite*: One Opera, Two
Librettos." *Donizetti Society Journal* 2 (1975): 117–129.

This article in general looks at the tradition of performing operas in
translation, particularly from the original French into Italian. Specifically, the Italian translation of *La favorite* by F. Jannetti is dis-

cussed. The author compares the texts of both the French and Italian versions and observes that the Italian text does not fit the music very well. In addition, important features of the plot have been changed in the Italian version, skewing the original intent of the work.

658. Loppert, Max. "*La favorite*." Opera on the gramophone, 56. *Opera* 44–3/4 (March–April 1993): 291–296, 416–425.

An updated and abridged version of the author's essay and discography that appeared in *Opera on Record* 3 (London: Hutchinson, 1984).

Discography:

659. *La favorite.* Gloria Scalchi, soprano;, Luca Canonici, tenor; Orchestra e Coro di Milano della RAI, Donato Renzetti, conductor. Ricordi/Fonit Cetra, 1992. RFCD 2015.

Recorded live, September 1991, Teatro Donizetti, Bergamo at the X Festival "Donizetti e il suo tempo." A recording of the critical edition by Rebecca Harris-Warrick.

660. *La favorite.* Ketty Lapeyrette, soprano; Robert Lassalle, tenor; Opéra-Comique, François Ruhlmann, conductor. Marston, 1998. 52010-2. Pathé Opera series, vol. 2.

Recorded in 1912.

Videography:

661. *La favorita.* Fiorenza Cossotto (Leonora), Alfredo Kraus (Fernando); NHK Symphony Orchestra and Chorus, Oliviero de Fabritiis, conductor. Bel Canto Society 569.

Sung in Italian; with Japanese subtitles.

Adelia, o La figlia dell'arciere (1841)

Premiere: Rome, Apollo, 11 February 1841

Autograph: *I-Nc*

Other Contemporary Sources:

662. *Adelia: Melodramma serio in tre atti* / ridotta da Pietro Corbi. Milan: F. Lucca, [184-?]. Plate nos.: 2990–3003.

Vocal score.

663. *Adelia: Opera seria in tre atti* / musica di G. Donizetti. Paris: Maurice Schlesinger, [1843?]. Plate nos.: M.S. 3399–M.S. 3400, M.S. 3465.

Vocal score.

Libretti:

664. *Adelia: melodramma serio in tre atti.* Naples: Dalla Tipografia Flautina, 1841. LC: ML 48.S2630.

665. *Adelia: Melodramma serio in tre atti.* Genoa: Dalla Tipografia dei Fratelli Pagano, canneto il lungo N.o 800, [1845?]. LC: ML 48.S11809.

Discography:

666. *Adelia.* Mariella Devia, soprano; Octavio Arevalo, tenor; Boris Martinovic, baritone; Stefano Antonucci, bass; Orchestra e Coro del Teatro Carlo Felice, John Neschling, conductor. Ricordi RFCD 2029.

Program notes by Roger Parker.

Rita, ou Le mari battu (1841)

Premiere: Paris, Opéra-Comique, 7 May 1860

Autograph: *I-Nc*; also performed as *Deux hommes et une femme*

Other Contemporary Sources:

667. *Rita ou, Le mari battu: Opéra comique en 1 acte* / poème de M. Gustave Vaëz, musique posthume de G. Donizetti. Paris: H. Lemoine, 1860. Plate no.: 5738.H.L.

Vocal score.

Discography:

668. *Rita.* Susanna Rigacci, soprano; Ugo Benelli, tenor; Romano Franceschetto, baritone; Orchestra da Camera dell'Associazione In Canto, Fabio Maestri, conductor. Bongiovanni, 1992. GB 2109/10-2.

Recorded live September 1990, Teatro Communale, Narni at Opera In Canto 1990.

Maria Padilla (1841)

Premiere: Milan, La Scala, 26 December 1841

Autograph: *I-Mr*

Other Contemporary Sources:

669. *Maria Padilla: Melodramma in tre parti* / parole di G. Rossi; riduzione di Gio. Toja. Milan: G. Ricordi, 1841 or 1842. Plate no.: 13551.

Vocal score.

670. *Maria Padilla: Opéra en 4 actes pour chant et piano* / paroles françaises de Hippolyte Lucas; musique de G. Donizetti. Paris: Schonenberger, [1841?].

Vocal score in French.

Libretti:

671. *Maria Padilla: Melodramma in tre atti.* Milan: Dall'I.R. Stabilimento Nazionale privilegiato di Giovanni Ricordi, cont. degli Omenoni N. 1720 e sotto il portico a fianco dell'I.R. Teatro alla Scala, [1851?]. LC: ML 48.S2728.

Articles/Dissertations/Critical Studies:

672. Ashbrook, William. "Donizetti and Romantic Sensibility in Milan at the Time of *Maria Padilla*." *Donizetti Society Journal 5* (1984): 8–19.

The aspect of romantic sensibility in Donizetti's *Maria Padilla* differs from that in Verdi's *Nabucco*. In Donizetti's opera, this sensibility is focused on the emotional conflicts of the characters, while in Verdi's opera, it is focused on patriotism and national identity. Using a variety of sources, this article surveys the social and cultural attitudes in Milan that produced these different approaches.

673. Joly, Jacques. "Due padri-tenori tra odio e follia: *La juive* e *Maria Padilla*." In *Opera & libretto* 2, 199–213. Florence: Olschki, 1993.

A comparison of the character Eleazar in Halevy's *La juive* with that of Don Ruiz in Donizetti's *Maria Padilla*. Originally presented 1 September 1990 at a conference entitled *"Ruoli" e "parti" nell'opera*.

674. Parker, Roger. "*Maria Padilla*: Some Historical and Analytical Remarks." *Donizetti Society Journal* 5 (1984): 20–34.

The premiere of Verdi's *Nabucco* is thought to have eclipsed that of Donizetti's *Maria Padilla* during the 1841–1842 opera season in Milan. Actually, Donizetti's work, which inaugurated this particular season, was able to prove itself as successful long before Verdi's work was produced. This article surveys several general issues that surround *Maria Padilla* (most interestingly, the hybrid vocal characteristics of the title role), and provides a model for a convincing analysis of the opera.

Discography:

675. *Maria Padilla.* Lois McDonall, soprano; Della Jones, Joan Davies, mezzo-sopranos; Graham Clark, Ian Caley, tenors; Christian du Plessis, baritone, Roderick Earle, Roderick Kennedy, basses; Geoffrey Mitchell Choir, London Symphony Orchestra, Alun Francis, conductor. Opera Rara, 1992. ORC 6.

Recorded June 1980, Henry Wood Hall, London. The aria of Ines "Eran già create in cielo" is also included on the 1998 anthology entitled *Della Jones Sings Donizetti* (ORR 203).

Linda di Chamounix (1842)

Premiere: Vienna, Kärntnertor, 19 May 1842

Autograph: rev., Paris, 1842; *I-Mr*

Other Contemporary Sources:

676. *Linda di Chamounix: Melodramma in tre atti* / di G. Rossi; posto in musica da Gaetano Donizetti. Milan: Ricordi, 1842. Plate nos.: 13932–13955.

Vocal score.

677. *Linda di Chamounix: Opéra italien.* Paris: Schonenberger, 1842. Plate no.: S. 1148.

Vocal score.

Libretti:

678. *Linda di Chamounix: Melodramma in tre atti.* Venice: Dalla Tipografia di Giuseppe Molinari in rugagiuffa S. Zaccaria N. 4879, [18—]. LC: ML 48.S2701a.

679. *Linda di Chamounix: Melodramma in tre atti.* Milan: Dall'I.R. Stabilimento Nazionale Privilegiato di Giovanni Ricordi, cont. degli Omenoni, N. 1720 e sotto il portico a fianco dell'I.R. Teatro alla Scala, [1852?]. LC: ML 48.S2701.

680. *Linda von Chamounix: Grosse Oper in drei Aufzügen.* Stuttgart: Bei Musikalien-Verwalter Fein, Gymnastumstrasse Nro. 43, [18—]. LC: ML 48.S2705.

In German.

681. *Donizetti's Opera Linda di Chamounix.* Boston: Published by Oliver Ditson & Co., 277 Washington Street, [18—]. LC: ML 48.S2704.

In English and Italian.

682. *Linda von Chamounix: Melodram in drei Akten.* [Dresden?: s.n., 1843?]. LC: ML 48.S2702.

In German and Italian.

683. *Linda von Chamounix: Oper in drei Akten.* Berlin: [s.n.], 1845. LC: ML 48.S2703.

In German and Italian.

684. *Linda: Nagy opera 3 szakaszban.* Pesten: Nyomatott Trattner-Károlyi betuivel, 1845. LC: ML 48.S11554.

In Hungarian.

685. *Linda di Chamouni, or, The Blighted Flower: An Original Operatic Burlesque Extravaganza.* London: T. Macy, 1869. Lacy's acting edition, 1302.

A libretto to a parody of Donizetti's opera created by Conway Edwardes.

686. *The Pearl of Savoy: A Domestic Drama in Five Acts.* New York: S. French, [1864?]. French's Standard Drama. The Acting Edition, 337.

Libretto to an adaptation of *Linda di Chamounix;* to which is added a description of the costumes, cast of the characters, entrances and exits, relative positions of the performers on the stage, and the whole of the stage business.

Articles/Dissertations/Critical Studies:

687. Lippmann, Friedrich. "Casta diva: La preghiera nell'opera italiana della prima meta dell'Ottocento." *Recercare* 2 (1990): 173–209.

Prayers found in eighteenth-century Italian operas are primarily addressed to non-Christian deities. In the nineteenth century, operatic prayers had become more numerous, expanding the earlier tradition to include invocations to the Manes (ancient Roman spirits of the dead). The types of prayers in early nineteenth-century Italian opera can be illustrated by looking at a number of musical examples found in works by Rossini, Verdi, Cherubini, and Spontini, as well as in Donizetti's *Linda di Chamounix* and *Maria Stuarda*.

688. Rattalino, Piero. "Unità drammatica della *Linda di Chamounix*." *Studi donizettiani* 2 (1972): 29–40.

This article retraces the history of the composition of the opera and provides various interesting issues that surround the work. As such, it assesses the aspect of dramatic unity in the opera and demonstrates the vitality and effectiveness of Donizetti's dramaturgy.

689. Senici, Emanuele. *Virgins of the Rocks: Alpine Landscape and Female Purity in Early Nineteenth-Century Italian Opera.* Ph.D. diss., Cornell University, 1998.

Chapter 3, "Linda and the Taboo of Virginity" (pp. 132–215) discusses Donizetti's *Linda di Chamounix* from the standpoint of mid-nineteenth-century psychiatry, Freudian psychoanalysis, and Lacanian and post-Lacanian theories.

Discography:

690. *Linda di Chamounix.* Edita Gruberova, soprano; Don Bernardini, tenor; Ettore Kim, baritone; Swedish Radio Symphony Orchestra, Friedrich Haider, conductor. Nightingale Classics, 1993. NC 070561-2.

Recorded September 1993, Berwaldhallen, Stockholm, Sweden.

Videography:

691. *Linda di Chamounix*. Edita Gruberova (Linda), Deon van der Walt (Carlo, Visconte di Sirval), Armando Ariostini (Antonio); Orchestra and Chorus of the Zurich Opera, Adam Fischer, conductor. Legato Classics, 1996. 8959. VHS.

Without subtitles. Recorded in performance.

Caterina Cornaro (1842)

Premiere: Naples, San Carlo, 18 January 1844

Autograph: *I-Nc*; also known as *La regina di Cipro*

Other Contemporary Sources:

692. *Caterina Cornaro: Tragedia lirica in un prologo e due atti* / di Giacomo Sacchéro; riduzione di P. Tonassi. Milan: G. Ricordi, 1845. Plate nos.: 17127–17145.

Vocal score; reprinted in *Gaetano Donizetti: Collected Works. Series 1: Operas. No. 2*. London: Egret House, 1974.

693. *Caterina Cornaro* / opera di Sacchéro; musique del Mo. Gaetano Donizetti. Partition réduite avec accomp. de piano. Paris: Richault, 1845.

Vocal score.

Libretti:

694. *Caterina Cornaro: Tragedia lirica in un prologo e due atti*. Milan: R. Stabilimento Ricordi, [18—]. LC: ML 48.S2651.

Articles/Dissertations/Critical Studies:

695. Gallini, Natale. "Inediti donizettiani." *Rivista musicale italiana* 55 (1953): 257–275.

Through the use of letters and other associated documents, the author works out the changes made to the final scene of Donizetti's *Caterina Cornaro*. Employing the same technique, the duet for Maria and Riccardo in *Maria di Rohan* and the cavatina "Io tal'or più rammento" in *Sancia di Castigla* are examined.

Discography:

696. *Caterina Cornaro*. Denia Mazzola, soprano; Marzio Giossi, tenor; Pietro Ballo, tenor, Orchestra "I Pomeriggio Musicale" di Milano, Gianandrea Gavazzeni, conductor. Agora, [1996?]. AG 046.2.

Recorded September 1995.

697. *Caterina Cornaro*. Montserrat Caballé, soprano; José Carreras, tenor: Enrique Serra, Lorenzo Saccamani, baritones: London Symphony Orchestra and Chorus, Carlo Felice Cillario, conductor. Foyer, 1991. 2-CF 2048.

Recorded at the Royal Festival Hall, London, 10 July 1972.

Don Pasquale (1843)

Premiere: Paris, Italien, 3 January 1843

Autograph: *I-Mr*

Other Contemporary Sources:

698. *Don Pasquale: Dramma buffo in tre atti: opera completa per canto e pianoforte* / G. Donizetti. Milan: Ricordi, 1843. Plate no.: m. 42051 m.

Vocal score; a second edition was published in 1871.

699. *Don Pasquale: Komische Oper in 3 Acten* / von G. Donizetti; die deutsche Übersetzung von Heinrich Proch. Vienna (Graben No. 1133): A. Diabelli, [1843?]. Plate nos.: 7644–7656.

Vocal score in German and Italian.

Libretti:

700. *Donizetti, Don Pasquale*. L'avant scène opèra, 108. Paris: L'Avant Scène, 1988.

Libretto in Italian with French translation in parallel columns (pp. 23–75); includes a discography (pp. 94–104) and a bibliography (pp. 112).

701. *Don Pasquale: Opéra buffa en trois actes* / livret de Giovanni Ruffini; musique de Gaetano Donizetti; traduction mot à mot accent tonique par Marie-Thérèse Paquin. Collection "Opéras et Lieder." Montréal, Québec: Presses de l'Université de Montréal, 1985. ISBN: 2760607291.

Opera libretto in Italian with word-for-word and line-by-line renderings into English and French (in the middle column) and French and English translations (in the outer columns); prefatory material and synopsis in English and French. Includes a bibliography (p. [133]).

702. *Donizetti's Opera Don Pasquale.* Boston: Oliver Ditson & Co., 277 Washington Street, [18—]. LC: ML 48.S2655.

In English and Italian.

703. *Don Pasquale: Opéra-bouffe en trois actes.* [Paris?: Imprimerie d'Éd. prix, rue Neuve-des-Bons-Enfans, 3, 1843?] LC: ML 48.S2654.

In French.

704. *Don Pasquale: Komische Oper in drei Aufzügen.* [S.l.: s.n., 18—.] LC: ML 48.S2657.

In German.

705. *Don Pasquale: Komische Oper in drei Akten.* Berlin: [s.n., 18—]. LC: ML 48.S2656.

In German and Italian.

706. *Don Pasquale: Dramma buffo in tre atti.* Milan: Dall'I.R. Stabilimento Nazionale privilig. di Tito di Gio. Ricordi, cont. degli Omenoni N. 1720 e sotto il portico a fianco dell'I.R. Teatro alla Scala, 18—]. LC: ML 48.S2653.

Articles/Dissertations/Critical Studies:

707. Allitt, John. "*Don Pasquale.*" *Donizetti Society Journal* 2 (1975): 189–198.

This article looks at where this particular opera belongs in Donizetti's soul and in the context of his other works. The author opines that the opera has two guiding principles: life as initiation and life as love. As such, he demonstrates how these principles and ideas of traditional thought are worked out through an extended discussion of the opera's plot.

708. Anselmo, Francesco Attardi. *Don Pasquale di Gaetano Donizetti.* Invito all'opera, 6. Milan: Murcia, 1998. ISBN: 88-425-2412-3.

Includes the libretto (pp. 129–206), a discography, and bibliography.

709. Ashbrook, William. "Eleven-day Wonder." *Opera News* 35/6 (December 5, 1970): 24–25.

Covers the compositional process of *Don Pasquale* by discussing the speed with which Donizetti composed and evidence of self-borrowing.

710. Cronin, Charles P. D. "Stefano Pavesi's *Ser Marcantonio* and Donizetti's *Don Pasquale.*" *Opera Quarterly* 11/2 (1995): 39–54.

Donizetti's notion of adapting for his opera buffa *Don Pasquale* (1843) Angelo Anelli's libretto for Pavesi's dramma giocoso *Ser Marcantonio* (1810) fits squarely within a long tradition of composers reusing plots of successful subjects. The texts and musical settings of these two operas are compared in order to identify aspects of *Don Pasquale* that are particularly characteristic of Donizetti's personal style and that reflect changes in the buffa genre during the first half of the nineteenth century.

711. Heuscher, Julius E. "*Don Pasquale, Fidelio,* and Psychiatry." *American Journal of Psychoanalysis* 52/2 (June 1992): 161–173.

Both Donizetti's *Don Pasquale* and Beethoven's *Fidelio* illustrate the human quest for authenticity. Through their music and dramatic presentation, these operas convey profound insights into philosophical and psychological truths. They could be especially helpful in psychotherapy by providing access to potentials that are ordinarily set off, enhancing the awareness of inauthentic attitudes, facilitating the acceptance of seemingly paradoxical aspects of human existence, and providing a sense of life's meaningfulness.

712. Maione, Rino. "Se questo è scemo di cervello (Il *Don Pasquale* di Donizetti)." *Rassegna musicale curci* 48/2 (May 1995): 18–22.

By juxtaposing Donizetti's *Don Pasquale* with Verdi's *Falstaff*, an understanding of Verdi's work as a tragedy overturned by comedy and Donizetti's work as lacking the tragic emotion of the comic is revealed. However, *Don Pasquale*'s overall theme of mockery runs a wide and diverse gamut. The author provides an extended analysis of the opera in terms of these ideas.

713. Messenger, Michael. "Donizetti's Comedy of Sentiment." *Opera* 24/2 (February 1973): 108–113.

Every operatic composer who has maintained a place in the standard repertory has contributed something unique to the genre and its development. Donizetti was no different, working within the conventions of nineteenth-century Italian opera, but bringing his personal style to every work. This style involved a matching of text and music. This article looks at *Don Pasquale* in light of the basic conventions of opera buffa, as well as the progressiveness of its structure. Also assesses Donizetti's other works in the comic vein from this viewpoint.

714. Rattalino, Piero. "Il processo compositivo nel *Don Pasquale* di Donizetti." *Nuova rivista musicale italiana* 4/1 (January–February 1970): 51–68; 4/2 (March–April 1970): 263–280.

A study of the composition of Donizetti's *Don Pasquale,* based on several sketches, reconstructed corrections from the autograph manuscript of the score, and modifications of Giovanni Ruffini's libretto by the composer. Reconstructs the creation of the melodic line in the first part of Ernesto's aria "Cerchero lontana terra" and in the duet between Ernesto and Don Pasquale ("Mi fa il destin mendico"), and examines Donizetti's various attempts to set the episode "Vado, corro," in the duet between Norina and the doctor in Act I. The second part of the essay, discussing transformations in the personality of each character, includes an unpublished variation of Don Pasquale's part (Ricordi piano-vocal score 42051, pp. 154/2/2 to 155/2/1). Changes in instrumentation made after the first performance are listed, as well as several printing errors.

715. _____. "Trascrizioni, riduzioni, trasposizioni e parafrasi del *Don Pasquale.*" In *Atti del 1° Convegno Internazionale di Studi Donizettiani*, 1015–1034. Bergamo: Azienda Autonoma di Turismo, 1983.

Opera productions in the nineteenth century were as much a commercial enterprise as an artistic one. The success of any given work was predicated on the quick dissemination of the work in various arrangements. Most important, and usually the first to appear, were vocal selections which were then grouped together and published as piano-vocal scores. However, other types of arrangements were produced in order to reach a wider audience. These were of three types: transcriptions and reductions for solo instruments or instrumental combinations, transpositions into keys other than the original, and paraphrases (often for piano). This article looks at these kinds of arrangements for Donizetti's *Don Pasquale*, comparing several of these adaptations to the original work. A list of the nineteenth-century publications of this type is provided.

716. Rosenthal, Harold. "*Don Pasquale.*" Opera on the Grammophone, 34. *Opera* 24/3 (March 1973): 203–215.

The most famous revival of *Don Pasquale* in this century is perhaps that at La Scala in 1904, which featured (as did the premiere performance of the work) the most-celebrated singers of the day. This selective discography discusses ten recordings of Donizetti's opera, covering 78 rpm as well as long-playing albums from 1933 to 1965.

717. Walker, Frank. "The Librettist of *Don Pasquale.*" *Monthly Musical Record* vol. 88 / 990 (November–December 1958): 219–223.

Summarizes the career of Michele Accursi, the Italian expatriate-working as theatrical agent in Paris, who recommended to Donizetti that Giovanni Ruffini be the librettist for *Don Pasquale*.

Discography:

718. *Don Pasquale*. Barbara Hendricks, soprano; Luca Canonici, tenor; Gino Quilico, baritone; Gabriel Bacquier, bass; Opéra de Lyon, Gabriele Ferro, conductor. Erato, 1990. 2292-45487-2.

Recorded 1–7 March 1990, Palais de la Bourse, Lyon.

719. *Don Pasquale.* Eva Mei, soprano; Frank Lopardo, tenor; Thomas Allen, baritone; Renato Bruson, bass; Munich Radio Orchestra, Roberto Abbado, conductor. RCA Victor, 1994. 09026-61924-2.

Recorded in 1993.

720. *Don Pasquale.* Beverly Sills, soprano; Alfredo Kraus, tenor; Alan Titus, baritone; Donald Gramm, bass; London Symphony Orchestra, Sarah Caldwell, conductor. EMI Classics, 1996. 7243 5 66030 2 8.

Recorded in August 1978, No. 1 Studio, Abbey Road, London.

721. *Don Pasquale.* Lynne Dawson, soprano; Barry Banks, tenor; Andrew Shore, Jason Howard, baritones; Clive Bayley, bass; Geoffrey Mitchell Choir, London Philharmonic Orchestra, David Parry, conductor. Colchester, Essex, England: Chandos, 1998. CHAN 0311(2).

Sung in English. Recorded 15–21 November 1997 at Blackheath Concert Halls.

Videography:

722. *Don Pasquale.* Alda Noni (Norina), Cesare Valletti (Ernesto), Sesto Bruscantini (Malatesta), Italo Tajo (Pasquale); Radiotelevisione Italiana, Milan, Albert Erede, conductor. Legato Classics, 1955. VHS.

In black and white; no subtitles.

Maria di Rohan (1843)

Premiere: Vienna, Kärntnertor, 5 June 1843

Autograph: rev. Vienna, 1844; *I-Mr*

Other Contemporary Sources:

723. *Maria di Rohan: Melodramma tragico in tre atti* / di S. Cammarano; riduzione per canto con accompagnamento di pianoforte di C. Czerny. Milan: G. Ricordi, 1843. Plate nos.: 14901–14917.

Vocal score; second edition published in 1870 or 1871.

724. *Maria di Rohan: Tragische Oper in 3 Akten* / Gedicht von Salvatore Cammarano; übersetzt v. J. Kupelwieser; Musik von Gaetano Donizetti; vollständiger Clavierauszug von Carl Czerny. Vienna: Ant. Diabelli, [1843?]. Plate no.: 7735.

Vocal score with German and Italian text.

Critical Edition:

725. *Maria di Rohan.* Edizione Critica delle Opere di Gaetano Donizetti. Milan: Ricordi, [forthcoming].

Edited by Luca Zoppelli.

Libretti:

726. *Il conte di Chalais: Melodramma tragico in tre atti.* Naples: Dalla Tipografia Flautina, 1844. LC: ML 48.S11811.

727. *Maria di Rohan: Melodramma tragico in tre atti.* Milan: Tipografia Truffi, Due Muri N. 1034, [1845?]. LC: ML 48.S2723.

728. *Maria di Rohan = Maria of Rohan: A Grand Opera in Three Acts.* [New York: Published by Palmer & Co., at C. Breusings, 701 Broadway, 18—.] LC: ML 48.S2725.

In English and Italian.

729. *Maria von Rahn: Tragische Oper in drei Akten.* Darmstadt: Druck der G. H. Jacoby'schen Hofbuchdruckerei, 1860. LC: ML 48.S2726.

In German.

730. *Maria von Rohan: Tragische Oper in drei Akten.* Berlin: [s.n.], 1847. LC: ML 48.S2724.

In German and Italian.

Discography:

731. *Maria di Rohan.* Edita Gruberova, soprano; Octavio Arévalo, tenor; Ettore Kim, baritone; Radio Symphonieorchester Wien, Elio Boncompagni, conductor. Nightingale Classics, 1997. NC 070567-2.

Recorded live, 3 and 6 December 1996, Großen Saal, Wiener Konzerthaus.

Dom Sébastien, roi de Portugal (1843)

Premiere: Paris, Opéra, 13 November 1843

Autograph: *F-Pc* (with unpublished additions)

Other Contemporary Sources:

732. *Dom Sébastien: Grand opéra en 5 actes* / paroles de E. Scribe. Paris: Escudier, 1843? Plate no.: L.E. 1807.

Vocal score.

733. *Don Sebastiano* / musica del M. G. Donizetti. Milan: Ricordi, 1844. Plate nos.: 15871–15888.

Vocal score in Italian; a second edition was published in 1886.

734. *Dom Sébastien: Opéra in Five Acts* / libretto by Eugène Scribe; music by Gaetano Donizetti. Early Romantic Opera, 29. New York: Garland, 1980. ISBN: 0824029283. LC: M 1500.D68 D4 1980.

A facsimile of the printed orchestral score published by the Bureau Central de Musique in Paris, 1843–1844. The introduction by Philip Gossett works out the genesis of the opera. A synopsis by Laura DeMarco follows.

Critical Edition:

735. *Dom Sébastian, roi de Portugal.* Edizione Critica delle Opere di Gaetano Donizetti. Milan: Ricordi, [forthcoming].

Edited by Mary Ann Smart.

Libretti:

736. *Dom Sébastien roi de Portugal: Opéra en cinq actes.* Paris: C. Tresse, éditeur de La France dramatique, Palais-Royal, Galerie de chartres, nos 2 et 3, derrière le Théâtre-Français; et chez Mme veuve Jonas, libraire de l'Opéra, 1843. LC: ML 48.S2658.

737. *Text der Gesänge aus Dom Sebastian von Portugal.* Hamburg: Gedruckt bei F. H. Nestler und Melle, [18—]. LC: ML 48.S2661.

In German.

738. *Dom Sebastian: Oper in fünf Akten.* Vienna: Gedruckt bei Ferdinand Ullrich, 1845. LC: ML 48.S2660.

In German.

739. *Don Sebastiano, re di Portogallo: Dramma serio in 5 atti.* Barcelona: Dalla Tipografia di T. Gorchs, strada del Carmen presso Università, 1848. LC: ML 48.S11812.

In Italian.

740. *Don Sebastiano, re di Portogallo: Dramma serio.* Milan: Tipografia Valentini e C., C. de' Borromei N. 2848, [1847?]. LC: ML 48.S2659.

Discography:

741. *Dom Sébastien.* Klara Takacs, soprano; Richard Leech, tenor; Opera Orchestra of New York, Eve Queler, conductor. Legato Classics, 1984. LCD 190–2.

In French; recorded in 1984.

742. *Don Sebastiano.* Fedora Barbieri, soprano; Gianni Poggi, tenor; Maggio Musicale Fiorentino, Carlo Maria Giulini, conductor. Italian Opera Rarities, [1990?]. LO 7726/28.

In Italian. Recorded in 1955.

743. *Rare Donizetti.* Margreta Elkins, soprano; Philharmonia Orchestra, James Judd, conductor. Opera Rara, 1979. OR 4.

Recorded January 1979, London. Includes the romance, "Que faire où cacher ma tristesse."

D. Incomplete Works

Olimpiade (1817)

> **Premiere:** Introduzione and aria [aria adapted from *Le nozze in villa*] in *Il piccioli virtuosi ambulanti* (opera buffa, 1), Bergamo, summer 1819, pasticcio perf. by students of Mayr's school
>
> **Autograph:** duet *I-BGi* (not autograph)

Articles/Dissertations/Critical Studies:

744. Commons, Jeremy. "The Authorship of *I picciolo virtuosi ambulanti*." *Donizetti Society Journal* 2 (1975): 199–207.

Using the printed libretto to this work as a guide, the author firmly establishes that Donizetti wrote only the introduction and adapted an aria from *Le nozze in villa* for inclusion as well. Other scholars have stated that the work was completely that of Donizetti, but it can now be told that this pasticcio was the work of Giovanni Simone Mayr. Includes a synopsis of the plot. Also published in Italian in *Studi donizettiani* 2 (1972): 83-89.

Discography:

745. *L'Olimpiade*. Susanna Rigacci, soprano; Daniela Broganelli, contralto; Orchestra da Camera dell'Associazione In Canto, Fabio Maestri, conductor. Bongiovanni, 1992. GB 2109/10-2.

Recorded May 1991, Teatro Communale, Narni. Includes the recitative, "Assistetemi O numi" and the duet, "Ne' giorni tuoi felici."

La bella prigioniera (1826)

Premiere: not performed

Autograph: 2 nos., pf acc., *I-BGi*

Discography:

746. *La bella prigioniera*. Susanna Rigacci, soprano; Paolo Pellegrini, tenor; Romano Franceschetto, baritone; Orchestra da camera dell'Associazione In Canto, Fabio Maestri, conductor. Bongiovanni, 1992. GB 2109/10-2.

Recorded April 1992. Includes the recitative, "Ella parlar mi vuole," and the duet, "Per pietà non mi scacciate," for Amina and Everardo; and the recitative," Olà...tosto discenda", and the duet, "Sciagurata, il tempo affretta," for Amina and Carlo.

Adelaide (1834)

Premiere: not performed

Autograph: inc. autograph *FPc* [partly used in *L'ange de Nisida*]

Articles/Dissertations/Critical Studies:

747. Harris-Warrick, Rebecca. "*La favorite*: Introduzione storica." In *La favorite: Opéra en quatre actes* /di Alphonse Royer, Gustave Vaëz e Eugène Scribe, XI–XXXII. Milan: Ricordi, 1997.

Discusses the importance of *Adelaide* to the genesis of *La favorite*, as well as outlining how the projected opera was constructed. In Italian.

L'ange de Nisida (1839)

Premiere: not performed

Autograph: composed 1839; also known as *Silvia;* rev. as *La favorite;* excerpts F-Pc

Articles/Dissertations/Critical Studies:

748. Ashbrook, William. "*L'ange de Nisida* di Donizetti." *Rivista italiana di musicologia* 16/1 (1981): 96–114.

Following the success of *Lucie de Lammermoor,* the French version of *Lucia,* Anténor Joly, the director of the Théâtre de la Renaissance contracted with Donizetti for a new opera for his theater which was to have been *L'ange de Nisida.* After providing a short history of the theater, Ashbrook thoroughly discusses the history of the work, using the composer's correspondence, manuscripts, and secondary literature. Three tables are provided at the end that show the transformation of the main characters in *L'ange de Nisida* into those of *La favorite,* the numbers in *La favorite* indicating whether they are taken from *L'ange* or other works by the composer, or newly composed, and the status of numbers in *L'ange* that weren't reused in *La favorite.* Translated into Italian by Luigia Minardi.

749. Harris-Warrick, Rebecca. "*La favorite*: Introduzione storica." In *La favorite: Opéra en quatre actes* / di Alphonse Royer, Gustave Vaëz e Eugène Scribe, XI–XXXII. Milan: Ricordi, 1997.

Discusses the importance of *L'ange de Nisida* to the genesis of *La favorite.* Includes a synopsis of the projected work. In Italian.

Le duc d'Albe (1839)

Premiere: as completed by M. Salvi and others, Rome, 1882; as completed by Thomas Schippers, Spoleto, 1959

Autograph: *I-Mr* (inc.)

Libretti:

750. *"Le duc d'Albe." Donizetti Society Journal* 5 (1984): 243–316.

First publication of the French libretto to the opera, with prefatory remarks by Fulvio Lo Presti. Includes a facsimile of three leaves from Scribe and Duveyrier's manuscript of the libretto.

751. *Il duca d'Alba: Opera in quattro atti.* Milan: Stabilimento Musicale ditta F. Lucca, [18—]. LC: ML 48.S2662.

In Italian.

Articles/Dissertations/Critical Studies:

752. Commons, Jeremy. "An Introduction to *Il duca d'Alba.*" *Opera* 10/7 (1959): 421–426.

Surveys the status of the opera as left unfinished at the time of the composer's death and the completion of the work by Donizetti's pupil, Matteo Salvi. By outlining what is innovative about the work in light of what Donizetti wrote before this work, the author also assesses the jarring juxtapositions of Donizetti's style with that of the more modern style of Salvi.

753. Koth, Stefan. *Beitrage zu Donizettis Il duca d' Alba.* Vienna: Freunde der Musik Gaetano Donizettis, 1987.

The genesis of Donizetti's four-act opera *Le duc d'Albe* (text by Eugene Scribe) is studied through letters and other contemporary sources. The music, the libretto, and the reviews of the premiere, delayed until 1882, are discussed.

754. Schlitzer, Franco. "Interessi ereditari: *La duc d'Albe.*" In *Mondo teatrale dell'ottocento,* 98–109. Naples: Fausto Fiorentino Libraio, 1954.

Works out, with the aid of surviving letters and other historical documents, the fate of Donizetti's *Le duc d'Albe,* left unfinished at the composer's death. Describes the state of the autograph manuscript and the completion of the score in Italian translation by Matteo Salvi.

Discography:

755. *Il duca d'Alba.* Ivana Tosini, soprano; Renato Cioni, tenor; Louis Quilico, baritone, Trieste Philharmonic Orchestra, Thomas Schippers, conductor. Opera d'Oro, 1998. OPD-1178.

Sung in Italian. Recorded live at the Spoleto Festival, June 1959, Thomas Schippers conducting.

Ne m'oubliez pas (1842)

Premiere: not performed

Autograph: 7 nos. F-Pc; *La fidanzata,* sketch of a tenor aria, F-Pc

Discography:

756. *Ne m'oubliez pas.* Margreta Elkins, soprano; Alexander Oliver, tenor; Christian du Plessis, baritone; Geoffrey Mitchell Choir, Philharmonia Orchestra, James Judd, conductor. Opera Rara,1979. OR 4.

Recorded January 1979, London. Includes five numbers: the romance, "Oh, la belle campagne," the ballade, "Heinach disait," the duet "Belle Henriette, il en est d'autres," the romance, "Ah, faudrait-il qu'elle appartien," and the duet, "Adieu, ma paupière est lassée."

Other Works

A. Critical Studies

757. Allitt, John S. *Donizetti's Songs: Written in the Bass Clef.* London: The Mayr & Donizetti Collaboration, 1992.

Limited edition of 250 copies. Not examined.

758. Barblan, Guglielmo. "La *Messa di Requiem* di Gaetano Donizetti." *Rassegna musicale* 18 (1948): 192–198.

A forgotten page in the history of Donizetti's works was recalled to the public in a 1948 performance of the composer's *Messa di Requiem,* under the baton of Gianandrea Gavazzeni. This work, written in the autumn of 1835, was dedicated to Bellini, whose premature death deeply affected Donizetti. In an effort to reestablish the importance of this work, an overview of the genre as practiced in the nineteenth century is provided, as well as Donizetti's efforts to distinguish the style of this sacred work from that of his operas. A brief analysis of the work and an overview of its reception is given.

759. Bellotto, Francsco. *I quartetti per archi di Gaetano Donizetti.* Tesi di laurea, Università di Pavia, Scuola di Paleografia e Diplomatica, 1988–1989.

Not examined.

760. Cagli, Bruno. "La musica vocale da camera." In *Atti del I° Convegno Internazionale di Studi Donizettiani,* 215–245. Bergamo: Azienda Autonoma di Turismo, 1983.

Little attention has been given to Donizetti's vocal chamber music. This can be attributed to the Donizetti Renaissance's greater interest in the stage works, as well as a prejudice against this particular genre based on its quality relative to other works. Donizetti's vocal chamber music comprises a vast corpus of works, much of which has not been precisely or completely cataloged. This article is predominantly bibliographical and lists the published collections of Donizetti's melodies, subdivided into three categories. These categories are those collections published during the composer's lifetime, those published posthumously in the nineteenth century, and those published in the twentieth century. Also includes a discussion of the text authors for these pieces and a catalog of the vocal music.

761. Capitanio, Fabrizio. "Un inedito donizettiano nella Biblioteca Civica: Canone infinito a 5 voci (1825)." *Bergomum* 89/3 (July–Sept 1994): 103–110.

A commentary on Donizetti's canon dedicated to his "carissimo fratello" Giuseppe Donizetti (1788–1856) and dated 10 October [1825]. An edition of the canon is included.

762. Cattaneo, Pieralberto. "Un abbozzo di un'opera sconosciuta di Donizetti." *Studi donizettiani* 3 (1978): 108–114.

Sketch studies for Donizetti's operas have been actively undertaken, most notably by Piero Rattalino (*Don Pasquale*), William Ashbrook (*La favorite*), and Philip Gossett (*Anna Bolena*). However, this type of study has virtually been ignored for Donizetti's sacred works. This article looks at several autograph folios housed in the library of the Conservatorio San Pietro a Majella in Naples which contain sketches for the composer's sacred music. A transcription of the sketches is included.

763. _____. "Contributo per un'analisi della produzione sacra di Gaetano Donizetti." In *Atti del 1° Convegno Internazionale di Studi Donizettiani,* 401–452. Bergamo: Azienda Autonoma di Turismo, 1983.

Donizetti's compositional method produced works that were fundamentally expressive, regardless of whether they were sacred or secular. This article globally discusses the vast body of sacred music that Donizetti composed between 1814 and 1845. The majority of this article (pp. 421–450) is a thematic catalog of the sacred works of the composer.

764. Cho, Gene J. "Donizetti's *Laudate pueri*: A quattro." *Donizetti Society Journal* 5 (1984): 89–133.

Includes a facsimile of the manuscript and a transcription of the score.

765. Commons, Jeremy. "Quixotic Quest." *New Zealand Libraries* 38/3 (June 1975): 136–144.

The study of opera within New Zealand is not the easiest of tasks, as the genre is perceived there as a relic of the nineteenth century. The author here provides valuable insight into researching early nineteenth-century Italian opera in various European libraries, conservatories, and archives. His method is a combination of learned notions of where to find the appropriate sources, combined with a certain amount of serendipity. Such a method builds a rich and detailed picture of the circumstances that surround a work's composition, dismissing old legends and placing the piece in a new authentic context. The author tells of his discovery of several unknown songs by Donizetti, of the manuscript to *Rosmonda d'Inghilterra,* and of several letters from the composer to the impresario Alessandro Lanari.

766. Croan, Robert J. *The Ensemble Song of the 19th Century: A Study of Representative Repertory for Solo Voice and 2 to 5 Instruments.* Ph.D. diss., Musicology: Boston University, 1968.

In the nineteenth century, ensemble songs appear as a special type of the various European art songs; the most common variety is related to the German lied. The most important composers of the genre are Schubert, Spohr, Meyerbeer, Brahms, Berlioz, Donizetti, Saint-Saëns, and Chausson. Composers chose this kind of accompaniment, instead of the solo piano or full orchestra, for a variety of reasons: 1) the practicality of alternative published parts, which may sell the music to a wider public; 2) the Romanticist's penchant for exploiting the tone colors of the obligato instruments; 3) the programmatic use of instruments for texts that dealt with shepherds, birds, hunting, etc. The violin is by far the most popular obligato instrument, but arbitrary ad libitum substitutions are common. Abstract abridged from *Dissertation Abstracts Online*.

767. Donella, Valentino. "Musica d'organo e organisti in Italia dalla decadenza alla riforma (secolo XIX e prima metà del secolo XX)." *Rivista internazionale di musica sacra* 3/1 (January–March 1982): 27–88.

Primarily a biographical study of organists in nineteenth- and early twentieth-century Italy, the organ works of several composers are also examined, including the organ exercises in fugal and contrapuntal techniques that Donizetti wrote during his student years in Bologna (1815–1817).

768. Gallota, Bruno. "La musica vocale da camera di Bellini e Donizetti." *Rassegna musicale curci* 48/2 (May 1995): 5–11.

The vocal chamber music of Bellini and Donizetti as compared to their operas suffers an unfortunate history. For Donizetti, a vast amount of these works survives (mostly in manuscript form) and provides an additional musical repertoire to explore. This article looks at the antecedents of Bellini's and Donizetti's vocal chamber music, especially in light of Rossini's contributions to the genre, and attempts to establish the historical and cultural contexts for these pieces. As such, the negative connotations associated with these works can then be eliminated.

769. Keller, Marcello Sorce. "Gaetano Donizetti: Un bergamasco compositore di canzoni napoletane." *Studi donizettiani* 3 (1978): 100–107.

Briefly analyzes three Neapolitan songs by Gaetano Donizetti. Shows that the composer adopted a variety of formal solutions to avoid the most common clichés of the Neapolitan musical vernacular.

770. _____. "*Io te voglio bene assaje*: Una famosa canzone napoletana tradizionalmente attribuita a Gaetano Donizetti." *Studi donizettiani* 4 (1988): 163–182.

The attribution of this famous Neapolitan song to Donizetti demonstrates the former closeness of art music and light music. When the song appeared, Donizetti was in Naples; however, his contemporaries thought that it was a popular song. We can now say that the melody is not of the type that is transmitted orally. Although it is not possible to ascertain who wrote the famous melody, it can be demonstrated that Donizetti was not its author. An English version of this article appears in *Music Review* 45–3/4 (August–November 1984): 251–264 and in Italian in *Nuova rivista musicale italiana* 19/4 (October–December 1985): 642–653.

771. Kim, Soo Yeon. *The Chamber Songs of Rossini, Bellini, and Donizetti.* A. Mus. D. thesis: University of Illinois at Urbana-Champaign, 1992.

Includes translations to song texts and scores to the songs, transcribed by the author.

772. Martinotti, Sergio. "La musica strumentale. Le liriche. Le composizioni sacre." In *Gaetano Donizetti,* 117–129. Milan: Nuove Edizioni, 1983.

The decline in the composition of musical genres other than opera in the late eighteenth and early nineteenth centuries in Italy provides the context in which to discuss Donizetti's nonoperatic works. This vast corpus of music deserves to be more closely looked at.

773. Marx-Weber, Magda. "Neapolitanische und venezianische Miserere-Vertonungen des 18. und frühen 19. Jahrhunderts." *Archiv für Musikwissenschaft* 43/1 (1986): 17–45.

A continuation of a study that first appeared in the *Hamburger Jahrbuch für Musikwissenschaft* 8 (1985), pp. 7–43. Donizetti's *Miserere in G Minor* is discussed beginning on p. 38. An index to the manuscript sources crucial to this study appears on pp. 40–45.

774. Sandelewski, Wiaroslaw. "*Rex Christe*: Nieznane polskie 'Donizettianum." *Muzyka* (Poland) 26/1 (1981): 55–64.

This piece for voice and piano, an arrangement of the arietta *La lontananza*, from the collection *Soiree d'automne a l'infrescata* (1837), is preserved in the Archives of the Cracow Cathedral (shelf no. 389) in an anonymous manuscript. Facsimiles of the manuscript and of the score to *La lontananza* are appended. A summary in English is included.

775. Schlitzer, Franco. "*Io amo la mestizia.*" In *Mondo teatrale dell'ottocento*, 54–57. Naples: Fausto Fiorentino Libraio, 1954.

Describes an album in oblong format owned by the countess Sofia de' Medici di Marignano that was used in the series of salons she hosted in Milan. The album contains works of several celebrated musicians of the nineteenth century, including Donizetti. In 1841 or 1842, Donizetti inscribed in this album the vocal line of an untitled romanza whose text incipit begins "Io amo mestizia" and dedicated it to the countess. Here, the author publishes for the first time the complete poetic text and a transcription of the vocal line.

776. Townsend, Douglas. "The Unsung Donizetti: The Composer's Forgotten Works." *Opera News* 45/15 (March 14, 1981): 16–18.

In 1797, two great composers were born—Donizetti and Schubert—both of whom left behind a tremendous output. Of these composers, there are still works that remain largely unknown: for Schubert, his operas, and for Donizetti, his nonoperatic works. From the beginning and throughout his career as an opera composer, Donizetti also wrote choral, instrumental, and nonoperatic vocal music (predominantly songs). His string quartets pale in comparison to their Viennese models. However, in their own right, they display a melodic and rhythmic inventiveness and a varied and colorful harmonic structure. This article surveys the nonoperatic works produced throughout Donizetti's life in an attempt to identify other works worthy of revival.

777. Weatherson, Alexander. "Lament for a Dead Nightingale: The Cantata *In morte di M. F. Malibran de Bériot.*" *Donizetti Society Journal* 5 (1984): 155–168.

The death of the mezzo-soprano, Maria Malibran, at the age of twenty-eight provided the impetus to memorialize her in a composite work, a *pasticcio* cantata, in which the individual movements would be written by different composers. The resultant work was performed only once, on 17 March 1837, and included music by Donizetti, Pacini, Mercadante, Pier-Antonio Coppola, and Nicola Vaccai. These composers were all associated with the career of the late singer. After providing an overview of these composite works in the nineteenth century, the author hypothesizes why these five composers were brought together for this work. Donizetti provided the sinfonia for the work, which, when analyzed, proves to be a wry portrait of Malibran, a testament to the magic she created onstage. The reexamination of this work illuminates the effect of the singer on Donizetti, and the link between them, which was Nicola Vaccai.

B. Discography

778. *Allegro in C Major for Strings.* Rossini Ensemble, Budapest; András Kiss, leader. [Hong Kong]: Naxos; Munich, Germany: Distributed by MVD Music and Video Distribution, p1992. Naxos: 8.550621.

Recorded at the Festetich Castle in Budapest in October 1991.

779. *Chamber Music.* Ex Novo Ensemble. Milan: Giulia; [Portland, OR]: Allegro [distributor], p1992. Giulia: GS 201018. Ottocento strumentale italiano.

Recorded in Ortisei, January 1992. Includes the Trio in E-flat Major for violin, cello and piano; the Sonata in C Major for flute and piano; the Trio in F Major for flute, bassoon, and piano; the Largo in G Minor for cello and piano; the Sonata in F Major for violin and piano; the Studio for clarinet; the Variations in B-flat Major for violin and piano; and the Trio in D Major for violin, cello, and piano.

780. *The Complete Piano Duets.* Larissa Kondratjewa, Reinhard Schmiedel, piano. Georgsmarienhütte: CPO, p1994. CPO: cpo999 163-2.

781. *The Complete Piano Music.* Pietro Spada, piano. Arts: RTS 47381—RTS 47383.

782. *Composizioni da camera per canto e piano forte.* Eva Mei, soprano; Fabio Bidini, piano. New York: BMG Music, p1995. RCA: 09026-68025-2.

Recorded 7–10 June 1994 at Bayerischer Rundfunk, Munich.

783. *Concertino for Clarinet* [In. 609, B-flat Major]. Lucien Aubert, clarinet; Virtuosi di Praga. Prague: ICN Polyart, 1992. ICN Polyart: ICN 008.

784. *Donizetti Songs Written in the Bass Clef.* Ian Caddy, bass-baritone; Melvyn Tan, fortepiano; Anthony Halstead, natural horn; Sebastian Comberti, violoncello. London: Meridian, 1989. Meridian: CDE 84183.

Includes the songs *Canto d'Ugolino,L'amor funesto, Trovatore in caricatura, Spirto di Dio, Viva il matrimonio, Le renégat, Noé: Scène du déluge, Le départ pour la chasse, Un cœur pour abri,* and *La hart.*

785. *Instrumental Concerti.* Camerata Budapest (orchestra); László Kovács, conductor. [Germany?]: Marco Polo; Munich: Distributed by MVD Music and Video Distribution, p1994. Marco Polo: 8.223701.

Recorded at the Festetich Castle, Budapest, 5–11 June 1994. Includes the *Sinfonia a soli instrumenti di fiato* in G Minor, the *Concertino* for flute and chamber orchestra in C Minor, the *Concertino* for oboe and chamber orchestra in F Major, the *Concertino* for violin, cello, and orchestra in D Minor, the *Concertino* for English horn and orchestra in G Major, the *Concertino* for clarinet and orchestra in B-flat Major, and the *Sinfonia per la morte di Capuzzi* in D Minor.

786. *An Italian Songbook: Bellini, Donizetti, Rossini.* Cecilia Bartoli, mezzo-soprano; James Levine, piano. New York: London Records, p1997. London: 455 513-2.

Includes Donizetti's songs *Il barcaiolo, Amore e morte, Ah! rammenta, o bella Irene, La conocchia,* and *Me voglio fà 'na casa.*

787. *Messa di Gloria e Credo.* Danielle Borst, soprano; Hélène Jossoud, mezzo-soprano; Jean-Luc Viala, tenor; Vincent Le Texier, bass; Choeur Régional Provence-Alpes-Côte d'Azur; Orchestre Lyrique de Région Avignon-Provence; Michel Piquemal, director. Adda, 1992. Adda: 581293.

Recorded on 1–3 November 1991 at the Chartreuse de Villeneuve-lez-Avignon, Centre National des Ecritures du Spectacle.

788. *Messe di Requiem; Messe di Gloria e Credo*. Renato Bruson, Veriano Luchetti, Samuel Ramey, Antonio Savastano, and Rita Susovsky; Orchestra Sinfonica e Coro di Roma della Rai; Gianluigi Gelmetti, conductor. Italy: Fonit Cetra, 1985. Musica/aperta. LMAD 3018. LP.

Recorded April 8 and May 28, 1983 at the Auditorium del Foro Italico di Roma.

789. *Musique sacrée inédite* = Unpublished Sacred Music. Vocal soloists; Chœurs de la Radiodiffusion Tchéque; Orchestre Symphonique de Prague; Edoardo Brizio, conductor. [Prague]: San Paolo; Paris: Distribution Studio SM, 1995–1996. San Paolo: D2484, D2569, D2582.

Vol. 1 contains the *Ave Maria* in F Major for soprano and chorus; the *Asperges me* in B-flat Major for chorus and orchestra; the *Kyrie* in D Major for soloists, chorus, and orchestra; the *Gloria in excelsis* in D Major for soloists (STB), chorus, and orchestra; the *Credo* in C Major for soloists (STB), chorus, and orchestra; the *Laudate pueri* in D Major for four solo voices and orchestra; and the *Salve Regina* in G Major for soprano and orchestra. Vol. 2 contains the *Credo* in D Major, the *Qui sedes*, the *Dominus a dextris* in D Minor, the *Docebo*, the *Nisi Dominus*, and the *Magnificat*. Vol. 3 contains the *Tuba miram*, the *Qui tollis*, the *Tecum principium*, the *Tantum ego*, the *Tibi soli peccavi*, and the *Dixit Dominus*.

790. *The Other Donizetti*. Jeremy Polmear, oboe, English horn; Diana Ambache, piano. London: Meridian, 1987. Meridian: CDE 84147.

Includes Donizetti's Sonata in F, Waltz in C, *Concertino* for English horn in G, and *Il barcaiolo*, as well as Pasculi's Concerto on Themes from the Opera *La favorita* and Fantasia on the Opera *Poliuto*, and Liszt's *Reminiscences de Lucia di Lammermoor*.

791. *Parafrasi dei Christus*. Maria Spindler, soprano; Greda Prochaska-Stolze, mezzo-soprano; Suk Chamber Orchestra; Leos Svarovsky, conductor. Lotos: LT 0013.

792. Quintets; Nocturnes; Study for Clarinet; Wind Music. Japan: Frequenz, p1986. Frequenz: CAQ 1.

Includes the *Introduzione* in D Major for strings, the String Quintet in C Major, the Quintet in C Major for guitar and strings, the *Nocturne* for winds and strings, the *Studio* in C Major for clarinet, the *Sinfonia* in D Major for winds, the *Larghetto* in F Major for winds, the *Moderato* in B-flat Major for winds and organ, and the *Marcia* in F Major for winds and percussion.

793. *Sonata for Flute and Harp*. Marc Grauwels, flute; Catherine Michel, harp. Hong Kong: Marco Polo, p1987. Marco Polo: 8.220441.

An arrangement of the *Larghetto* for violin and harp in G Minor [In. 614].

794. *String Quartets nos. 7–9*. The Revolutionary Drawing Room (period instruments). Georgsmarienhütte, Germany: CPO, 1995. CPO: 999 170-2.

Recorded at Heathfield Church, East Sussex, 24–26 January 1994.

795. *String Quartets nos. 10–12*. The Revolutionary Drawing Room (period instruments). Georgsmarienhütte, Germany: CPO, 1996. CPO: 999 279-2.

Recorded at Heathfield Church, East Sussex, 19–21 July 1994.

796. *String Quartets nos. 13–15*. The Revolutionary Drawing Room (period instruments). Georgsmarienhütte, Germany: CPO, 1996. CPO: 999 280-2.

Recorded at Heathfield Church, East Sussex, 18–24 November 1994.

797. *Serenata: Songs by Italian Opera Composers*. Patricia Wright, soprano; David Vine, piano. Wellington, N.Z.: Atoll; Academy Opera Trust, 1998. Atoll: A9803.

Recorded 29–30 January 1998 in the Music Theatre of the School of Music, University of Auckland, N.Z. Includes Donizetti's *Mi voglio fa 'na casa*.

Name Index

Here are listed names of authors, editors, translators, arrangers, performers (vocalists, instrumentalists, conductors, etc.) and performing bodies (orchestras, chamber ensembles, choruses, etc.). NB: Numbers in this index refer to item numbers, not page numbers.

Subject Indexes

Numbers refer to items in the bibliography, not pages.

About the Author

James P. Cassaro is Head of the Theodore M. Finney Music Library at the University of Pittsburgh. Previously he was the Assistant Music Librarian at Cornell University, and he has served on the library staff at North Texas State University and the University at Buffalo. He holds the B.A. in Music from the University at Buffalo (1978), an M.L.S., also from Buffalo (1980), and the M.A. in Musicology (1993) from Cornell University. His master's thesis, "A Critical Edition of Jean Baptiste Lully's 'Ballet des Saisons': Historical Background, Manuscript Sources, Livret," will appear in the composer's collected works, to be published in 2001. Cassaro has published widely on topics in music librarianship as well as in American music, and was recently elected Vice-President/President-Elect of the Music Library Association.

Composer Resource Manuals
GUY A. MARCO, *General Editor*